D0843376

Aging Across the United States

CHARLES LOCKHART AND JEAN GILES-SIMS

Aging Across the United States

Matching Need to States' Differing Opportunities and Services

The Pennsylvania State University Press
University Park, Pennsylvania

Library of Congress Cataloging-in-Publication Data

Lockhart, Charles, 1944– .
    Aging across the United States : matching need to states'
    differing opportunities and services / Charles Lockhart and
    Jean Giles-Sims.
        p.   cm.
    Includes bibliographical references and index.
    Summary: "Compares services and opportunities for older
    Americans by region and state. Examines the criteria of
    recreational lifestyle, meaningful contributions and supportive
    communities, affordability and safety, health and high-quality
    medical care, and accessible, high-quality long-term care"—
    Provided by publisher.
    ISBN 978-0-271-03756-1 (alk. paper)
    1. Older persons—United States—States.
    2. Aging—United States—States.
    I. Giles-Sims, Jean.
    II. Title.

    HQ1064.U5L63 2010
    305.260973—dc22
    2010021723

The Pennsylvania State University Press is a member of the
Association of American University Presses.

It is the policy of The Pennsylvania State University Press to
use acid-free paper. Publications on uncoated stock satisfy the
minimum requirements of American National Standard for
Information Sciences—Permanence of Paper for Printed
Library Material, ANSI Z39.48–1992.

This book is printed on Natures Natural, which contains
50% post-consumer waste.

In Loving Memory of Our Parents:
Wilbur and Dorothy Grindell
Charles H., Gertrude, and Elizabeth Lockhart

CONTENTS

FIGURES

TABLES

The state ranking tables (A.1–A.40) appear in the Appendix

PREFACE

This study grew out of recent troubling and often sad experiences with our parents, to whom we dedicate this book. Across something more than a decade we watched, initially from the sidelines, but increasingly over time from the field of action, as they became progressively more physically frail, cognitively limited, or both. Lengthy portions of this process occurred in different states, and we were repeatedly surprised by how much the experiences in one state differed from those in another.

We decided to learn more about the underlying reasons for these differences. So academics happily engaged in research on comparative public social policy and aspects of family sociology involving much younger persons became gerontologists with the encouragement and assistance of others.

So, what—in brief—have we learned? First, older citizens form a heterogeneous population with different priorities associated with successive stages of aging. Second, the American states turn out to be specialists, rather than generalists, with regard to supporting these various priorities. So, third, sequentially realizing the shifting priorities of an older couple often entails a pair of cross-state moves as they age, moves designed to match their current priorities to different states' distinctive strengths.

In developing this book from these three fundamental points, we have enjoyed the assistance of a number of persons. While we each found the process of learning and, particularly, writing as spouses to pose numerous unanticipated challenges to our relationship, each of us grew to appreciate more fully the other's talents and capacities. Neither of us could have produced this book on her or his own.

Murray A. Straus encouraged us to examine cross-state differences in what he called "state elderly-friendliness" systematically. An early version of our thinking on this topic appeared in *Publius: The Journal of Federalism* 35, no. 3 (2005): 425–47. This terminology has gradually morphed into the "state senior friendliness" found in this book. Some authors are now using the term "age-friendly states" to express a similar concept. The late Marc Miringoff provided a wonderful example for us to loosely emulate in his *The Social Health of the Nation: How America Is Really Doing* (with Marque-Luisa Miringoff) (New York: Oxford University Press, 1999). Frank Caro, Christine L. Day, and Sandy Thatcher read the manuscript and made numerous helpful suggestions, prompting improvements.

This book centers on state rankings on forty indicators (eight for each of five dimensions) of state senior friendliness. We are grateful to a number of institutions, such as the U.S. Census Bureau and the Inter-University Consortium for Political and Social Research at the University of Michigan, which either create or maintain the data on which these rankings are based. We cite these and a number of other institutions that provided data frequently throughout the text. Here we wish to express our gratitude to persons at various institutions who have been particularly helpful in making data available. Thanks especially to Gretchen Straw, AARP; Elizabeth Gough, American Foundation for Suicide Prevention; Gina Flores and Alan Schafer, Arizona Health Care Cost Containment System; Robert Clair, U.S. Census Bureau; Tara Balsey, Centers for Disease Control; Lori Anderson, Deborah Kidd, and especially Janet G. Freeze, Centers for Medicare and Medicaid; Bob Mollica, National Academy for State Health Policy; and Steve Eiken, Thomson Medstatt.

Sanford G. Thatcher, director of Penn State University Press, expressed an interest in our research and provided crucial support as the book developed. Erin Greb, a cartographer at the Gould Center for Geography Education and Outreach at Penn State, created the maps scattered throughout the text from our tables. Kathryn Yahner ably managed the transformation of our manuscript into a book.

Born in 1944 and 1945, we often find ourselves thinking about the questions in the book with respect to our own lives. Unsurprisingly, given our generation, we sometimes need help with the computers that younger generations find intuitive. Trey Ivy, Jason Packer, Amanda Giles, and Andrea Sims provided this help with extraordinary good humor when we faced the limits of our computer savvy. Each of us had previously worked with qualitative methodologies, and the current project required us to update and deepen our statistical analysis skills. Kristen Klopfenstein and Cathy Coghlan helped us immensely in overcoming data analysis problems and provided us with the skills to manage the data analysis for this book ourselves.

Ralph Carter, Pat Kinkaid, Mary Volcansek, and Nowell R. Donovan at TCU all supported an academic leave in the spring term of 2007 that facilitated our completing the manuscript in a timely fashion.

During the writing of this book, Jean's good friend Dee Sharlip became ill and required extensive medical care. All of us face these risks in the short or long term, and we hope that we all will find a graceful way to face them. The humor of Gregg Franzwa, Richard Galvin, and other members of the "optimists" has, thankfully, enabled Charles to survive the stresses of shifting trends in academic management for decades. Our three children—Andrea, Gregory, and John—and our whole family motivate us to make the world a better place for future generations in whatever small way we can.

Garrison Keillor's amusing stories about the residents of an imaginary small northern Minnesota town who fantasize in February, not about sex, but about living in Florida remind us of one way in which where we live influences our well-being as we grow older. Indeed, once they retire, many Minnesotans spend their winters in Florida or other states with milder winter climates and a range of outdoor recreational opportunities. Some Minnesotans move entirely to these other states, at least during their early retirement years. But later in retirement they develop different needs, and among persons eighty-five or older, Minnesota actually has net *in-migration*. That is, more persons in this age group, many of them long-term Minnesotans who departed early in retirement, move into the state than move out.[1]

Why would young retirees leave and then return to Minnesota as they grow old? The short answer is that at older ages many retirees need high-quality medical care, encouraging and financially accessible long-term care, and help from younger family members or friends more than mild climates and various recreational facilities.[2] Some states offer enticing climates and recreational possibilities to young retirees, but other states provide better-quality medical care services to older retirees.

This study focuses on the surprising range of benefits people seek and can find in moving from one state to another as they grow older. We examine how some states help retirees maximize their "young-old" years—facilitating their enjoyment of leisure or finding meaning in life or conserving resources—while other states offer older or sicker Americans better chances for superior medical care or more desirable forms of long-term care. Fortunately, more than in the past, many retired persons can now choose where they live. A large proportion of seniors can, and a great many do, move from state to state to meet their changing needs. On the basis of research conducted over a number of years, we offer a synthesis of empirical facts or data and a theoretical explanation of variation in states' support for diverse basic issues that confront retired Americans whose priorities change as they age.

Incidentally, researchers writing about older Americans disagree about what terms to use.[3] Following AARP, we use *older adults, older Americans, older residents, seniors,* and frequently, given the focus of our topic, *retirees* to refer to persons in their late fifties and up. We also occasionally use *young-old* and *old-old* to distinguish persons from the mid-fifties through the sixties from those in their eighties or older. Each of these terms has drawbacks in particular contexts. For instance, some seniors still work rather than being retired. And some young, healthy retirees—perhaps in their mid- to late fifties—likely resent the label *senior*. Overall, we think that these terms represent the most appropriate options. We try to select particular terms to fit the context at various junctures, and if we occasionally offend some readers, we regret doing so.

In the following chapters we assess each state's strengths and weaknesses in areas of major concern to older Americans. These areas include gaining support for a recreational lifestyle, fostering supportive communities and opportunities for finding meaning in life through volunteer work for various civic organizations, locating inexpensive yet comfortable and safe places to live, acquiring support for healthy habits and enjoying high-quality medical care, and obtaining access to affordable, high-quality long-term care. We address these issues from two vantage points by combining the macroperspective or "big picture" of states' social, economic, and political realities with the microperspective of the lived experience of individuals in families that have their own unique characteristics. Some readers may choose to begin by reading this introduction, the initial vignette and conclusions sections of chapters 1 through 5, and the Epilogue as well as by examining the maps that are scattered across chapters 1 through 6.

How We Came to Conduct This Study

Every family tells a particular story of parents, grandparents, uncles, aunts, or family friends encountering the pitfalls of the years from retirement to old age. Many painful stories illustrate that few contemporary older Americans foresee the challenges they will face as they grow still older, so these stories also testify to the importance of better preparation. Our own parents' struggles ignited the passion and need to know that fueled this research.

Jean's parents ran a small tourist business on the south shore of Cape Cod for twenty years before her father's arthritis, his bout with a nasty liver virus that nearly killed him, and her mother's diabetes led them to put that chapter of their lives in the rearview mirror and—in their early sixties—head to Florida to avoid the long, cold, gray New England winters. Her father loved the warmth, the beaches, the airy and affordable houses, and the grapefruit. In Florida, her parents joked about heavy coats and snow shovels. Over the years her father bought ever bigger and shinier motor homes, and her parents made their long-awaited trip around the United States as well as taking many shorter jaunts. Her mother found new friends and got herself spiffed up in new duds and—for a brief time (thankfully)—in slightly blue hair. Her parents loved to dance, and each Saturday evening they dressed up, danced, and laughed like kids. During her visits, Jean even remembers hearing sexual innuendoes that brought red to her cheeks. For her parents, life was good after nearly fifty years of hard work, community dedication, and raising a family of five children.

Then the inevitable decline set in. Her mother's first stroke occurred in Maine as her parents were packing up the house they had bought for the six months they spent in New England each year. Her mother was saying a stressful good-bye to family heirlooms and moving away from the kids and grandchildren who lived across New England. She had been neglecting her diabetes and high blood pressure, and one day Jean's father came up from his workshop in the basement and found her mother was not "right." Moving to Florida scared Jean's mother, who feared losing contact with her children and grandchildren and the feeling of home that came with her New England roots. But her father loved Florida and was also in decline with arthritis, which led to double knee replacements and a lot of back pain. To compensate her mother, Jean's father oversaw the construction of "the house of her dreams" in Florida as her parents reached eighty.

But the timing of this move and the home construction created too much stress. Her parents spent the following autumn living with children in New England so that her father could have heart valve replacement and bypass surgery in Boston. His long recovery and return to Florida were accompanied by another major stroke for her mother. Jean's parents began a life of almost daily physicians' appointments with a series of different specialists. Their medications multiplied across these appointments, and no one coordinated their care. Then her father fell asleep at the wheel and drove through the yard and into the garage of a neighbor whose children were playing nearby. Her father's subsequent minor strokes and then a bigger one signaled the end of their independent lives shortly thereafter.

As each crisis occurred, Jean packed up her work and flew from Texas or Maine to help—six times over three years. Finally, time and distance made her parents' care unmanageable. Jean and her brothers in New England searched for a place to move their mother and father. Jean's husband packed up her parents' house and put it on the market. In a harrowing trip from the hospital in an ambulance to wheelchairs and dementia on American Airlines, they all flew to Boston, where one of Jean's brothers met their parents and settled their mother in a retirement center and her father in a nearby rehabilitation facility, both near the family and support her parents now needed.

As Jean and her family tried to help her parents, they visited an elder law attorney and investment counselors, contacted the Area Agency on Aging, and talked with a number of physicians. They often felt frustrated by the difficulty of getting information about various financial, housing, and medical options, and as Jean's parents moved from retirement housing to assisted living to a nursing home, new issues arose. But they did settle on a single geriatrician who coordinated her parents' care and culled their medications, improving some of their medical problems in the process. Jean's parents never expected to run out of money, but their expensive care and long lives eventually exhausted their savings. Near the end, Medicaid became their primary source of support.

Jean's parents' overall physical decline continued with her mother's heart attacks, myelodysplasia, and cancer and her father's dementia, disruptive behavior, eventual nursing facility residency, and final stroke. Her father died while Jean flew from Texas to New England, and her mother entered the hospital the same evening with a recurrence of cancer obstructing her intestines. A couple of days of testing and talking, aided by the trusted geriatrician, led to a decision not to treat the cancer and to discontinue insulin. Jean's mother died peacefully exactly one week after her father had, with six family members at her side. Overall, Jean's parents did pretty well, but earlier planning could have avoided some of the stress and improved the quality of life they experienced during their final years.

Other families we have talked with tell broadly similar stories about the challenges of how and where to grow old. One family's parents moved to Arizona to play golf, and then the father developed Alzheimer's. Another's parents moved to Las Vegas to play the slots but lost both money and health. Still other parents moved to a retirement village in South Carolina, but gradually all their friends died and they suffered alone in old age. These stories suggest that we need to look at the needs of older people in stages, stages defined by changes in persons' most pressing needs. The American states differ in the degrees to which they support these various needs, and we think that the trick is to match retirees' shifting priorities to states' varying strengths and capacities.

Our own questions about what we want as we grow old sometimes keep us awake at night. We are hardly alone, just ahead of the leading edge of the baby boom generation, whose 78 million members (born from 1946 to 1964) will, over roughly the coming five decades, age from sixty to nearly ninety.[4] Virtually every family will be coping with the issues of lifestyle, expenses, and care. Each state and the federal government will be struggling with how to provide, regulate, and finance the services needed for this and following generations. For individuals, the information in this study illustrates the needs and the availability of opportunities and services as well as provides guidance for choosing where to live at various stages of aging. For relevant professionals and policy makers, the study shows the relative strengths of some states that may offer models for emulation. For all Americans, the study provides a straight-talk introduction to what are likely to become some of the major personal, political, and economic concerns of the twenty-first century.

Americans Growing Older

Consider some basic demographics of our aging society. In 2005, 12.4 percent of the American population was sixty-five or older and another 17 percent was between fifty and sixty-four.[5] Projections for 2020 place 16.3 and 18.9 percent of the population in these two categories, respectively. As a percentage of the total population, then, these two cohorts are expected to grow nearly 20 percent in fifteen years. The total population is projected to grow by 13 percent during the same time period, so the rate at which these cohorts of older Americans are increasing outpaces the rate of the overall population's growth by a considerable margin.

Among the population sixty-five or older, minority groups contribute just a bit less than one-fifth (18.5 percent) of the total. After age forty, women outnumber men in the American population, but their numerical predominance grows sharply until, after eighty-five, they become slightly more than twice as numerous as males. For both genders, rates of living with a marital partner decline with age, but whereas the rate for men declines from about 74 to 67 percent as they age from sixty-five to seventy-four to seventy-five and older; the rate for women drops from 54 to 29 percent across the same age range. So while just over 30 percent of Americans sixty-five or older live alone, somewhat over two-thirds of these persons are women.

Chronic illnesses (e.g., in declining frequency, high blood pressure, arthritis, heart disease, and diabetes) afflict large proportions of Americans sixty-five or older, and these proportions grow as age increases. These conditions contribute to disability among seniors, so that, among those over sixty-five, nearly 60 percent of men and just over 70 percent of women have activity limitations with respect to ordinary daily actions. These limitations become more severe with age, so that while the proportions of men and women needing assistance with everyday activities in the sixty-five-to-sixty-nine age cohort are about 42 and 43 percent, respectively, these proportions rise to 68 and 77 percent for the eighty-and-over cohort. Almost inevitably, then, significant numbers of men and women spend the last portion of their lives in various forms of long-term care such as nursing facilities, and the percentages increase with age. For men, the percentage rises from about 3 percent in the seventy-five-to-eighty-four age cohort to around 12 percent for those eighty-five and older. For women, the increase is from around 5 to about 20 percent. Overall, about 1.5 million older persons reside in nursing facilities.

The median household income for persons sixty-five or older was slightly less than $24,000 in 2003. This was a bit over half (55 percent) the median income for all American households (about $43,500) that year. In spite of this discrepancy in median income, Americans sixty-five or over had a poverty rate (10.2 percent) slightly lower than that for the American population as a whole (12.5 percent) in 2003. For better or worse—surely the latter—it is Americans under eighteen who bear the brunt of poverty in the United States, with a rate of 17.6 percent. However, most Americans sixty-five or older live on limited incomes. In the vast majority of instances these are incomes less, frequently far less, than they were accustomed to during their working years.

In terms of wealth (net worth), the holdings of Americans' sixty-five and older compare reasonably well with those of the fifty-five-to-sixty-four age cohort, the group generally in the prime of their economic lives. Median wealth among sixty-five-or-older households stood at just under $109,000 in 2000, whereas the median figure for the fifty-five-to-sixty-four cohort barely topped $112,000. But considering the length of retirements that many persons in the baby boom generation can expect, neither of these figures bodes well for the economic security of future retirees. Further, when the equity in persons' residences is excluded, these figures drop to $23,369 and $32,304, respectively. So most Americans will likely experience sharply reduced income levels in retirement as well as quite limited amounts of accumulated financial resources to cover various emergencies.

America's elders are distributed unevenly among the states. Nationally, 12.2 percent of the population was sixty-five or older in 2000. But some states had particularly large proportions: in declining percentages, Florida (17.6), Pennsylvania (15.6), West Virginia (15.3), Iowa (14.9), North Dakota (14.7), Rhode Island (14.5), Maine (14.4), South Dakota (14.3), and Louisiana (14.0). Other states had unusually low percentages: in increasing percentages, Alaska (5.7), Utah (8.5), Georgia (9.6), Colorado (9.7), Texas (9.9), and California (10.6). While there are exceptions (e.g., Florida), the states with particularly high percentages tend to be located in the Upper Midwest and Northeast; while the states with the lowest percentages (again with exceptions, e.g., Alaska) tend to be southern, particularly southwestern.

As we introduced above, most older Americans live in the community, rather than in institutions, but the proportions of those who are institutionalized vary across the states. In fourteen of the fifty states, 5 percent or more of the sixty-five-or-older population reside in nursing facilities (in descending order: Iowa (6.5 percent), North Dakota, South Dakota, Connecticut, Kansas, Nebraska, Louisiana, Rhode Island, Massachusetts, Minnesota, Ohio, Indiana, Illinois, and Missouri [5.0 percent]). Ten of these fourteen states form a contiguous group in the Midwest, and Louisiana is the only clearly southern state among the fourteen. Most of these states include relatively high proportions of elderly persons among their total population.

Nationally, older persons numbering about three times (4.5 million) the nursing facility population participate in their states' Medicaid Home and Community-Based Services aged/disabled waiver programs, while living at home; spending days in adult day care; or living in congregate residential care facilities, including assisted living.[6] People living in these three venues generally receive, through this program, care that is less extensive than that available in a nursing facility. Family and friends also provide an uncertain but likely large number (around 8 million) of older Americans with similar assistance informally. As these statistics suggest, the aging population presents a broad range of needs, and social and political institutions as well as individuals would do well to plan for these eventualities.

Why Is Planning for Retirement Becoming More Important and Difficult?

We hope that this study raises consciousness among both the general public and relevant professionals and public officials and stimulates critically important advance thinking and planning about retirement. The grandparents of current mature working-age persons probably did not need to do much retirement planning. They did not live as long or have many options for moving. The generation that came of age in World War II did not engage in much retirement planning either, but now aging baby boomers frequently find themselves with distressing problems that arise from their parents' inadequate retirement planning. Several changes in American society explain why retirement planning is so important today for individuals as well as social and political institutions.

First, Americans live much longer than in the past. For instance, when the Social Security Administration initially issued checks in the early 1940s, social planners did not expect many people to reach the age (sixty-five) at which persons became eligible for these pensions. Average life expectancy for men and women now stretches more than a decade longer, into the mid- and upper seventies, respectively, and persons who reach sixty-five can expect to live, on average, into the late eighties.[7] So for the baby boomers, now perched on the verge of retiring, increasing life expectancy expands the retirement stage of life from a few years at most to around a couple of decades.

Second, many people now retire before they reach sixty-five. Whereas the vast majority of American men and women between the ages of twenty-five and fifty-four now work (84.6 and 73.4 percent, respectively), in the sixty-to-sixty-four age group labor force participation drops to 54.2 percent for men and 39.8 percent for women.[8] So for many people retirement lengthens at both ends. Increasing lifespan, addressed in the preceding paragraph, adds to the back, and the early retirement trend described in this paragraph adds to the front.

As a consequence of Americans' living longer and leaving work earlier, retirements can span close to three decades, and the purposes and needs of retirees change considerably across this period. For instance, a healthy and affluent couple in their late fifties may focus on recreation, but their priorities will likely transform into protecting assets and acquiring encouraging medical and possibly long-term care as they confront their early eighties.

Third, the American states have long varied in how well they support the different needs and hopes of older Americans. Yet recent decades of social and economic conservative influence at the national level have stalled a trend of reducing cross-state differences in policies of particular interest to older Americans that had generally held sway from Roosevelt's New Deal through Johnson's Great Society. Conservative initiatives have shifted public social program responsibilities (and the financial burdens that go with them) to the states. States, in turn, react to these new responsibilities in varying ways, so differences in the ease with which older Americans in the states obtain access to essential services are substantial and—in some instances—growing.

Fourth, the members of the baby boom generation who will retire over the coming decades surely rank among the healthiest and most affluent retirees in American history. They have also traveled more and moved their households from one state to another more frequently. So both their condition and their experiences prepare them well for taking advantage of the distinctive strengths of different American states that meet retirees' shifting priorities as they age.

Because of these four trends—living longer, retiring earlier, differences in state policies affecting seniors, and more capable retirees—making the most of one's retirement entails planning on a scale rarely necessary among previous generations. The length of many current retirements argues for careful deliberation about a range of household financial matters as well as thoughtful reflection on how to spend one's time. When retirement lasted only a year or two, careful financial planning was less necessary, and lying on a couch watching television (or more likely, listening to the radio) seemed a reasonable reprieve after a lifetime of hard physical labor. Now that retirement can frequently last a quarter century, people need to plan both what to do with their time as well as how to finance it, but few understand how state variations help or hinder them when it comes to reaching their goals.

Currently a number of fine guides offer help with the two retirement concerns noted above, figuring out what to do in retirement and how to finance it.[9] We address these issues in this study only when opportunities vary across states. We provide information about how well or poorly the various states support different objectives; further, we point out a few basic implications that may help in effective retirement planning. We focus our analyses on the amazing degree of cross-state variation in our society. Generally speaking, retirement guides do not address these differences.[10] We hope to inform readers about state environments that provide the most help in realizing encouraging outcomes with regard to the shifting needs and priorities that seniors face in successive stages of retirement.

Five Basic Issues Seniors Confront

Seniors' priorities generally include dealing successfully with one or more of five basic issues. Save for the poor fellow of legend who retires on his sixty-fifth birthday and dies of a heart attack before the following dawn, most seniors confront at least some of these issues, particularly after retirement. Seniors' well-being hinges largely on finding and acting constructively on answers to these questions. A broad range of people will find these questions relevant, but these issues frequently hold greater pertinence for seniors. Different issues likely represent higher priorities in the lives of individual seniors at different stages of aging. Characteristically, younger retirees find one of the first three questions most relevant. Across time, the importance of the fourth and then eventually the fifth questions usually increase.

(1) *Where can retirees best find a life of companionship and active recreation?* Most academics find the following point painful to confront and contemplate: many people are not fond of school. A substantial majority tolerate it long enough to graduate from high school. A growing minority achieve a bachelor's degree. And community colleges offer assorted forms of largely occupational training to a growing number of people who fall between these two educational levels. But as any instructor knows, a large proportion of students do not master the material, and many students feel—at least initially—immensely relieved to graduate and move on to what looks like freedom. Even those students who

carry fond memories of their school years generally, though not always, base them on good times with their classmates.

But the world of work often turns out to be discouraging in its own right. Many Americans confront a daily grind of inflexible hours and work activity they find personally meaningless—as Marx labeled it, "a degrading scramble after money."[11] Many engage in a scramble to enjoy life off the job. Researchers disagree about whether Americans spend more time on the job than they once did or more than comparable workers in other societies.[12] But they generally agree that work is organized and focused so that large proportions of employees have to enjoy life in the gaps between work periods, though some of these may be found at work (joking around the water cooler) rather than off the job.

The strictures of school and work foster in many people who are looking to retire a longing, most of all, for a life of leisure. They want to go somewhere pleasant and spend their time engaging in some form of active recreation that they enjoy. We can surely understand this as one—not the only—reasonable reaction to having spent, say, seventeen of one's sixty-five years in school and another forty-three working at something onerous. People conceptualize a recreational lifestyle in many different ways, but one version attracted a considerable following and became virtually a social convention across the second half of the twentieth century. It focused on moving in retirement to a generally sunny climate with mild winters and pursuing outdoor recreation: playing golf, fishing, bird-watching, and so on. Needless to say, some states support this objective more thoroughly than others.

(2) *Where can retirees best find a meaningful life and supportive communities?* Not everyone favors pursuing a life of play after being at the beck and call of others for six decades. Many wish to add meaning to their lives by doing something they see as more constructive—for themselves (e.g., starting their own business) or others (e.g., contributing their expertise to civic organizations that support goals they share)—than simply having fun. Others may try to do both, in varying degrees. A retired attorney who plays golf daily from his house by the fairway in an Arizona golf course community may also lend his expertise pro bono to help solve some of the community's legal issues with an adjacent commuter airport. Likewise, a retired public administrator, now living in Minneapolis, may seek and acquire a regular task of providing outreach sessions on long-term care insurance to various groups for her local Area Agency on Aging office but still go swimming with a longtime friend nearly daily in the indoor pool of a local club. The difference lies in priority. What is one's life organized around: enjoying a recreational activity or finding meaning through the provision of a service of benefit to others? As was true for fun in the sun,

states vary considerably in the opportunities they afford for meaningful community service.

Some states' social environments facilitate the search for community and, particularly, opportunities for contributing to these communities in personally fulfilling ways far more than others. Some states have long-standing traditions of hierarchical institutions (slavery in the South or patronage political parties in regions of the Northeast and Midwest).[13] As Robert Putnam and his colleagues have shown, these institutions not only repress meaningful participation in society for many while they exist, but also leave a cultural heritage of repression in the wake of their demise that impoverishes civic life for lengthy periods.[14] It takes little imagination to recognize that Minnesota, where 73 percent of those who were eligible voted in the 2004 presidential election, affords more meaningful opportunities for civic participation than does Texas, where only 46 percent engaged in this simple civic act.[15] As we will see in chapter 2, Minnesota's seniors also exhibit a range of citizen activism, and this helps to explain why Minnesota ranks near the top in providing so-called circuit breaker property tax credits to seniors, whereas seniors in Texas reveal far lower levels of activism, and Texas ranks near the bottom in state circuit breaker property tax relief for older residents.

(3) *Where can retirees best afford to live (and be safe)?* Many retirees live on relatively modest incomes that increase only with the cost of living. Nationwide, 34 percent of people sixty-five or older live below 200 percent of the federal poverty level.[16] Sixty-five percent of Americans sixty-five or older receive more than half their income from Social Security (technically, Old Age, Survivors, and Disability Insurance [OASDI], but hereafter generally just Social Security).[17] So many retired Americans live on limited incomes, and these incomes routinely fall below those the retirees received while they were working.[18] Extremely affluent individuals generally enjoy sufficient income to maintain their former lifestyles and simply save less. But most retirees must choose between two options. They can reduce their cost of living where they are now by purchasing fewer (or in some instances less expensive) goods and services. Or they can move to a place with a lower cost of living—for goods and services similar to those they are currently consuming. The states (and naturally, regions within them) vary sharply on cost of living. Retirees from New England tend to move to the Southeast to enjoy a lower cost of living and less congestion, in addition to a milder climate. On the other side of the country, people move from California to Nevada and other western states to reduce their cost of living and the frustrations that go with the congestion of large metropolitan areas.[19]

Retirees can often find less expensive neighborhoods in their local area, but these may offer a less desirable ambiance or even entail worries about crime.

Many older Americans feel vulnerable to and fear crime. Thus many seniors make cross-state moves to achieve a lower cost of living without noticeable sacrifice in ambience and safety. Sadly, state-level statistics show that the most expensive states also tend to have the lowest levels of crime. But among relatively inexpensive states, crime levels vary considerably, particularly for the forms of property crime that tend to predominate among elderly crime victims. So we consider crime rates along with cost of living to identify inexpensive states also affording relative safety.

(4) *Where will retirees have the greatest opportunity for being healthy and finding the best medical care?* States differ in the healthiness of their overall populations. On rankings derived from a number of components, for instance, Minnesota boasts the healthiest population, with an overall score of 25, and Louisiana has the least healthy, with an overall average score of −21.3.[20] In spite of considerable and growing cross-state migration among Americans, most people living in any given state have lived in that state for some time. So we should expect, and in chapter 4 we will find, that the health habits of states' sixty-five-or-older populations also vary sharply and similarly to the healthiness of states' total populations. Thus, retirees can choose to live in states with a range of supports for healthy living. Further, seniors are generally more vulnerable to health problems than are other adults and need conscientious preventive care. Additionally, many seniors with acute or chronic illnesses require periodic or regular therapeutic treatment. Surprisingly, the average quality of the medical care delivered to seniors via the Medicare program also varies a great deal across the states. Practicing healthy habits and receiving high-quality medical care generally become increasing high priorities as people age, and we consider how states differ in providing supports for healthy living and in the quality of the medical care seniors receive.

(5) *Where can retirees find accessible, affordable, high-quality long-term care?* Finally, many Americans age eighty or older need various forms of long-term care. States' programs to help with the extraordinary costs (currently averaging well over six thousand dollars a month for nursing facilities) of professional long-term care differ sharply. States also differ widely in their efforts to ensure quality of long-term care by regulating providers. States offer different mixes of long-term care options, and the complexities of long-term care insurance are numerous and subtle. In our experience most current seniors and the about-to-be-senior baby boomers tend to be poorly informed about these aspects of long-term care. Thus we seek to help relevant professionals and public officials as well as older Americans generally become better informed. In the case of the latter our efforts may help to enable more pleasant final years of life.

Research Issues and Strategy

We take up three topics in this section. Initially, given obvious intrastate variation, why do we focus on states rather than individual communities? We offer four responses. The first might best be termed *parsimony*. There are fifty states, but thousands of communities. Researchers in the popular press who focus on communities tend to do so with a particular vision of retirement priorities in mind. But as we explained in the previous section, retirees confront multiple distinct basic issues, and the relative priority of these issues shifts as individual retirees age. There are, no doubt, a few communities that are good bets on several of the issues we introduced above, but most of these communities are so expensive as to lie far beyond the reach of the vast majority of retirees. Across the five basic issues, we think that we can generalize more effectively about states than others do about communities while at the same time posing a broader and more realistic view of retirement issues. Our second response is that comparable data exist for states to a far greater extent than they do for state subdivisions, including individual communities. A variety of institutions collect and—as necessary—disaggregate data to afford cross-state comparisons. These include, but are not limited to, the Census Bureau, the National Center for Health Statistics, the Centers for Medicare and Medicaid, and private-sector organizations such the United Health Foundation.

Third, and possibly most important, a variety of state policies that are particularly important in the lives of older Americans vary considerably across states but are generally relatively invariant within states. These include but are not limited to Medicaid and senior tax relief policies. Fourth, distinctive state histories, institutions, and cultures impart cross-state differences that have surprised us. When we began this work five years ago, we had no idea that, for instance, the medical care provided for Medicare patients in various states or the average number of days that state residents were physically unhealthy in the previous month would differ as much as they do. Surely these matters differ within states too. But extensive interstate variation exists in spite of these intrastate differences. For an average resident, state of residence carries a surprising range of implications, and this seems to be particularly the case for the elderly, whose lives are more closely tied to state-level policies than are those of most other age groups.

Our next topic involves our three guiding objectives. First, we wanted to provide breadth of data about where individuals can grow old most comfortably. U.S. seniors represent a heterogeneous population. Data about state recreational facilities of interest to relatively young, healthy, and affluent retirees will not help older persons whose highest priorities involve finding adequate medical care and vice versa. We wanted our data to speak to as full a range of basic senior concerns as possible. Our extensive sources are cited throughout the text, and our Epilogue brings these various sources together in one convenient list for the use of older Americans as well as professionals and public officials interested in seniors and their issues.

Our second objective was to provide a synthesis of a massive amount of data in order to help seniors as well as relevant professionals and policy makers become more keenly aware of cross-state differences. While some of these data are complex, most are "hiding in plain sight" in public documents. We examined a broad range of indicators, discarded many, and funneled those that remained into a manageable five-dimensional concept of "state senior friendliness" (SSF).

Our third objective involves the writing. While we are confident that this book is sophisticated enough to merit the time of relevant professionals and public officials, we have tried to make it accessible also to seniors themselves and to the friends and family members who care about them. Characteristically, our text explains both what the data show and what this means in terms of major implications for seniors as well as for professionals and public officials engaged in social planning to accommodate burgeoning growth in the senior population.

Our third topic takes up the analysis in chapter 6. In chapters 1–5 we present "raw" data. In chapter 6 we standardize this data (z-scores) for our analyses. We engage in two sorts of explanations in this chapter. First, we seek to identify the origins and strive to justify the structure that we have placed on the SSF concept. The origins take us into the nature of the American senior population at any given point in time, the changes that aging brings to the priorities of the individual members of this population over time, and the distinct strengths and weaknesses of the American states. Second, we offer an explanation drawn from the literature on cross-state policy differences as to why states support distinctive aspects of what we call SSF so differently.

Organization of the Book

In the following five chapters we sequentially address in detail each of the five issues we introduced in a previous section. These empirical chapters represent the describing-the-world purpose of science. We use data gathered from the most appropriate contemporary sources to compare the fifty states on a number of relevant indicators. These data provide the macroperspective, or big picture, both for the strengths and weaknesses of individual states across the issues and for the relative capacity or ranking of all fifty states on indicators relevant to each issue. One of our most pervasive discoveries indicates that regional groups of states often display similar capacities. But the states that provide a supportive environment for seniors with respect to one issue often flag in comparison with other states in supporting another issue.

This macroperspective misses important features, so we want to add three caveats. First, the macroperspective fails to provide much insight about the lived experience of individual seniors and their families: the microperspective. So we begin each of the next five chapters with a contrasting pair of vignettes of older persons—generally couples—and their particular concerns. We return to the characters in these vignettes in the conclusions section of each of these chapters. We drew these vignettes from the experiences of a range of older Americans, not from interviews with individual couples. Each pair of vignettes contrasts the pitfalls of handling a particular question poorly with a more successful example. Then each chapter moves to data on broad social patterns. Finally, the concluding section of each chapter relates these broad patterns to the lived experiences portrayed in the vignettes.

Second, particularly as seniors become older and increasingly frail, institutional care in hospitals becomes more common and a nursing facility or another form of long-term care becomes the norm for some. In these situations, a local community social support system can be invaluable. Patients who have such support fare better when they enter hospitals than those without family or friends to foster what Dennis McCullough calls "circles of concern" to help look after them.[21] Patients with community support from family or friends have better chances of receiving what—after reflection—are the treatments they prefer, and they suffer fewer honest mistakes in care and less conscious casualness on the part of professional caregivers in hospitals and nursing facilities and in related situations, including those of assisted living or home-based care. Further, supporting a senior's medical or long-term care experiences often requires a loving, capable adult child or close friend.

For this reason, we have built such people into some of our vignettes, and we encourage seniors to include them in their plans for retirement. For example, an older retiree who lives in New Hampshire and needs a complicated medical procedure may know that the medical care provided to Medicare patients in New Hampshire is as good as it currently gets (New Hampshire is ranked first among the states). But at seventy-eight she no longer has any broadly capable friends and needs the help of her son's family in Louisiana or that of her daughter in Iowa. She ought to think carefully about the capacities of medical care providers near her children in these two states. The retiree would need to have considerable faith in her son to overcome the disadvantage of Louisiana's fiftieth-place ranking on the quality of medical care delivered to Medicare patients. But the advantage of having family community support might reasonably tip the decision on the venue of her operation toward her daughter's location in Iowa (ranked sixth on the scale) so long as suitable medical personnel and facilities for the procedure in question existed nearby.

Third, in the course of our study we characterize states in terms of forty distinct indicators. While these indicators offer a reasonable basis for comparing states in terms of our five questions, they do not exhaust the factors that are important to the lives of individual older Americans. For instance, particular individuals may have good reasons—such as a rich supportive network of family or long-term friends—for ignoring the implications of the state differences that we highlight. Unfortunately, high-quality cross-state data for Home and Community-Based Services forms of long-term care are only beginning to become available. Consequently, our measures for the dimension of SSF pertaining to acquiring accessible, high-quality long-term care rely heavily on nursing facility data.

In chapter 6 we consolidate the indicators used in conjunction with the five issues and analyze why states differ. This chapter represents the explaining-the-world purpose of science. The explanation focuses on two distinct matters. First, we explain the roots of this multidimensional character. We begin by determining state rankings on the five issues areas by using the four basic indicators for each issue that we introduced in chapters 1–5 to form scales of state issue supportiveness. We find that states that are quite supportive of seniors on one issue frequently do quite poorly in comparison to other states with regard to supporting another issue or issues, and we conclude that SSF is a multidimensional concept. We calculate the relations among the dimensions and further validate these distinct dimensions through their relations with indicators we designate as "so-what" variables. These variables represent particularly relevant social outcomes associated with states' support of particular SSF dimensions.[22] Second, we offer an explanation of why certain groups of states differ in their supportiveness of various SSF dimensions. In so doing we draw on the literature of cross-state policy differences that focuses on indigenous state characteristics such as cultural or ideological predisposition, political party competition, material capacity (e.g., state personal income per capita), the dimension of citizen need (e.g., percentage of a state's population eighty-five or older), as well as patterns of interstate emulation (e.g., on the basis of shared circumstances).[23]

The multidimensional character of the SSF concept fits certain behavior patterns among current seniors, and we recommend consideration of these patterns by older Americans generally. For instance, early in retirement it is reasonable for healthy, affluent New England retirees—who are predisposed to do so—to head for the Southeast to enjoy milder winters and yearlong outdoor recreation, as many do. Alternatively, it seems appropriate for healthy, but not so affluent, New England retirees to consider places in West Virginia as more inexpensive, relatively safe and uncongested locations in which they can conserve their resources. Places in Nevada or Arizona fit into a similar sensible rationale for California retirees. But the New England retirees ought to recognize that they are moving from regions that support senior healthiness and high-quality medical and long-term care quite well to regions that are far less supportive of these concerns. So as they continue to age, it might be reasonable for them to consider yet another move back to states that are more supportive of the concerns that generally take on greater prominence in the lives of older retirees. The California retirees confront a more difficult situation in that none of the three states in question—California, Nevada, and Arizona— ranks highly on the average quality of medical or long-term care. So as these retirees age, another move to a new, unfamiliar location—in Colorado, Utah, or Oregon—represents the counterpart of moving back to New England. If California retirees knew this in advance, some of them might alter the location of their initial move to Utah or Oregon.

Cross-state moves often carry high psychological and financial costs. In a better world the federal government would provide older Americans with a national program of long-term care in addition to the existing national program for acute medical care (Medicare). Such a program could reduce differences in long-term care accessibility even if it would not eliminate cross-state variations in quality similar to those we find for Medicare acute care in chapter 5. However, reductions in current cross-state variation in accessibility and quality of long-term care do not appear on the national political horizon. So in the meantime, older residents of many states need to weigh the costs of moving against the benefits of better care in other states. We hope that the analyses in this study will inform older adults about how states support various dimensions of SSF differently and that they will pressure states to improve, particularly in sustaining health and supporting high-quality medical care as well as accessible, high-quality long-term care. We discuss this matter further in chapter 6.

We conclude the study with a brief Epilogue. This portion of our narrative returns to the lived experience portrayed in our vignettes to stress several of our central points and to place them in a broader social context.

1

Contemporary Americans in their late fifties through their sixties, the "young-old," express widely varying orientations toward retirement. In this chapter and the two that follow, we examine state support for three common but sharply distinct broad objectives for retirement: the attainment of fun, of meaning, and of safe affordability. This chapter addresses the first basic issue we presented in the Introduction: where can retirees best find a life of companionship and active recreation? Naturally, people long to live differently. Some Minnesotans actually enjoy ice fishing and would not winter in Florida or Arizona for anything in the world. Others prefer indoor activities such as chess or bridge that can be pursued in a broad range of locales and social circumstances. But still others search for new places to live and different things to do when they "vote with their feet," often seeking mild winters and sunny weather that accommodate numerous outdoor recreational activities.[1] In this chapter we compare the U.S. states on their support of outdoor recreational opportunities and chances for making new friends with whom active young retirees can essentially play. We start by considering the choices of two different couples in vignettes that illustrate both the pitfalls and opportunities retirement poses for those baby boomers aspiring to a "second childhood."

Jerry and Arlene Senter

Jerry and Arlene Senter, seventy-one and sixty-seven, respectively, live near Mason City, Iowa, where they worked and raised two sons. Jerry retired five years ago and wanted to get out of the northern plains, but Arlene felt attached and obligated to her mother, Emma, who lived in a nursing facility nearby, even though she did not recognize Arlene—or anyone else for that matter. They talked about moving to Arizona and transferring Emma to a nursing facility there, but at the time Arlene feared that her mother would not adjust well to new surroundings. She realized that this fear was not rational; her mother would probably not know the difference. But Arlene worried about her own guilt if her mother became more disoriented over time in Arizona. Now, Arlene wonders if she let her mother's condition become an excuse for not squarely facing the uncertainties associated with a serious change in her own life.

Emma died about three years after Jerry retired, but Arlene still felt obligations. Her brother lived in Chicago and her sister in Indianapolis, and they either could not or would not come to help with Emma's estate. Arlene took early retirement and began clearing out her mother's house and settling her estate, which took over a year. Shortly after she finished these lengthy tasks, Arlene took a hard fall on their icy driveway one winter morning and broke a leg. It took her nearly a year to regain her strength and have confidence about walking again. By the time she had recovered physically, she seemed to have lost her interest in going out. She became enthralled with soap operas and game shows.

Jerry helped Arlene clear out her mother's house and with related matters, hoping for more fun and time together at the end. After working in a series of offices for more than forty years, he dreamed of time outdoors in a mild climate, playing golf or fishing. Northern Iowa's winters are long and hard. Jerry tried walking inside during the winter at the local shopping mall, but a group of teenagers who hung out there began following him, harassing him as— putting it as politely as possible—a hapless geezer. They drove him off, and he gave up walking in the winter. Summers in the Mason City area are generally hot and frequently humid. Jerry hates the heat and humidity combination, so he has retreated into the house and television as well.

Most of the friends that Jerry and Arlene acquired through child rearing, community activities, and several jobs over the years have now retired and moved. While a couple of them are "snowbirds," living in Arizona or south Texas in the winter and returning to Iowa for the summers, most have simply moved away to different locations in Florida, Arizona, New Mexico, and Utah. Jerry and Arlene rarely see or communicate with these friends except through yearly Christmas cards.

So Jerry and Arlene often feel lonely and isolated. They spend much of their time cooped up in their house. Even when they go out, they rarely join—or even see—friends; mostly they go out to run errands, go to church, or see a physician. Their sons, who live in Pennsylvania and Colorado, call occasionally but visit only once a year. Jerry and Arlene could, of course, move now. But they cannot seem to find the motivation or energy. Several years of progressively more limited activity and social interaction have left them both feeling less adventurous than they were when Jerry retired, and they were rather risk adverse even then. They seem to have aged more in the past five years than in the previous couple of decades. They accept their current lives, and they cannot find the initiative and energy to pursue new possibilities.

About a month ago Jerry suffered a stroke, likely caused by high blood pressure, which he neglected because he did not want to take medication. He currently receives rehabilitative physical therapy, and he will probably recover use of his leg and all or most of the motion in his right arm. But he and Arlene have pretty much lost the freshness and hope that once infused their dreams about retirement. They are not all that old, but they fear that they are simply waiting—on the northern Iowa prairie—for whatever happens next.

Many of us can probably think of people who are in situations similar to Jerry and Arlene's. They have dealt with some tough breaks: Emma's dementia and Arlene's broken leg. They faced circumstances beyond their control, but they also made choices that lacked foresight and initiative. After all, most of their friends got out of Iowa in retirement and now enjoy life more fully.

Art and Karen Munro

Now consider how one such couple, Art and Karen Munro, constructed a more encouraging retirement. Art and Karen, both sixty-seven, also spent their adult lives living and working in the Mason City area. But they looked forward to retirement, began early to look around, and took off as soon as they could.

Karen's mother, Janet, needed help with long-term care, but two years before they retired Karen worked out a sharing arrangement with her younger sister, Sandra. Janet lived in a nursing facility near Mason City, and Karen visited her several times a week to keep her company and check on the quality of her care. Then when Art and Karen retired, they transferred Janet to a nursing facility in Denver, Colorado, where Sandra lives. Karen worried about this transfer, but Sandra actually welcomed the chance to spend more time with their mother before the latter died a few months ago.

During their last few years at work Art and Karen became increasingly excited about finding a new home—a place preferably warmer and drier where they could both spend time outdoors much of the year. Their local librarian showed them how to explore different areas on the Internet. As their next step, they vacationed during their last several years of work in a number of possible communities to get the feel of the places. They fell in love with a small town just west of Roswell, New Mexico, in the foothills of the Sacramento Mountains (a southern outcropping of the Rockies). The area offers mild winters because of its southern location and mild summers as a result of its altitude. Area lakes and streams afford boating and fishing opportunities in a scenic setting, and golf courses, tennis courts, public lands with hiking trails, and other recreational opportunities abound.

Art and Karen contacted a Roswell realtor immediately. She kept an eye out for houses within their modest budget. When Art and Karen retired within weeks of each other, they already had a buyer for their Iowa house, and they bought their small but cozy house in New Mexico within the month. They spent several weeks in Iowa, packing and attending a series of good-bye parties with friends, including Jerry and Arlene. Then they moved to New Mexico and began a new life.

This new life has worked out wonderfully for them. They love the New Mexico scenery and have made a number of friends among other newcomers to the Roswell area. Art and Karen each have Social Security, and Art receives a small private pension, so their annual retirement is just over 60 percent of the median U.S. household income (slightly below fifty thousand dollars), or about thirty thousand dollars. To date, they live very comfortably without dipping into their modest savings. The Roswell area attracts a number of people from other places, so Art and Karen play golf, share dinners, and go to church with other young retirees they find interesting. They both love their new small boat. Karen joined a local crafts group and now makes pottery in the covered work area at the back of their home. Art fishes and frequently goes bird-watching in the national forest.

Art and Karen host friends for dinner a couple of evenings a week, and friends invite them out at least that often. They rarely miss their life in Iowa; they are too busy and involved. For them, this is an almost ideal retirement. If they remain healthy and active, they can reasonably expect to enjoy another dozen or so good years. So thankfully, Karen is pretty health conscious. She makes appointments for periodic checkups and flu shots for each of them and monitors Art's blood pressure and medication. Currently, no cloud looms on the horizon. Art and Karen are not waiting for the other shoe to drop; they're living a full, active, and socially engaged life in a beautiful natural environment. Their Christmas cards say, "We Love It Here!"

Retirement as a "Second Childhood"

After World War II, many Americans gradually came to expect a leisure-filled retirement to do what they wanted, where and with whom they chose. In this view, retirement amounts to a sort of second childhood, free from the routines associated with school and work. The declining portion of retirees holding secure defined-benefit pensions threatens the viability of this common American ideal for a good number, but it continues to be a reality for others. This reality carries some subtle hazards. For instance, however appealing playing may initially appear, many mature adults want more meaning out of life. We recognize this and focus on it in chapter 2. Additionally, without the discipline of the labor market some retirees do not make the effort to play actively or socially and thus become sedentary and isolated, as Jerry and Arlene have, and these conditions often play havoc with both the quality and quantity of life. Prior planning can help keep these hazards at bay. In contrast to Jerry and Arlene, who began talking about changing their life after Jerry retired, Art and Karen found a location that offered the activities and social interaction they wanted and created a plan to achieve what they desired prior to retiring.

For Art and Karen, the move has worked out well—at least for their current needs. Some people cannot face a long-distance move at the outset of retirement, perhaps because of the separation from family and established friendships that this transition entails. Others may fear the difficulty of making new friends at this stage of their lives. As we will see in later chapters, even Art and Karen may eventually have to consider another move, possibly back to Iowa, as their health deteriorates and their needs for high-quality medical and accessible, high-quality long-term care grow. But with luck, Art and Karen will enjoy more than a decade of far greater quality of life than will Jerry and Arlene. Their recreational lifestyle keeps them active and socially engaged.

Assessing a State's Support of Outdoor Activity and a Recreational Lifestyle

States offer different levels and types of outdoor recreational opportunities. We assess four central indicators of this supportiveness: climate, retiree social support, retiree capacities, and the attractiveness of state recreational facilities. We support our discussion of how states vary on these indicators with maps (figures) in this and each of the following five chapters. Tables of the data on which the maps are based appear in the Appendix (tables A.1 through A.7).

State Climate

We consider climate first because older Americans often seek sunshine and warmth as a backdrop for their outdoor living and recreation. Multiple options exist for measuring state climates. We think that what most older persons with the goal of an outdoor recreational lifestyle are looking for is mild (particularly in winter), sunny weather. Generally, and up to a point, lower humidity is preferable to higher. So we begin by comparing states on mean annual daily temperature and number of days with clear sky. Virtually all state climates vary internally on both factors, so we use a weighted average of variation in the two elements considered as equal contributors. Then we add or subtract a more modest amount to the temperature-and-sun score based on varying levels of humidity. As figure 1.1 illustrates, all the states that score highly on our climate index are, to no one's surprise, southern, from California and Arizona in the West to South Carolina in the East.[2] The "Sunbelt" is aptly named. Northern, especially northeastern and north-central, states score poorly on our climate index.[3] Many of the states in the bottom ranks are well know for their gray and icy winters that stretch from October to April.

Sunshine feels good on our bodies, enhances the beauty of the world around us, and often raises our spirits. Research indicates that people feel less depressed when they spend more time outside in the sun.[4] Warmth is good up to a point. However, states with relatively mild winters can be blisteringly hot in the summer. So we count off for the sort of mean annual daily temperatures associated with the summers that states such as Arizona are known for, but give these states credit for their generally mild winters. Additionally, we consider two caveats. First, regions of some western—and particularly West Coast—states enjoy, by virtue of altitude or other factors such as on-shore Pacific breezes, warm but not sizzling temperatures in summer. Second, generally speaking, states differ more on the coldness of their winters than on the heat of their summers. Maine is generally far colder than Florida throughout a long winter, but summer heat differences tend to be more modest.

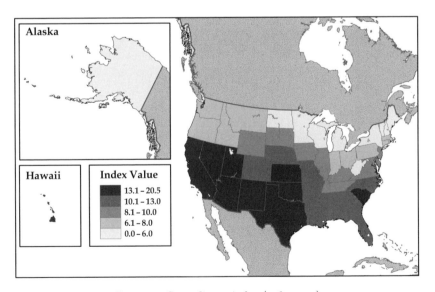

Figure 1.1: State climate index (1961–1990)

Senior Companionship

The retirees who migrate long distances to sun and warmth are dispropor-
tionately relatively young (as retirees go)—late fifties through the sixties. They
commonly share two other characteristics as well: affluence and spouses or
other partners. These couples frequently look to share recreational experiences
with others. A number of outdoor activities (e.g., tennis) require another
person or persons and, while other activities may not be inherently social, our
experience is that generally people golf or go hiking, hunting, fishing, and even
bird-watching with others. These others do not necessarily come from their
own households, but having a housemate who shares—or at least indulges—
one's interests facilitates the activities. One spouse may encourage or prod the
other to engage in physical activities, and the latter may do the same for the
former with respect to social activities. So, these individuals have an advantage over retirees who live alone in participating in many outdoor recreational
activities. Couples also tend to have higher household incomes and greater net
worth than singles. Thus our second indicator estimates the proportion of a
state's senior population that is at least available for couples' activities: the proportion of a state's sixty-five-or-older population who do *not* live alone. If a
state really supports outdoor activity and a recreational lifestyle, we should find
that its population—some acquired recently from other states (more later)—
ought to reflect a relatively low rate of older state residents living alone.

Figure 1.2 offers support for this contention in that states that are known
as recreational lifestyle destinations for mobile retirees (e.g., Hawaii, Florida,
Arizona, and Utah) maintain the largest percentages of seniors having household partners.[5] On the other end of the scale, states in which the fewest seniors
have household partners, we find north-central states such as the Dakotas,
Nebraska, and Wisconsin. These are states that—as we shall see shortly—young
retirees leave in large numbers.

Critical Mass of Active Seniors

Having a "critical mass" of active retirees is a prerequisite for supporting some
recreational opportunities, such as the golf course–centered housing develop-
ments that seem to pop up everywhere in Arizona and Florida. So the third
indicator that we use for assessing a state's capacity for supporting outdoor
activity and a recreational lifestyle seeks to estimate the proportion of a state's
senior population that is capable of engaging in outdoor recreational activity.
We approach this task in two ways. The first is to add the number of sixty-five-
or-older persons who reside in a state's nursing facilities (per one hundred

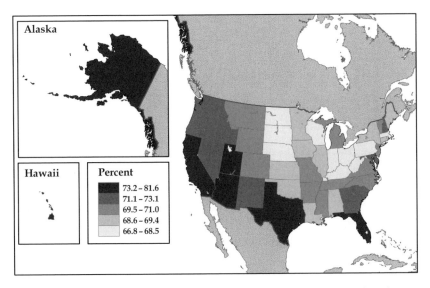

Figure 1.2: State residents sixty-five or older who do not live alone (2005)

state residents sixty-five or older) to the number of sixty-five-or-older persons who participate in a state's Medicaid Home and Community-Based Services aged/disabled waiver program (per one hundred state residents sixty-five or older). These latter persons receive assistance with activities of daily living in their own homes, adult day care centers, congregate residential facilities other than nursing homes (frequently referred to as residential care facilities), or assisted living complexes. Then we subtract this total from one hundred to derive an estimate of what percentage of each state's sixty-five-or-older residents are at least capable of (not disabled from) pursuing outdoor recreational activities. This estimate draws only on persons who have been thoroughly vetted for disability, so it produces a conservative accounting of a state's older residents available for following any active form of recreational lifestyle. In all the states, many noninstitutionalized seniors whose status remains below the horizon of state long-term care officials are unable to follow active physical pursuits.[6]

Fortunately, the Census Bureau surveys the American population in sufficient depth to make annual estimates of the number of older residents in each state who classify themselves into one of five disability categories but seek no publicly financed professional help with their limitations. So a second way we estimate the proportion of a state's seniors who are eligible, so to speak, for pursuing outdoor activity and a recreational lifestyle is to draw on these data. Unfortunately, these data come from ordinary citizens' self-reports of their conditions; there is no vetting by outside professionals. Additionally, some of the disabilities the Census Bureau asks citizens about involve matters, such as hearing loss, that would not disqualify a person from a recreational lifestyle. Thus a person who wore a hearing aid, but who was otherwise quite fit, would likely be categorized among the disabled. Accordingly, these data are apt to produce a generous estimate of the proportion of a state's elderly population whose disabilities disqualify them from joining other seniors in a range of outdoor physical activities.

To solve this dilemma of having two estimates—one quite conservative, the other excessively liberal—we build our indicator on the average of the two estimates for each state. Figure 1.3, based on this average, supports the validity of this approach. The states with the highest proportions of sixty-five-or-older persons capable of pursuing outdoor activity are, once again, the states quite famous for their support of outdoor activities (e.g., Arizona, Florida, Nevada, Utah, and Hawaii).[7] However, this time the states with the lowest proportion of seniors capable in this sense are not northern, as were the states at the bottoms of the rankings in figures 1.1 and 1.2, but rather south central. As we explain in chapter 4, states in this region tend to support the healthiness of their populations poorly and offer Medicare beneficiaries relatively low quality medical care—characteristics that fit with their exhibiting exceptionally high levels of disability among seniors. Nonetheless, for affluent and healthy young retirees looking for fun in the sun, surely one of the things "the matter with Kansas"

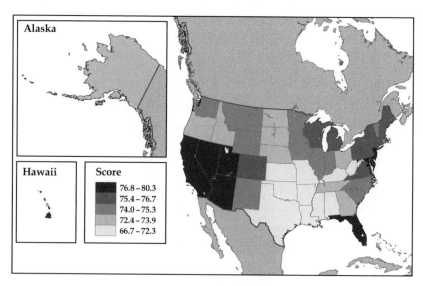

Figure 1.3: State residents sixty-five or older who are not disabled (2005)

would be its rank (forty-second) in the proportion of its older residents physically prepared to engage in outdoor recreation.[8]

State Recreational Facilities

Our fourth indicator of a state's support of outdoor activity and a recreational lifestyle assesses the recreational opportunities a state furnishes, using the proportion of a state's gross state product (GSP) attributable to a particular form of tourism (overnight stays and round-trip travel of one hundred miles or more). This measure of the significance of recreational opportunities to a state's economy gives us an indication of the attractiveness of these opportunities, both to state residents and to persons from other states.

Figure 1.4 reveals state rankings on the attractiveness of a state's recreational resources to state residents and out-of-state tourists.[9] Once again, those states that excel at attracting young, healthy retirees include those western states for which domestic tourism looms relatively large in GSP: Nevada, Hawaii, Montana, Wyoming, and New Mexico. Florida also appears among the top five, and other southeastern Sunbelt states fill out most of the other top-tier ranks.

While the states that rank highly in tourism as a percentage of GSP share recreational opportunities that attract both tourists and young retirees, they also tend to have relatively modest economies overall. Of the states in the top-ten ranks of domestic tourism as a percentage of GSP (in descending order,

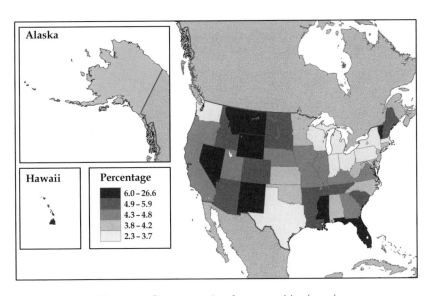

Figure 1.4: State recreational opportunities (2004)

Nevada, Hawaii, Montana, Florida, Wyoming, Mississippi, New Mexico, Vermont, Louisiana, and South Carolina) only Florida ranks in the top half of states in GSP size. States with low ranks on domestic tourism as a percentage of GSP include states such as New York, which attracts large numbers of tourists, though a smaller proportion for enjoying outdoor recreational activities, but has an extensive, diversified economy in which tourism barely registers.

Overall

State rankings on some indicators employed in later chapters can be changed through human motivation and effort, for example, the quality of medical care delivered to Medicare beneficiaries in a state. But differences between the states on at least a couple of the four central indicators introduced above arise from factors neither state officials nor the population can alter. In contrast to Arizona, for instance, people in Connecticut suffer cold, dark winters with slippery pavements. Thus both tourists and healthy, financially secure, recently retired migrants choose Arizona rather than Connecticut as a locale for supporting outdoor recreational activities. The people of Connecticut could more easily make the mighty Connecticut River run uphill than gain ground on Arizona in these regards. Similarly, Nevada relies on tourism to support its current population, and it is difficult to imagine how the state might emulate New York in quickly diversifying its economy to any significant degree.

Additional Indicators

The four factors that we introduced in the preceding section serve as strong indicators of a state's ability to support recreational lifestyles involving outdoor activities, but now we want to consider three other indicators related in different ways to this consideration: the patterns of younger and older retirees moving to and leaving the various states and the relative frequency of senior suicide among the states.

Net State Migration Among Persons Sixty-five to Seventy-four

Seniors vote with their feet on the popularity of the American states as retirement havens. In chapter 6 we employ a state's net in-migration among persons sixty-five to seventy-four to help to validate the four variables in the previous section as predictors of a state's support of outdoor activity and a recreational lifestyle. For the moment, we will limit ourselves to a discussion of figure 1.5.[10]

This map is based on immigration rates derived by (1) subtracting a state's out-migration for a particular age group from its in-migration for the same age group, producing net migration for this group; (2) dividing this net migration by the state's population for the same age group; and (3) multiplying by 1,000 for ease of data presentation. The states that attract the greatest number of incoming young retiree migrants (as a proportion of the state's population in this same age group) are familiar from the indicators that we discussed in the previous section. Nevada, Arizona, and Florida are the top three, so they deserve their reputation as playgrounds for the "young-old." Other southern—particularly southwestern and southeastern—states appear in the top ranks in figure 1.5.

Familiar northern states fill the low ranks in figure 1.5, ranging from Alaska in the West to Connecticut in the East. But northeastern and north-central states, including Iowa, which the Munros left and in which the Senters remain trapped, predominate. For several of the states with low ranks in figure 1.5—Connecticut, New York, and New Jersey—concerns for reducing cost of living and congestion add themselves to the goal of avoiding cold, gray, icy conditions during the winter months as grounds for out-migration among young retirees. These three states cost more to live in than many others, and their extensive urban areas are densely populated, creating congestion problems, even if they are close to great museums, theaters, and other cultural attractions. In chapter 3 we focus on these as alternative incentives for leaving these states (and similar ones in other parts of the country, e.g., California).

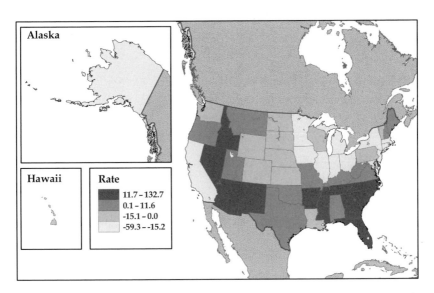

Figure 1.5: Net state in-migration of persons sixty-five to seventy-four (1995–2000)

Net State Migration Among Persons
Eighty-five or Older

Figure 1.5 reports on relatively young retirees. We now turn to still older Americans. Do retirees stay in their new locations in western and southeastern states once they have aged a decade or two? Figure 1.6 deals with this question with rates calculated in the same manner as explained above. Although the data on which figures 1.5 and 1.6 are based (see tables A.5 and A.6, respectively) correlate at 0.36, showing that states' rates of migration for the sixty-five-to-seventy-four cohort resemble their rates for the eighty-five-or-older cohort, interesting shifts appear among some states. (Correlation coefficients range from 1.00 [indicating a perfect positive relationship with the two variables rising and falling together] to –1.00 [signifying a perfect negative relationship in which, as one variable increases the other decreases and vice versa].) Some, though not all, of the northern states with high rates of out-migration among younger retirees turn positive with net in-migration among the older retirees. The most extreme example of this is Alaska, which ranks at the bottom in figure 1.5 but virtually at the top in figure 1.6. Alaska loses younger retirees in droves, but it appears that a sizeable proportion of these émigrés—who are still alive at eight-five—return to the state.[11] Colorado, New Hampshire, Maine, Maryland, Washington, Wyoming, and other states offer similar, though not so dramatic, examples of this pattern. Later chapters develop some likely explanations of

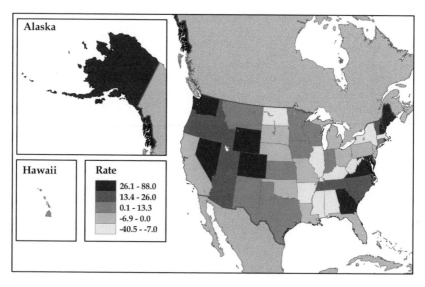

Figure 1.6: Net state in-migration of persons eighty-five or older (1995–2000)

this combination of migrating south among younger retirees and returning north among the advanced elderly.

State Senior Suicide Rate

Figure 1.7 compares rates of suicide among persons sixty-five or older across states. Seniors have the highest suicide rates of any age group, and theory suggests that social isolation, low income, and illness contribute to these high rates.[12] Still, particularly for low-population states, the total numbers remain small and tend to vary from year to year. So figure 1.7 is based on the average of the years 2000, 2001, and 2002. The rate represents the number of suicides per one thousand sixty-five-or-older state residents.[13] These rates arise from a number of factors, including both individual traits and characteristics of individuals' social environments.[14] Nonetheless, it is hard to ignore that several of the states with high rates of elderly suicide also offer enticing climates. Further, only modest percentages of their senior populations either live alone or suffer disability. Additionally, these states provide extensive outdoor recreational activities and attract young retirees. In contrast, states with low rates of senior suicide tend to rank on the opposite end of the continua on all five of these factors.

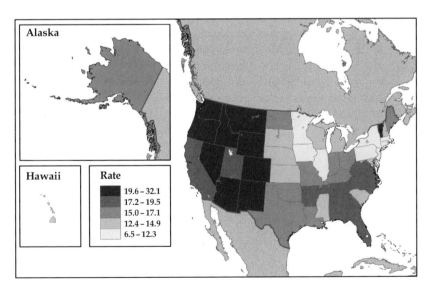

Figure 1.7: State sixty-five or older suicides per 1,000 sixty-five or older state residents (average 2000–2002)

Positive correlations between state elderly suicide rates and these five factors associated with a state's support of outdoor activity and a recreational lifestyle illustrate the "ecological fallacy." Without individual-level data, we do not know to what degree the sixty-five-or-older persons who are committing suicide in a state are also people who moved to the state early in retirement. However, the correlations offer food for thought. Do retirees who migrate across states to find a second childhood experience a sufficiently meaningful, supported, and fulfilling life? Or might they discover playing away one's life somewhat vacuous, fostering either the anomie or fatalism to which Durkheim attributed two of the four roots of suicide?[15] Certainly, our next chapter suggests that some seniors look for more than just relaxation and fun in their retirement.

Conclusions: Back to the Senters and the Munros

Remember how disillusioned Jerry and Arlene felt in contrast to the joy Art and Karen found after they moved. For those whose predisposition, health, and financial position point them toward seeking a recreational lifestyle in retirement (and Art and Karen are pretty average financially, but they are healthy, and they plan well), several Western states support this goal. A number of southeastern states, particularly Florida, also have much to offer in this regard. Art and Karen moved to one of these western states to find a mild climate, scenic landscapes, a broad range of recreational opportunities, an inexpensive and uncongested social environment, and other newcomers with whom they could make new friends fairly easily. Given their dreams and goals, it is no wonder that Art and Karen are happy. Their success in carving out a delightful retirement can be duplicated by many others. With advance planning others can find similarly encouraging, though likely different, realizations of a recreational lifestyle distinct from that of the Munros.

Characteristically, northern states—particularly in the Northeast and Upper Midwest—support year-round outdoor activities and a recreational lifestyle less well than many southern states. Jerry and Arlene, for instance, feel trapped on the northern Great Plains. In this location, they face cold, gray weather and icy pavements in winter and hot, humid summers, all discouraging them from leading the life that they had imagined retirement would offer. Further, they are pretty isolated socially at least in part because many of their friends chose to leave for more encouraging retirement venues. We empathize with their plight and hope that others draw on our suggestions to plan—prior to or very early in retirement—in order to avoid their predicament.

Young retirees in reasonably good health, having adequate financial resources and a willingness to move, can easily find recreational opportunities, as figure 1.5 illustrates. But the choice of moving to New Mexico that brought Art and Karen highly rewarding years may not work well for the entirety of their retirement. When Art or Karen experience serious deterioration in their health, they will likely be well served to move again. Only three (Colorado, Hawaii, and Utah—see chapter 4) of the ten states ranked at the top in supporting outdoor activities and a recreational lifestyle also appear in the top ten positions when we consider supporting healthy seniors and high-quality medical care. So states that serve the needs of many young and healthy retirees often lack high-quality services central to the needs of older retirees. For example, New Mexico, where Art and Karen now live, ranks near the top of states in its support of recreational lifestyle opportunities, but it ranks around the middle of the states with regard to the healthiness of its senior population and the quality of medical care delivered to Medicare patients.

Several western states, particularly Nevada and Arizona, that rank high on recreational opportunities offer much lower levels of senior health and quality of medical care. Yet they continue to attract a large number of those eighty-five or older from other states. However, the health and medical care shortcomings of these states suggest that such moves are often shortsighted. Older retirees may make the moves unwittingly—as Jean's parents did—and discover the downside only after their health deteriorates, making a subsequent move to a state offering better medical care extremely difficult or simply unrealistic. Our research suggests that the young retirees who follow the example of Art and Karen and move for recreational opportunities are generally well advised to recognize the potential drawbacks of their new state of residence in time and plan effectively once again to move to another state that better serves their changing needs as they continue to age later in retirement.

2

MAKING MEANINGFUL CONTRIBUTIONS AND
FINDING SUPPORTIVE COMMUNITIES

To remain healthy and happy, most older people continue to need meaning in their lives and social involvement that keeps them connected with others.[1] Elders who retire from their normal full-time employment often miss the structure, identity, companionship or community, and sense of shared purpose that employment can—but does not always—provide.[2] Some seek part-time employment or start their own businesses. And, as we discussed in the previous chapter, many retirees turn to social recreational activities outdoors in mild climates and make friends golfing, fishing, or hiking. But working for pay and leisure activities do not always provide the meaning or connections that older persons want. When their lives lack activities that they find meaningful, older persons may become socially disengaged, and—as we suggested in the last chapter—suicide rates may escalate.

About one-quarter of older citizens make acquiring meaning and social support through civic involvement and community attachment a central objective of their retirement.[3] Civic involvement denotes individuals' memberships in churches, charities, and related civic organizations as well as time spent in volunteer activities associated with these formal organizations such as working on community projects like those of Habitat for Humanity. These activities enable their participants to help other people, and the vast majority of participants (78 percent) say that this is their primary objective and an important source of meaning in their lives.[4] Research on civic involvement often focuses on how these activities build and sustain the social fabric of communities. Our interest here is more on the value and meaning that being involved brings to older persons.

Community attachment includes these secondary-group activities, but primary associations with others are more central to this concept. Some of these personal attachments arise, of course, through the activities of civic involvement, but they often also entail family members and friendships that predate those acquired through community organizations. Many people understand the words *my community* in terms of a collection of other people with whom they share experiences and affection. This sense of belonging grows with home ownership and length of residence, but the breadth of personal networks and the amount, type, and intensity of involvement with their members appear to be crucial.

Many older persons—63 percent in a recent survey—volunteer regularly to find meaning and support.[5] The most common outlets for these efforts are religious organizations, but many seniors support other organizations by raising funds, organizing and running events, making phone calls, and helping with meals and transportation. Often older people help their families, particularly in caring for grandchildren. They also frequently assist friends who are sick or who have disabilities. Their own accounts indicate that volunteering provides a sense of shared purpose, companionship, and attachment to their communities.

The AARP's recent survey of older Americans, as published in *Beyond 50.05 Survey,* finds that nearly four-fifths of the seniors sampled felt involved with and attached to their communities. But the slightly over one-fifth that fails to share this feeling represents a slight increase from a previous survey of about a decade earlier.[6] Sociologists and gerontologists find that, as civic involvement and community attachment increase, so too do satisfaction with life, overall well-being, and even physical health. For instance, as we move from those who say they are "not very attached" to their communities to others who say they are "very attached," the proportion of people who say they are "satisfied with their lives" rises from 52 to 88 percent.[7] As Aristotle pointed out, humans are—for the most part, at least—social animals, and most need regular and meaningful social interaction.

In this chapter we provide data on the amount and intensity of older persons' civic involvement and community attachment across the American states. We also explain how aspects of societal context influence the level of civic involvement and community attachment. Finally, we show how societal context, civic involvement, and community attachment collectively contribute to distinctive state political cultures. These cultures vary in the degree to which they support the need for meaning and community. As in the previous chapter, we use a contrasting pair of vignettes to help in showing how and why these differences occur.

Arnie and Muriel Hestir

Arnie and Muriel Hestir are both in their early seventies. Arnie retired more than a decade ago from a small factory located near Atlanta, Georgia, which manufactured vehicle components under contract to Chrysler Corporation. He took reduced Social Security benefits at sixty-two. Muriel hung on for another few years, working long hours as a receptionist/secretary for a pair of attorneys in order to get full Social Security benefits at sixty-five.

The home they have owned for nearly forty years was once in a solidly middle-class neighborhood of owner-occupied houses, but many of their former neighbors have moved away, and the new absentee landlords now rent mostly to short-term tenants. Arnie and Muriel try to be friendly to their new neighbors, but the young struggling families have scarce time to reciprocate, and they have little in common with the Hestirs. Arnie and Muriel feel increasingly isolated in their neighborhood. They would like to move, but their modest retirement incomes and the declining value of their house represent serious limitations. They have not been terribly ambitious about looking, but they have yet to find a viable alternative. They see themselves as stuck in a declining neighborhood and tend to retreat increasingly into their own home.

Their children—a son and a daughter—seem to be doing pretty well, and they both live in the Atlanta area. But they each have several children, and their time, energy, and material resources go into their children rather than being diverted toward Arnie and Muriel.

The Hestirs no longer have any friends to speak of outside their neighborhood, and this increases their sense of social marginalization. Arnie lost track of most of the people he had worked with seven years ago when Chrysler shifted to an overseas supplier. Arnie's former company had folded at this point and several of his closest friends left the Atlanta area, seeking better opportunities elsewhere. Muriel was one of two office assistants hired by the law partners, and she never made close friends at work. The attorneys were clearly above her social level, their clients paid little attention to the office staff, and she never connected well with the series of younger women in the other staff position.

Neither Arnie nor Muriel has ever been much involved with formal organizations apart from their jobs. Neither is a natural "joiner," and they even became less involved with their church as work and child rearing increasingly occupied their time. In the past, they had relied on family and friends from the neighborhood or Arnie's work, but for practical purposes these persons have now virtually disappeared from their lives.

Arnie and Muriel appreciate each other's company, but they increasingly feel isolated and lonely. Further, they see no clear purpose to their lives apart from occasional visits from their grandchildren. They seem to simply be hanging on from day to day. They have virtually no civic involvement or community attachment. They dropped their daily newspaper as a cost-saving measure when they retired, and their knowledge of local issues and events comes largely from snippets on the television evening news. They even watch the news with decreasing frequency, as they do not recognize it as having much relevance to their lives. Their immediate neighborhood has changed so much that it has become the "other," rather than theirs. This scares them as they age and become more vulnerable in various ways. When they do occasionally encounter acquaintances their age—out shopping or at a movie theater—the others seem as withdrawn as Arnie and Muriel themselves, and little mutual interest develops among them. In short, they feel almost completely estranged from the social world around them. Decisions affecting their lives (e.g., the decline of their neighborhood) rest in the hands of others; and they have few resources for improving their current precarious social position. They fear that this situation will worsen as they age, yet they despair about doing anything that would improve their circumstances.

They are increasingly socially disengaged and frightened. Their isolation and fear has led to fatalism and depression, compounding declining health. They recognize that if either of them had a health crisis, their current situation would not provide the connection and support they would need. But they have no idea what they would do. It is no wonder they have so little attachment to the strange and forbidding social environment that they perceive enveloping them.

Nancy Currier

We might expect a single woman like Nancy Currier to face an even more distressing social environment than that of the Hestirs. Nancy is sixty-eight; she retired about two years ago. Her husband, Alex, suffered from the early onset of serious dementia, and for nearly twelve years, until his death three years ago, this was a serious drain on their combined material resources as well as on Nancy's emotional and physical energy. A demanding full-time job and a cognitively disabled spouse left Nancy little time to develop and sustain friendships. Her only child, a daughter, had emigrated to the United Kingdom in the 1980s and developed a reputation as a commercial photographer, leaving Nancy essentially on her own for years.

Nancy grew up in Minnesota and earned a Master of Social Work at the University of Minnesota in 1962. For the last twenty years that she worked, she was a midlevel regional administrator in the Missouri Department of Health and Senior Services, working in Springfield. On her retirement Nancy took a step that separated her from virtually everyone she knew: she moved back to Minneapolis, where she had gone to college. So with her spouse deceased and her daughter in Great Britain, and her having moved interstate to a major metropolitan area where she knows virtually no one, is Nancy's life devoid of meaning and does she long for community? Not at all!

Nancy settled in a modest Minneapolis condominium and began volunteering at the Minneapolis office of the Area Agency on Aging (AAA).[8] Because of her work in Springfield with the new prescription drug coverage being added to Medicare, she had become reasonably well versed in the bewildering complexities of this innovation. She realized that many older Americans would need help understanding how to parse the program's intricacies so as to enroll effectively. Nancy not only volunteered with the AAA as a speaker for interested groups on this topic; she offered to initiate contact with groups on the AAA's mailing list to inquire if their members were interested in hearing her presentation.

In a short time Nancy was giving presentations three or four days a week and had a string of these events scheduled weeks into the future. She found, as she expected, that individual women frequently came up to ask questions after her presentations. Some of these women were her age and inquiring about their own situations, but others were younger, trying to help elderly parents figure out what to do with regard to Medicare prescription coverage. Out of every twenty or so women whom Nancy encountered in this way, she made friends with one, and a few of these connections have developed into sustaining friendships.

Nancy's civic involvement enables her to help large numbers of people understand more clearly how to enroll effectively in the Medicare prescription drug program, and she derives considerable satisfaction from providing this help. Occasionally, she gets up feeling tired and achy, particularly in her knees, but she actually feels better after one of her presentations. For her, this civic involvement has become an important purpose or reason for living. And this very activity—which brings her into contact with a large number of people— has provided her with community attachment, a group of good friends, some her age, others younger.

Finding Meaning and Fostering Community

In terms of a meaningful life and a community of supportive friends, Nancy Currier enjoys what the Hestirs lack. In part, the differences between her circumstances and theirs derive from personal characteristics. Nancy likely has more relevant expertise and seems to be more imaginative about applying it. But, as we shall show, the contrast between Nancy and the Hestirs arises as well from differences in their social contexts. Georgia and Minnesota differ on the social distances that separate varying socioeconomic strata, both among the population generally and among older persons. This difference contributes to variation in the degree to which the two states' populations, and particularly their seniors, display civic involvement and community attachment. These latter differences, in turn, culminate in sharply different cultures, one sustaining relatively doctrinaire, elite or top-down directives to a frequently disengaged and compliant population, the other fostering relative pragmatic egalitarianism drawing on the support of numerous grassroots initiatives. Although states differ sharply in the provision of meaningful volunteer opportunities, the Corporation for National and Community Service (http://nationalservice.gov)—which sponsors Senior Corps, among other organizations—represents a convenient source for information about a portion of the opportunities available in each state.

Assessing a State's Support of Meaningful Volunteering and Supportive Communities

Putnam's Social Capital

We begin with a measure of state populations' general civic involvement and community attachment. If, as we suggest, the populations of some states are generally better prepared to be actively involved in and attached to their communities, then there ought to be evidence of different levels of these activities among states. To test this hypothesis, we turn first to a measure of the civic involvement and community attachment levels of a state's general population: Robert Putnam's index of social capital. Putman initially developed his state-level index in conjunction with his popular *Bowling Alone*.[9] He uses the term "social capital" to denote activities similar to those that we have termed *civic involvement* and *community attachment* and that collectively are sometimes referred to as *civic engagement*. Putnam's initial measure drew on data spanning nearly the quarter century prior to 2000. We draw on his updated measure, the Comprehensive Social Capital Index II. This index includes several categories of civic involvement and community attachment: attending club meetings, working on community projects, entertaining friends at home, volunteering time to nonprofit groups, and spending time visiting with friends.[10]

As in chapter 1, we find a pattern of regional differences. Figure 2.1 reveals a North-South distinction for Putnam's social capital index.[11] So states in New England, the Upper Midwest, and the Northwest rank near the top of the scale, and states across the southern United States rank near the bottom. On average, then, the residents of many northern states are more actively engaged in volunteer efforts in their communities than are their counterparts in most southern

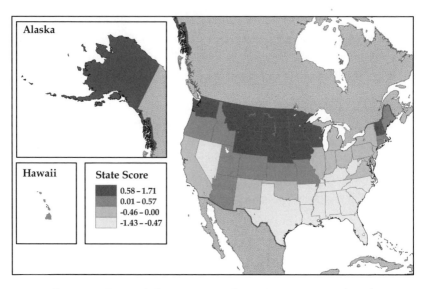

Figure 2.1: Putnam's Comprehensive Social Capital II Index (2000)

States within the map legend:

Alaska

Hawaii

State Score
- 0.58 – 1.71
- 0.01 – 0.57
- -0.46 – 0.00
- -1.43 – -0.47

states. Similarly, northern residents are more thoroughly attached to other members of their communities through social activities than are the residents of southern states.

Percentage of Sixty-five-or-Older Persons Voting in the 2004 Presidential Election

Putnam's index covers a state's population generally. It would be good to have a complementary indicator focused on the sixty-five-or-older population. This sort of information exists for elections, and presidential elections generally elicit the highest rates of participation. Accordingly, our data come from the 2004 presidential election, the latest one for which state-level, age-specific data are available. If, as we contend, the populations—with special attention now on older persons—of northern states are better positioned to engage in civic activity than their counterparts in the southern United States, then we should find that they participate more thoroughly in elections.

The North-South pattern is not as clear as in figure 2.1, but it is still present in figure 2.2.[12] The percentage of a state's older population voting in this election correlates positively and statistically significantly with Putnam's social capital index at 0.61. States in New England, the Upper Midwest, and the Northwest again rank at the top of the spectrum, although a few states in each of these regions have slipped downward in the ranking. In this regard, New York exhibits a surprisingly low rate of voting among older persons. With the exceptions of Alabama, Louisiana, and New Mexico, states in the South rank near the bottom of the spectrum of electoral participation among seniors.

Income Equality

How do these state and regional differences in civic involvement and community attachment arise? In the 1960s political scientists discovered that narrower divisions among social strata or classes facilitate increases in activities similar to those that we are calling civic involvement and community attachment among a society's citizens.[13] One common means of measuring these divisions is the Gini index of income inequality. This index measures deviations from an equal distribution, so a higher reading indicates more income inequality. We have reversed the Gini scale for the states on which figure 2.3 is based, so darker shades indicate greater income equality. This index, then, can be understood as an indicator of the degree to which a state's general population is positioned or prepared for civic engagement of various sorts. If state income inequality is high, sharp status differentials are apt to create different lives and greater social distances among the population. This tends to hinder constructive interaction across social strata and may foster a situation in which those at the top of the

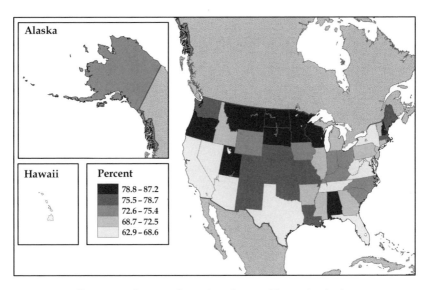

Figure 2.2: State residents sixty-five or older voting in the
2004 presidential election

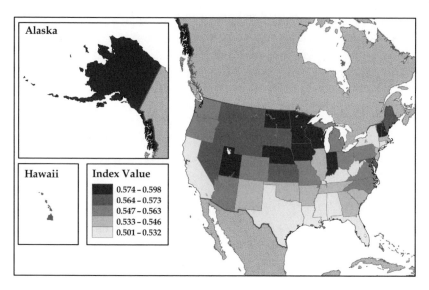

Figure 2.3: State income equality (Gini index reversed) (1999)

socioeconomic hierarchy dominate while those below comply passively, but perhaps resentfully. On the other hand, if state income inequality is relatively low, then members of various social strata are able to interact more equally and—generally under these circumstances—more productively in terms of producing public and private activities that serve the interests of a broad swath of the population.

Once again, figure 2.3 indicates that northern states—particularly those of northern New England, the Upper Midwest, and the Northwest—generally have relatively high degrees of income equality. Southern states routinely have relatively high levels of income inequality.[14] Georgia and Minnesota are fairly typical examples of this division. The most obvious exceptions to these generalizations come from a series of northern states that have either large urban centers in combination with extensive small town/rural areas (California, Illinois, and New York) or widespread urbanization (Connecticut, Massachusetts, and Rhode Island). Income inequality tends to expand under each of these conditions.

Percentage of Sixty-five-or-Older Persons Living Above the Federal Poverty Level

The inequality indicator above is focused on the population generally. We need to include also an indicator limited to seniors. Older Americans enjoy an income distribution that is much more similar to that of the population generally than they did prior to the introduction of Social Security pensions and Medicare, but differences exist. Unfortunately, state-level, age-specific Gini indexes are not available. We rely instead on the percentage of states' sixty-five-or-older populations who are living on incomes above the federal poverty level. Given the strong association between income and political participation in the United States, it is reasonable to suppose that older Americans living below the poverty level are much less commonly actively involved and attached to communities outside their own families.[15]

Like figure 2.3, figure 2.4 reveals a largely North-South pattern for poverty among older individuals.[16] The correlation between these two indicators is statistically significant at 0.52. New England and the Northwest generally, as well as portions of the Upper Midwest, have fairly low rates of poverty among older residents. Southern states, with the exceptions of Arizona and California, have higher levels of poverty among seniors. There are several exceptions to this generalization in the North. Colorado, Illinois, Indiana, North Dakota, South Dakota, and Wisconsin all have higher levels of poverty among older people than do other northern states, but they all still have levels below those common among southern states.

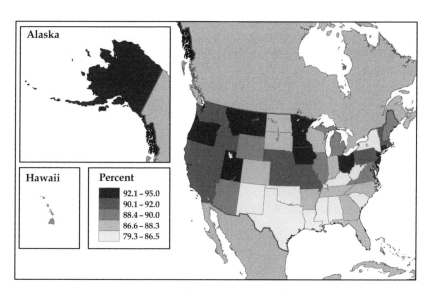

Figure 2.4: State residents sixty-five or older above the
federal poverty level (2005)

Overall

Collectively, these four indicators portray a consistent pattern. A number of states, generally but not entirely in northern regions, each exhibit relatively high levels of social equality within their populations. States in another group, generally but not entirely in southern regions, each reveal lower levels of social equality within their populations. While there is some slippage, the former, states with a relatively high level of social equality, also reveal much higher levels of civic engagement both among their populations generally and among their older citizens than do the states with relatively low levels of social equality. For instance, states' scores on Putnam's index correlate at 0.69 with the state's Gini index (reversed) and at 0.53 with the percentage of the state's sixty-five-or-older population living above the federal poverty level. The percentage of a state's older population voting in the 2004 presidential election correlates positively at 0.48 with income equality and at 0.21 with the proportion of seniors living above the federal poverty level. (The first three of these correlations are statistically significant.)

We cannot infer causation from correlation, but the researchers whom we have referenced across the preceding few pages have developed and tested a theory, and repeatedly replicated evidence supporting it, that explains why relative income equality as well as a relative lack of severe privation foster civic engagement.[17] Briefly, relative income equality facilitates civic engagement by reducing social distances among members of distinct social classes, cultivating a sense of equality and easing efforts to work together with people from different backgrounds. Further, individuals who feel secure that their material needs are met are much more likely to turn their attention to community matters than those lacking this security.

In short, the populations of some states are better positioned for civic involvement and community attachment than are the populations of other states, and citizens—including seniors—in the former states engage in civic involvement more extensively and develop more extensive personal attachments to their communities than do their counterparts in the latter states. So the social context in Georgia hinders Arnie and Muriel Hestirs' efforts to sustain community attachment, while Nancy Currier thrives in Minnesota's social context.

Additional Indicators

As in other chapters, we use the first four indicators that we present to assess how well states support a basic issue that seniors confront. In this chapter the issue is finding a meaningful life and supportive communities. However, we consider three additional relevant indicators in this section. As before, the first additional indicator is the one that we called our "so-what," or social outcome, indicator in our Introduction. That is, it is an indicator of something encouraging—particularly for older residents—that occurs when a state registers high scores on the four indicators described in the previous section. The other two additional indicators relate in ways worth discussing to this social outcome indicator.

State Political Culture

Even before the formation of our current union in 1789, observers of American political life displayed an interest in cultural variation among the states.[18] Madison, for instance, thought that the different interests among the states would hinder the development of what he considered the greatest threat to republican government: a majority faction.[19] And de Tocqueville commented on regional, if not strictly state, variations in his famous commentaries on the United States in the 1830s.[20] In the past fifty years, Daniel J. Elazar has likely produced the most important work on the political cultures of the American states.[21] So we begin with him, but because his basic distinctions and data are around forty years old, we update aspects of his work across the final portions of this chapter.[22]

Elazar distinguishes three distinct cultures and characterizes the American states in terms of mixtures of them. An *individualistic* culture, which seems to be particularly prominent in the United States, treats political life similarly to economic life, like a market.[23] Efficiency is a central objective, and innovations are continuously sought and generally justified in its name. The emphasis is on the private production of wealth, which, as Smith noticed, can be facilitated by at least a limited range of public services: external security, a stable currency, the rule of law to limit competition to price rather than dueling skill, courts to hold persons to their contracts, development of basic economic infrastructure, and even education to combat the "mental mutilation" that the marketplace inflicts on workers.[24] So even individualists (adherents of the individualistic culture) require a limited commonwealth. But they emphasize the freedom of the private sector, and for them good government means a modest and vital, yet often less than virtuous, public sector to facilitate the more noble activities of producing and distributing goods and services privately. For Elazar, New York and most of the adjacent states exemplify this culture more thoroughly than the two alternatives that we take up below.

A second culture focuses more on the public sector, the commonwealth, rather than a private economy, but does so from an elitist or hierarchical perspective of domination of society by a select few. Elazar calls this the *traditionalistic* culture. Mary Douglas and Aaron Wildavsky subsequently developed an improved theoretical schema for explaining relations among Elazar's three cultures and refer to this as the hierarchical culture.[25] We adopt their terminology. Hierarchists (adherents of the hierarchical culture) tend to cling to long-standing procedures and goals and in contrast to individualists accept innovation only reluctantly. For them, good government means maintaining the existing order, an order that serves particularly the objectives of political elites. For Elazar, most of the states of the former Confederacy exemplify this culture more than the two alternatives, particularly in the dominance of large African American populations by European American elites. Other states with similar ethnically based hierarchies (e.g., New Mexico) also exhibit the dominance of this culture.

Elazar labels a third culture *moralistic*. He portrays this culture as prioritizing the commonwealth over the market, in contrast to the culture of individualism. But, as opposed to hierarchy, moralism does so in an inclusive and pragmatic manner. Douglas and Wildavsky call this moralistic culture *egalitarianism*, and we follow their terminology. As portrayed by Elazar, good government for egalitarians involves maintaining an open search for innovations that might provide benefits for broad segments of the public. This government is inclusive, encouraging contributions from all interested parties, and nondogmatically strives for compromises that extend the benefits of governmental innovations to the broadest possible portions of the public. In Elazar's view this egalitarian culture emphasizes the encouraging aspects of individualism and hierarchy (efficiency and commonwealth focus, respectively) while sidestepping the most discouraging tendencies of these cultures (a private rather than a public focus and hierarchical social relations, respectively). Naturally, then, it is for him the preferred culture. Elazar's research shows that this culture is more prominent than the two alternatives in certain—generally small population—states across the northern sector of the United States (e.g., Oregon, Maine, Minnesota, Vermont, Washington, and Wisconsin).

Thompson, Ellis, and Wildavsky emphasize the distinctive strengths and contrasting weaknesses of each of these three cultures. Indeed, they argue that we are best served in social units that represent all three, so that the strength of one culture may counter—to some degree—a corresponding weakness of another.[26] Nonetheless, egalitarian cultures aid vulnerable members of society the most. Egalitarians tend to further this objective by reducing extremes of wealth and poverty largely by raising the socioeconomic circumstances of the bottom ranks of the socioeconomic hierarchy. It is inevitable that some members of society will be poorer than the rest. In a society dominated by individualists, those at the bottom are left pretty much to their own devices. In contrast, a society with strong egalitarian representation will extend collective help to these persons, integrating them, for instance, into a national health insurance program assuring virtually all citizens relatively equal access to a broad range of medical care. Egalitarians also encourage citizens to participate in grassroots organizations, raising overall civic involvement.

So one of the results of a state's fostering greater income equality, general material adequacy, and active community participation is an egalitarian state political culture. This culture is senior friendly in that it further fosters the very sort of activities—civic involvement and community attachment—that facilitate its development. As Thompson, Ellis, and Wildavsky argue, relations between social structures such as income distributions or participation rates and culture are symbiotic.[27] An egalitarian culture nurtures income equality and widespread participation. And income equality and widespread participation foster an egalitarian political culture.

Figure 2.5 shows how the states were characterized by Elazar in the mid-1960s. Our index awards scores increasing in numerical value from hierarchy/traditionalistic through individualism to egalitarianism/moralistic. So states exhibiting egalitarianism most strongly appear at the top of the ranking in table A.12 and have the darkest shading in figure 2.5.[28] North-South distinctions, familiar from figures 2.1 through 2.4, appear even more prominently here. With the exception of the southern section of California, all the predominantly egalitarian states lie north of the thirty-seventh parallel (that is, between Colorado

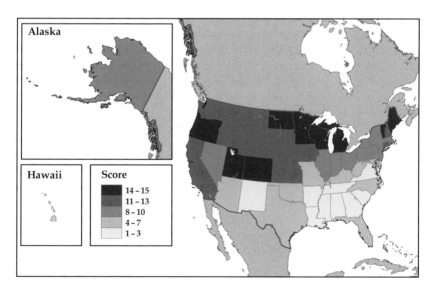

Figure 2.5: State political culture as per Elazar-Douglas-Wildavsky (mid-1960s)

and New Mexico), which is often considered to mark the northern edge of the Sunbelt. Virtually all the predominantly hierarchical states lie south of this boundary. Individualistic states appear on either side of this line, but largely on the northern side. Similarities in the patterns of shading between figures 2.1 through 2.4 on one hand and figure 2.5 on the other suggest that a predominantly egalitarian state culture is associated with efforts to cultivate civic involvement and community attachment.

Contemporary State Political Ideology

As we mentioned above, Elazar's data are more than forty years old. Given changes in life experiences and population across such a time period, we could reasonably imagine that states' political cultures have also changed.[29] Figure 2.6 shows how states compare on the Berry, Ringquist, Fording, and Hanson index of citizen political ideology.[30] This index measures political liberalism, so darker shades in figure 2.6 indicate more liberal state populations. Fortunately, the authors update this index of state political ideology on an annual basis, although there is a time lag between the current year and the last year of available data. The North-South distinction clearly demonstrated in figures 2.1 through 2.5 is just barely discernible in figure 2.6, and Elazar's ranking correlates with Berry, Ringquist, Fording, and Hanson's at only 0.22.

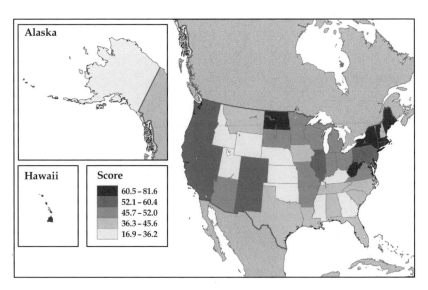

Figure 2.6: Berry, Ringquist, Fording, and Hanson state citizen liberalism (2004)

Does the liberal-conservative continuum, so prominent in the contemporary "red" and "blue" labels for the American states, adequately represent the factors included in either Elazar's or Douglas and Wildavsky's conception of political culture? Minimally, the liberal-conservative continuum ignores important distinctions that are central to the three culture models. The distinction between economic conservatives (individualists) and social conservatives (hierarchists/traditionalists) likely offers the most important example of such an oversight. Elazar, Douglas, and Wildavsky recognize these forms of conservatism as separate, distinctive cultures, but the liberal-conservative continuum conflates the two.

This oversight is important because, while economic and social conservatives agree on some issues, they disagree on others. For instance, civil rights matters (e.g., age discrimination in employment) generally pit an alliance of egalitarians/moralists (liberals, in the contemporary American context) and individualists (economic conservatives) *against* hierarchists/traditionalists (social conservatives). Yet individualists generally join ranks with hierarchists against egalitarians on property rights disputes (e.g., inheritance taxes), whereas egalitarians and hierarchists often form coalitions *against* individualists on social policy questions (e.g., the generosity of Social Security retirement pensions). Nonetheless, figure 2.6 offers the suggestion that events of the past forty years have altered states' political cultures. The relative positions of Georgia and Minnesota—relevant to the situations of the Hestirs and Nancy Currier—have, however, remained fairly stable across this period.

District Electoral Competition and Democratic Legislative Control

Barrilleaux, Holbrook, and Langer offer another, but also limited, way of comparing states' current political cultures with Elazar's calculations of the 1960s.[31] They contend that Democrats are most likely to reveal their true (liberal or egalitarian/moralistic) colors in supporting generous state-level public social programs, including those relevant to seniors such as generous use of Medicaid to support long-term care expenses, when two conditions are met. First, they hold power by controlling a state's legislature, and second, they face close competition from Republicans in the electoral districts for that legislature and thus need to maintain the loyalty of their base among the citizenry. So comparing the states on this measure ought to provide, minimally, an index of how states support various vulnerable groups, including seniors. The data for Barrilleaux, Holbrook, and Langer's index come from a range of years.[32] They are less recent than Berry, Ringquist, Fording, and Hanson's yet not as old as Elazar's.

Figure 2.7 contrasts the states on this measure. There is some resemblance between figure 2.5 (the relative influence of Elazar's three cultures among the states) and figure 2.7. Southern states generally hold low positions in the rank-ordering, as figure 2.7 depicts. Further, a few states with high ranks in figure 2.5 retain them in figure 2.7 (California, Maine, Minnesota, Oregon, Vermont, and Washington). However, New Mexico and West Virginia exhibit low scores in figure 2.5, but high scores in figure 2.7. Indeed, Elazar's ranking correlates with Barrilleaux, Holbrook, and Langer's at only 0.14. Berry, Rindquist, Fording, and Hanson's ranking and that of Barrilleaux, Holbrook, and Langer, however, correlate at a statistically significant 0.65, in an encouraging sign that each picks up portions of the same concept, presumably contemporary American liberalism. But as we mentioned above, the contrast between contemporary American liberal and conservative ideologies does not capture all that Elazar perceived in the distinctions among his three political cultures. So questions remain about how the American states differ in terms of Elazar's cultures today. Nonetheless, states with more thoroughly egalitarian/moralistic cultures or liberal political ideologies generally support social programs for seniors more extensively than others.

Conclusions: Back to the Hestirs and Nancy Currier

The Hestirs and Nancy Currier, similarly to the Senters and the Munros in the previous chapter, bear some personal responsibility for their respective problems and successes. In chapter 1 the issue involved finding an enjoyable life of active recreation. In this chapter our protagonists seek to develop activities and relationships that create meaningful civic involvement and community attachment. But, as before, contrasting features of the social contexts contribute to failure and success as well. The Hestirs, similarly to the Senters, face more difficult circumstances in achieving their goals. Let us examine these differences.

In Georgia and several other southern states, income is distributed relatively unequally across the population. This important index suggests that greater social distance separates various strata or classes of society. Increasing social distance, in turn, hinders people from different strata from meeting together as relative equals to discuss common problems and to search for mutually acceptable solutions. Problems are likely more frequent when incomes are less equal and a smaller proportion of persons has the resources to meet their needs. Further, mutually acceptable solutions are more difficult to achieve when incomes are sharply unequal, since they are apt to require redistribution, by which some people essentially pay for the improved conditions enjoyed by others. Minnesota

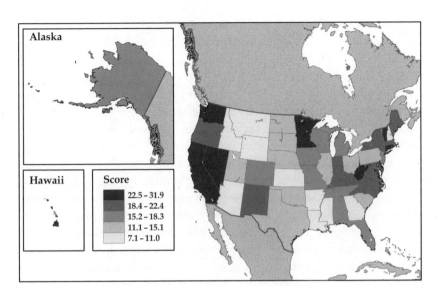

Figure 2.7: State district electoral competition X state
democratic legislative control (1980s)

and other northern states exhibit relatively high income equality and other indicators of social similarity across their populations. Accordingly, in these states citizens share problems more widely, discuss problems more equally, and create solutions benefitting broad swaths of the population more easily.

Further, Georgia and some other southern states have relatively high levels of poverty and near poverty, among both their general populations and their older residents. Individuals who are preoccupied with meeting their own material needs can only rarely spare the attention and other resources to focus broadly on their communities. In a number of northern states larger percentages of the population achieve financial security and contribute to solutions for shared problems. Nancy Currier benefits, while the Hestirs suffer, from these two discrepancies in social context between Minnesota and Georgia.[33]

Unsurprisingly, then, Minnesota exhibits a higher score on Putnam's index of social capital and has a higher percentage of its senior population voting in the 2004 presidential election. Citizens in the two states, including older residents, react predictably to the distinct social contexts surrounding them. Nancy Currier emulates—at least generically and perhaps unconsciously—the volunteering and voting activities of other Minnesota residents around whom she grew up. The Hestirs follow behaviors modeled for them by other Georgians across their lifetimes, but the two models differ sufficiently so that the Hestirs end up being socially disengaged and lack sustaining relationships.

These social structural patterns (income distributions and rates of social involvement) cultivate, as suggested above, distinctive state political cultures. Cultures differ within states as well as between states. Minnesota is not composed solely of citizens with an egalitarian political culture or Georgia of residents adhering to hierarchy. But as Elazar calculated and Berry, Ringquist, Fording, and Hanson would appear to confirm, a higher proportion of citizens in Minnesota adhere to egalitarianism than in Georgia.[34] In contrast, those who prefer and follow a hierarchical way of life likely form a larger proportion of the population in Georgia than in Minnesota.

These differences suggest that people of retirement age might want to consider leaving their existing communities and move to another state for the sake of finding satisfaction in civic involvement and community attachment. Volunteer opportunities in nonprofit organizations exist almost everywhere, but the accessibility and nature of these opportunities differ across the states. Egalitarian political cultures tend to support meaningful volunteer positions, affording opportunities to apply judgment and draw on the volunteer's personal and professional experiences. Hierarchical political cultures often offer less meaningful volunteer positions that resemble the "it's the boss's way or the highway" work positions that many employees retire to escape. These positions offer few opportunities to apply the individual discretion that Nancy Currier enjoys as a volunteer.

Nancy Currier moved from one state to another and into a major city where she had only a few preexisting personal acquaintances. Yet she found a meaningful way to give to this community, through which she also created a rich supportive network of friends. We hope that her successful example will serve as a model to others. It is not clear from figures 2.1 through 2.7 whether if Nancy Currier had stayed in Missouri, rather than moving to Minnesota, she would have experienced the same degree of success. Finding an encouraging locale in which to make meaningful contributions can lead to acquiring a supportive community.

3

Once people retire, their incomes usually decline, sometimes quite sharply, while their expenses remain much the same. With more free time, retirees face new temptations to spend money. And anyone with a long-term mortgage knows that taxes and insurance become the predominant elements of the payment by the time the mortgage is paid off.[1] Clever retirees have long recognized the benefits of moving from one state to another to reduce their expenses.[2] In this chapter we focus on states that offer seniors affordable yet safe residential options.

A century ago those relatively few Americans who lived until they were no longer able or allowed to work often confronted dire financial circumstances. Most were dependent on their own accumulated resources or those of their extended families, and few acquired savings sufficient to last them any length of time.[3] Some lived with their children in multigenerational households that often shepherded a family business such as a farm. Sometimes this solution worked well for all—or at least most—concerned. But in other cases it raised difficult, persistent interpersonal issues and served to lower the standard of living of others in the household, including the older person's grandchildren. Many older people lived, if not in the poorhouse, then at least in its shadow.[4] These poorhouses, or almshouses, existed in virtually all communities. Local authorities contracted with the lowest bidder to house and feed people who were unable to support themselves. Generally, once in an almshouse a person remained there unless able to demonstrate an ability to support her- or himself in the community. (This policy served to keep those often perceived as riffraff off the streets.) In the almshouse, younger vagrants often preyed upon the elderly. All in all, the almshouse was a terrifying apparition, and many older people worried ceaselessly about ending up in the local poorhouse.

The Social Security program, adopted in 1935 and issuing its first checks in 1942, eventually changed this situation considerably for the better. The general circumstances of older people further improved with the 1965 passage of Medicare, the federal medical care insurance program primarily for Social Security beneficiaries. These programs contributed importantly to a situation that, by 2003, left those who were sixty-five or older with a somewhat lower poverty rate (10.2 percent) than that of the American population generally (12.5 percent).[5]

These improvements in the circumstances of older Americans deserve our applause. Nonetheless, most contemporary seniors live on fairly limited incomes, often considerably less than those they enjoyed while working full time. Social Security pensions represent the largest single source of income for Americans sixty-five and older (39 percent of total income in 2001).[6] But a single woman with an average lifetime income who retired in 2001 at sixty-five, when she was first eligible for the full benefit, received a pension just barely over $1,000 a month ($1,051) or $12,612 a year.[7] The federal poverty level for a household with one person was $8,590 in 2001.[8] So Social Security will sustain this elderly woman above the poverty level. But the federal poverty level is not a generous standard in comparative perspective, and Social Security will clearly not provide this woman with much luxury.[9] Indeed, a person with a maximum earnings history who waited until seventy to apply for benefits received $1,879 a month or $22,548 a year in 2001, only about half the median household income for that year.

Of course, the maximum earners often have some sort of private pension (a defined-contribution plan would be increasingly likely) as well as other private assets and possibly earnings to supplement Social Security. But many people rely solely on their Social Security benefits. In 2001, 20 percent of Social Security recipients had no other source of income; for another 13 percent Social Security provided 90 percent or more of their income; for another 32 percent Social Security represented between 50 and 89 percent of their income. So Social Security constitutes less than 50 percent of income for only 35 percent of the recipients.[10]

In 2003, the median household income for those 65 or older was about $24,000. This amounts to slightly more than half the median household income for the population generally of about $43,500 in the same year.[11] Median income among retirees declines with age: for instance, in 2003 it was $32,746 for households in the sixty-five-to-sixty-nine cohort but only $19,470 for those in the seventy-five-and-older cohort. Female and minority households report much lower incomes. So many retirees would benefit from finding a locale with a relatively low cost of living.

In addition, the retirement outlook for the future looks less encouraging than the present situation. People retiring across the past decade enjoy more lucrative Social Security benefits than will those who follow in the next decade, and a higher proportion of the former receive one of the corporate defined-benefit pensions that became common after World War II. The baby boom retirees and particularly those who follow them will, by comparison, suffer some loss in Social Security benefits (e.g., as a result of becoming eligible a year to two later) and also less supplemental pension income because employers have widely replaced defined-benefit pensions with individual defined-contribution schemes such as 401(k)s and individual retirement accounts (IRAs). Nearly 70 percent of those who avail themselves of these defined-contribution options come from the top 20 percent of the income distribution and use these devices primarily to lower the taxes on their high current incomes. A smaller proportion of lower-income workers enroll in these schemes, and the contributions of those who do enroll are modest. Indeed, only about 50 percent of current American workers have access to 401(k)s, and of these only about 40 percent contribute to them. In 2004 the median value of these accounts stood at less than twenty thousand dollars, considerably less than the median household income of current retirees.[12]

Further, as we indicated in the Introduction, apart from the equity in their homes, households in the fifty-five-to-sixty-four age cohort, generally people in their peak earning years, held a median household net worth in 2000 of only $32,304, and households in the sixty-five-or-older cohort reported just $23,369.[13] So the plentiful advice on how to maintain one's nest egg in retirement misses the mark for many current retirees, and persons retiring in the next couple of decades will likely have little in the way of nest eggs to maintain. More apropos for most older persons is information on how to maintain as much as possible of their current standard of living on sharply reduced incomes supplemented only modestly by limited net worth. A move to a region with a lower cost of living benefits many retirees in this situation.

Older adults' financial needs and capacities often differ somewhat from those of the population generally. A relatively new initiative seeks to assess older citizens' financial situations more specifically: the Elder Economic Security Initiative with its standard or index (http://www.wowonline.org/ourprograms/eesi). So far, the initiative is active in only about a dozen states, so the cross-state comparisons it supports are currently quite limited. But the initiative provides data of considerable interest to older adults on some states, and for a few of these, county-level data are available.

In seeking a less expensive social environment, seniors understandably do not want to sacrifice safety. Surveys often identify fear of crime as a major concern of older persons. Gradual declines in strength and mobility may contribute to the propensity of older people to be more conscious and fearful of crime than are adults of younger ages.[14] A move within a community might reduce an older person's cost of living, but it might concomitantly induce a sharply increased fear of crime. People can often more easily duplicate many of the desirable features of one neighborhood, even a relatively expensive neighborhood, in another, more inexpensive neighborhood by looking across state boundaries. Sadly, however, expensive states frequently exhibit relatively low crime rates, while inexpensive states often experience higher crime rates. Thus, combining state indexes of affordability and relative freedom from crime in a single index would present conflicting patterns in a muddled fashion.

So we engage in a two-step process in this chapter to cover both affordability and safety. First, we deal with inexpensiveness, showing how the various states differ in being friendly to seniors living on modest incomes. Then we show how the states that are relatively supportive of seniors in this regard vary in the level of crimes most relevant to older Americans, identifying states that exhibit relative affordability and comparatively low property crime rates. As before, we introduce these issues with a pair of contrasting vignettes.

Carl and Jessica Sanford

Carl Sanford worked for several decades for an insurance company in New York, commuting from his home in south-central New Jersey, where he lived with his wife and children. After the children went off to college, his wife, Jessica, took a job as the appointments secretary in a fancy women's hair salon in their community. Jessica took this job more for connection with other women than because the Sanfords needed the income. Carl was well paid; during his last several years of work, he earned nearly $200,000 a year, a little over four times the median household income in the United States at the time. Jessica's job added only another $20,000. They decided to retire as soon as Carl was eligible for full Social Security benefits. Carl didn't expect any further promotions; his interest in his work had declined, and the daily commute seemed progressively more difficult. They thought that their retirement income would allow them to spend more time with each other and their friends, going out for lunch and playing golf. Yet in spite of their affluence, they have found it increasingly difficult to make ends meet across the three years since they retired, he at sixty-five, she at sixty-two.

Part of their problem arises from the decline in their income in retirement. As a maximum earner retiring with full benefits, Carl initially received about $18,500 a year from Social Security, but Jessica, who earned far less and who retired as soon as she could obtain access to Social Security at sixty-two, gets only around $9,000. By American standards, Carl enjoys a generous, defined-benefit pension from his former employer. He gets 50 percent of his average income across his last five years on the job, or about $83,000 a year. Jessica has no retirement income apart from Social Security. Sending three children to college has left the Sanfords without extensive personal savings. They have about $200,000, which is invested in a diversified manner. They think of these funds as reserves for serious problems later in life: medical emergencies and long-term care. But they have already drawn on these funds to meet some months' normal expenses. So, three years ago, when they were both still working, their household income was just short of $220,000. Now, despite unusually good retirement support, their income is about $110,000. This represents between three and four times the median income of retirees in the sixty-five-to-sixty-nine age cohort, so once again the Sanfords are fortunate. They also find themselves strapped for money to enjoy their leisure time.

The other part of their problem stems from trying to maintain a lifestyle to which they had become accustomed during their last years at work. Their biggest expense is housing. Although they paid off their mortgage several years ago, current and rapidly rising New Jersey property taxes and insurance rates, in addition to expensive association fees, utilities, and maintenance, mean that they currently spend nearly as much per month on their house as they did when they last had a mortgage payment. They also find themselves restless with more time on their hands. They spend more on lunches along the shore and on golfing with their friends. They also take a number of modest trips. These entertainment expenses actually exceed those from when they were employed. Other expenses, of course, have fallen; Carl no longer makes an expensive daily commute, and they both need fewer, less expensive clothes. But the expenditures required for the life they want to live have not fallen 50 percent as their income has. When they were employed, they deposited small monthly contributions to savings, but now find themselves routinely relying on shortcuts to live within their income, skimping on home maintenance, keeping cars longer than they once did. They even sometimes turn down offers to get together with friends in order to save money. They recognize that this situation will likely get worse as their current excellent health declines or some other sort of emergency with financial implications occurs.

So although they live well now, they worry about money and the future. As prices for nearly everything they purchase rise, they recognize that their current lifestyle becomes progressively less tenable. They fret, and the tension takes a toll on their relationship. These worries effectively take much of the fun out of a lifestyle that they anticipated enjoying.

Jim and Sonia Tate

On its face, the retirement income situation of Jim and Sonia Tate appears considerably less encouraging than that of the Sanfords. But as we shall see, the Tates made some early decisions to match their retirement expenses to their income. During most of their adult lives, the Tates lived in central Connecticut, another expensive region similar to the Sanfords' location in New Jersey. To cut expenses, the Tates moved—shortly after their retirement—to West Virginia. But this step gets us a little ahead of their overall story, so we shall back up and pick up a series of relevant points.

Jim worked as a commercial banker in Waterbury, and Sonia taught in a private elementary school in a neighboring town. Their pre-retirement income was somewhat less than the Sanfords'. In the last years before his retirement Jim earned just slightly over $100,000 per year, and Sonia just short of $60,000, for a combined income of roughly $160,000. The couple expected a retirement income slightly in excess of $100,000: $18,500 from Social Security for Jim and $13,000 from Social Security for Sonia plus nearly $70,000 from the generous pension program for executives at Jim's bank. So they recognized the need to cut back their expenses in retirement. Unfortunately, five years ago, before they each retired at sixty-five, Jim's bank experienced financial difficulties and defaulted on its support of its largely unfunded pensions. Thus Jim's "private" pension is actually coming from the federal government's pension insurance program, the Pension Benefit Guaranty Corporation (PBGC), which reduced his benefits to about 50 percent of what he expected.

Consequently, in their first year of retirement their income fell to less than two-thirds of what they had anticipated: $31,500 from Social Security and $35,000 from the PBGC, or $66,500. The Tates still receive a sizable retirement income by contemporary American standards, but an income far lower than they expected. In order to maintain their anticipated and desired standard of living, Jim and Sonia needed to stretch each dollar of retirement income a good deal further. Moreover, they had accumulated little retirement savings, as a consequence of having paid for their daughter's and son's college expenses. These extraordinary costs drained most of their personal savings and left them with little to supplement their retirement income. What were they going to do?

It turned out that the Tates received some good news as well. Their mortgage-free house had appreciated substantially in value. When their next-door neighbors sold their house at just about the time the Tates retired—for what the Tates considered an amazing sum—they got an idea. Why not sell their home and move to a less expensive area?

Their realtor encouraged them to put the home that they had purchased for $35,000 in 1968 on the market for $560,000. They cleared almost $500,000 from the sale. They had frequently vacationed in the region surrounding Shenandoah National Park in northern Virginia and were familiar with and liked the town of Clarksburg, West Virginia. When they examined the housing market there, they found prices around half those of Connecticut real estate.

They took their time finding a neighborhood with many of the same character-istics of the one they had enjoyed for so long near Waterbury. Then they found a house they liked: smaller than their Connecticut home, but with a number of modern conveniences that their Connecticut home lacked. They purchased it for a bit over $200,000 and moved.

Jim and Sonia have found that, similarly to housing prices, nearly everything costs less in West Virginia than in Connecticut. Since they moved to the Clarks-burg area five years ago, their money seems to go nearly twice as far as it did around Waterbury. So far, their $300,000 of savings created by their house ex-change remains undisturbed, quietly collecting interest. They live less luxuri-ously in some respects than when they were both employed; for instance, their children now travel to visit them rather than the reverse. But they always knew that their retirement income would not equal their employment income, and they live much as they expected to prior to the sharp decline in Jim's pension.

Each of them joined some local groups, made friends in the area, and feel increasingly at home. Now around seventy years of age, they expect to enjoy at least another decade in West Virginia. But while that state has proved inex-pensive, they fear that it cannot compete with Connecticut on the quality of medical care or the quality and accessibility of various forms of long-term care. Eventually, Jim and Sonia may need to consider moving closer to their children in New England. At that point, the $300,000 that they cleared on their house exchange will come in quite handy to help pay for housing and medical care in this later stage of retirement.

Finding Affordability and Safety

Jim and Sonia Tate faced more difficult financial circumstances, yet they manage to live happily on their retirement income. But with greater resources Carl and Jessica Sanford struggle to make ends meet. The Tates achieved this goal by cut-ting their expenses *without* reducing their standard of living below their expec-tations. Their experience demonstrates a lesson for most retirees. Generally speaking, contemporary Americans receive retirement incomes lower—often much lower—than their employment incomes in the years preceding retirement. Further, only a small proportion of older Americans accumulate sufficient liq-uid assets to augment their retirement incomes substantially on a regular basis. So most retirees need to reduce their expenses sharply. This inevitably pro-duces some painful consequences. However, if retirees move to a location with a lower cost of living, they can avoid a significant amount of this pain. We make no claim that moving from one region of the country to another will forestall all financial problems. But selective cross-state moves generally reduce expenses more satisfactorily than moving from one part of a given state to another.

Additionally, intra-state moves aimed at achieving greater affordability often raise problems for the second focus of this chapter: safety. Moving to a less expensive location in the same state may mean joining a less secure community. By moving across regions, the Tates found a neighborhood near Clarksburg that offered safety and ambience similar to those of their previous neighborhood around Waterbury. In the sections that follow we take up acquiring affordability and safety sequentially.

Assessing a State's Support of Affordability

Percentage of the Population That Is Nonmetropolitan

Metropolitan areas tend to be more expensive than smaller towns and rural regions. Urban property is typically more in demand and thus expensive, and the associated tax and insurance expenses also tend to be higher. Transportation needs are frequently more extensive. While certainly exceptions exist, retail overheads and thus prices for a range of goods and services also run higher. So we first assess the affordability of a state through the percentage of its population that is "nonmetropolitan." By *nonmetropolitan* we mean the proportion living outside "urban clusters" of more than fifty thousand population.[15]

Figure 3.1 shows how states vary on this indicator.[16] Darker shades mean higher proportions of the population living in communities of less than fifty thousand. This map shows no clear regional pattern, but states with huge metropolitan centers (e.g., California, Florida, Illinois, and New York) as well as states with high population density (e.g., Connecticut, New Jersey, and Rhode Island) rank low on this indicator. Whereas states without major cities (e.g., Maine and Vermont in New England, the Dakotas in the Upper Midwest, Montana and Wyoming in the Northwest, Arkansas and Mississippi in the Southeast, and West Virginia in the mid-Atlantic region) hold high ranks on this indicator. As we shall see below, our data also show that the percentage of a state's population that is nonmetropolitan serves as a surprisingly good indicator for the affordability aspect of state senior friendliness.

Median Mortgage Payment (Reversed)

According to the Bureau of Labor Statistics, housing constitutes the largest single expense category for most American households, averaging about one-third of total household expenditures.[17] Slightly over 80 percent of Americans

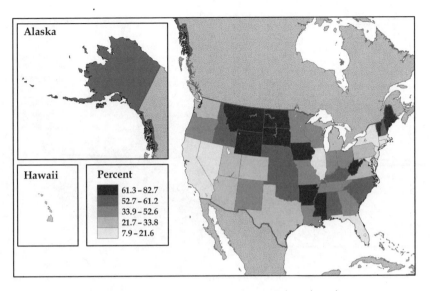

Figure 3.1: Nonmetropolitan state population (2000)

sixty-five or older own their homes.[18] At any given time a relatively large—but currently declining—proportion of older Americans have paid off their mortgages, so housing costs may well represent a lower portion of household expenses for many of them. Yet the combined impact of housing-related expenses—property taxes, insurance, condominium or association fees, utilities, maintenance, and occasional renovation (perhaps for wheelchair accessibility or ramps to replace stairs)—still represent a significant chunk of the budget of many older Americans. As a result nearly 35 percent of older American households report spending at the average one-third or more of their household income on housing-related costs.[19] In any case, housing prices in a state are indicative of other costs. (Indeed, states' median mortgage payments correlate at 0.80 [statistically significant] with their overall costs of living.) So we use this statistic as our second indictor of state affordability. To use mortgage payment levels as a measure of affordability, rather than expensiveness, we have to reverse them. So we subtracted a state's median mortgage payment from two thousand dollars.[20]

Figure 3.2 shows how states vary on this indicator. Because we have reversed this indicator, darker shading indicates *lower* median mortgage levels and greater affordability. This indicator correlates at 0.75 (statistically significant) with the percentage of a state's population that is nonmetropolitan as discussed above. So it is unsurprising that many of the same states rank at the top and bottom on both these indicators. Arkansas, the Dakotas, Mississippi, West Virginia, and Wyoming all appear once again among the leaders, and California, Connecticut,

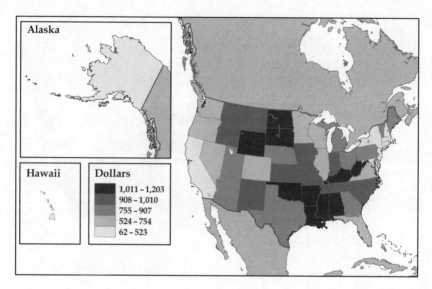

Figure 3.2: Median state mortgage payment (reversed) (2005)

New Jersey, New York, and Rhode Island lag behind most states on housing affordability.

The Federal Medical Assistance Percentage

A state's federal medical assistance percentage (FMAP) indicates the percentage of a state's Medicaid expenses paid by the federal government. This percentage is based (nonlinearly) on the relationship between a state's per capita income and the per capita income of the United States. The percentage falls as state's per capita income rises but cannot fall beneath 50 percent. So in one sense, this percentage reflects comparative state income levels. As such it focuses attention on differences among the poorer states, since the twelve states with the highest per capita incomes are all at 50 percent.[21] The FMAP likely also registers relative state Medicaid use, since states with high rates of federal cost sharing have incentives to expand their Medicaid programs. This is because federal cost sharing means that a given amount of state expenditure goes further than in other expenditure areas.[22] Overall, this index measures how well an older person with a limited income can fulfill her or his needs for goods and crucial services in a state.

Figure 3.3 portrays variation among the states on this indicator. The pattern at the upper end of the scale in figure 3.3 resembles that in figure 3.1 with a correlation of 0.63 (statistically significant) between the FMAP and the percentage of a state's population living in a nonmetropolitan setting. The FMAP also correlates statistically significantly with a state's median mortgage payment (reversed) at 0.82. The pattern at the lower end of the scale is somewhat less similar to figures 3.1 and 3.2 through the inclusion of six states such as Minnesota that have high enough incomes to share the bottom FMAP rank with familiar states such as California, Connecticut, New Jersey, and New York. The similarities at the upper end (higher FMAP, lower income end) suggest that, where prices are low, incomes are also relatively low. Or, perhaps, we should reverse this, that where incomes are low, prices are also relatively low. This latter formulation shows that persons with sharply reduced retirement incomes can stretch their incomes to cover more purchases in states such as West Virginia. We shall return to this theme below.

Median Sixty-five-or-Older Household Income (Reversed)

All three of the indicators discussed so far are based on states' general populations. We need an indicator focused on the sixty-five-or-older segment of the population. For this we use the median sixty-five-or-older household income. And since, as before, we are looking for how affordable a state is, we reverse this statistic. So the shadings in figure 3.4 represent forty-five thousand dollars minus the state's median sixty-five-or-older household income. Thus darker shading indicates lower incomes.[23]

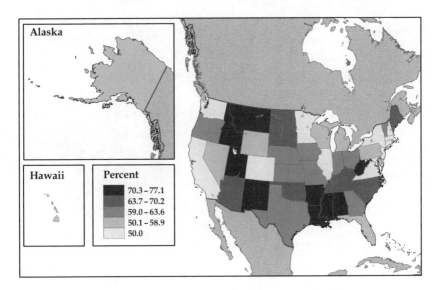

Figure 3.3: State federal medical assistance (2005)

Figure 3.4 shows a surprising range of variation in these median incomes, given that Social Security places a floor (a series of floors, actually) beneath the incomes of sixty-five-or older persons. These floors create a redistributive "replacement effect." That is, the replacement rate (the percentage of a person's previous earnings that Social Security replaces) increases as the recipient's previous income level declines. So while higher-income persons generally receive larger pensions than do lower-income persons, these larger pensions represent a smaller percentage of their former earnings. Consequently, Social Security tends to even out—in limited degree—the income variations produced by market economic interaction. In spite of this leveling effect, familiar states appear at the top with lower incomes (e.g., Arkansas, Mississippi, the Dakotas, and West Virginia) and at the bottom with higher incomes (e.g., California, Connecticut, and New Jersey) of this ranking. The variation revealed by figure 3.4 on this indicator correlates statistically significantly with variation in the percentage of a state's population that is nonmetropolitan (0.55), the median state mortgage payment (0.75), and the state's FMAP (0.59).

Overall

These four indicators of state variation in the cost of major household purchases (i.e., housing) and variation in state income levels, both among older Americans and the population generally, tend to run together. States with low

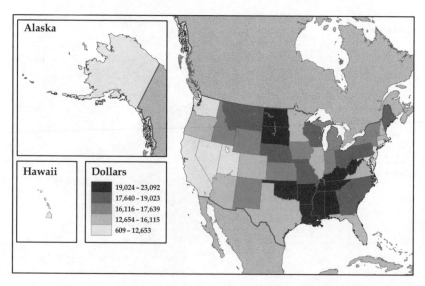

Figure 3.4: Median state sixty-five or older household income (reversed) (2005)

incomes tend to have low costs. Further, variation in incomes and costs roughly mimics variation in the proportion of a state's population living in communities of fewer than fifty thousand persons. When a relatively high proportion of a state's population lives in such communities, incomes and costs tend to be fairly low, but when most of a state's residents live in larger communities, then incomes and costs increase. Many retired persons, particularly those in expensive states such as California, Connecticut, New Jersey, and New York, would benefit from finding a location in which their expenses would be much lower. One way to achieve this objective would be for them to move to any of the most darkly shaded states in figure 3.1. Significant portions of these relatively nonmetropolitan states offer relatively low costs that allow persons with limited incomes to live fairly well. Attractive communities within low-income and low-cost states offer retirees good options on affordability.

Additional Indicators

We use the four indicators above to assess states' senior friendliness in terms of affordability. Now we examine three additional indicators. The first of these is our "so-what," or social outcome, indicator. But we deviate from the practice of previous chapters with regard to the remaining two indicators. These two indicators are focused on the second, independent concern of this chapter: safety.

State Cost of Living (Reversed)

In states with predominantly nonmetropolitan populations, relatively inexpensive real estate costs, and modest incomes among seniors and the general population, we would predict generally low overall costs of living. Berry, Fording, and Hanson provide the best current measure of cost of living for the American states.[24] As with a couple of the indicators in the previous section, we have reversed their measure so that higher numbers (darker shadings in fig. 3.5) indicate *lower* costs of living.

Figure 3.5 divides states on a largely North-South basis. Most mid-Atlantic (including West Virginia), southeastern, and southwestern (excluding California) states have relatively low costs of living. Northern states, with the exceptions of Idaho, Montana, and Wyoming have relative high costs of living. This map differs from figures 3.1 through 3.4, but table A.19 in the Appendix reveals a rank-ordering rather similar to those underlying these other figures. Indeed, the cost-of-living indicator correlates statistically significantly with the four others: nonmetropolitan (0.45), median mortgage (0.80), FMAP (0.71), and median

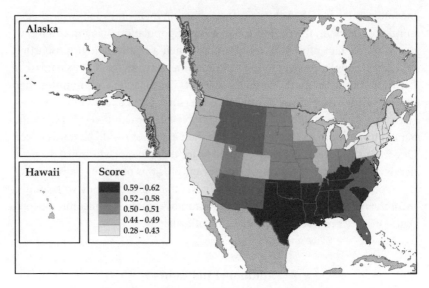

Figure 3.5: State cost of living (reversed) (2003)

sixty-five-or-older household income (0.45). The cost-of-living map, then, re-inforces the information provided by figures 3.1 through 3.4. It also suggests that older Americans from the northeastern and north-central regions move to various southeastern states in retirement for reasons beyond seeking mild winter climates. These moves offer relief from social congestion and high prices, providing the more relaxed and affordable socioeconomic environments that fit the needs of many retirees. Many Californians move to Nevada, Arizona, and New Mexico for similar reasons.

Affording Safety

Many people increasingly fear crime as they move from middle-age to senior status. Persons experiencing mobility problems and more extensive physical frailty likely feel more vulnerable to forms of malfeasance. Ironically, crime victimization generally decreases as people age. The highest rates occur among adolescents (e.g., 1.6 personal thefts per 1,000 cohort members), rates decline for working-age adults (e.g., 1.0 personal thefts per 1,000 cohort members), and rates drop still further among seniors (e.g., 0.4 personal thefts per 1,000 cohort members).[25] Many older Americans mostly fear violent crimes, the kind that appear on their local television newscasts with monotonous regularity. In fact, while their actual rates of victimization remain low, older Americans experience forms of nonviolent property crime more than any forms of violent crime.[26]

ELDERLY HOMICIDE

Older Americans experience extremely low rates of violent crime generally, and homicides among them occur rarely. Nonetheless, we analyze state variation on homicides among seniors because the statistics are more complete and generally accurate than the notoriously incomplete statistics for other crimes. Figure 3.6 is based on table A.20 in the Appendix. We mention the table here in an effort to emphasize the general lowness of the rates appearing in the figure. In 2004, New Mexico, the state with the highest rate of homicides among persons sixty-five or older, had a rate of 0.063 senior homicide victims per 1,000 state residents sixty-five or older. This translates roughly into 1 homicide for every 16,000 New Mexico seniors. At the other end of the spectrum, several states (Delaware, Iowa, and Wyoming) had no senior homicides in 2004.

An imperfect North-South pattern of regional variation appears in figure 3.6.[27] A number of southern states report slightly higher homicide rates among older Americans than those of most northern states, but several northern states (e.g., Michigan, Nevada, South Dakota, Utah, and Vermont) differ from the general pattern. This pattern of homicides with senior victims contrasts with the generally strong performance of southern states on affordability. While most of the relationships are not statistically significant, states' homicide rates among citizens sixty-five or older correlate positively with all five of the affordability

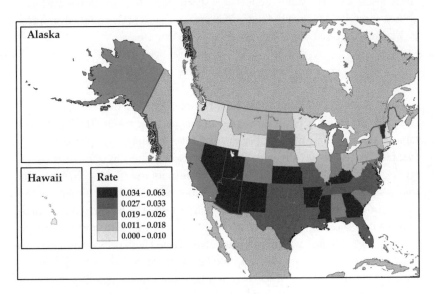

Figure 3.6: State sixty-five or older homicides per 1,000 sixty-five or older residents (2004)

indicators that we discussed above. Thus, affordable states tend to have higher rates of homicides among older citizens. Nonetheless, several states that are quite senior friendly in terms of affordability also exhibit relatively low rates of senior homicide, including Idaho, Iowa, Montana, North Dakota, West Virginia, and Wyoming.

PROPERTY CRIME

For the vast majority of seniors, homicide is an extremely remote contingency, but older citizens may experience property crime. The Bureau of Justice Statistics' definition of property crime includes burglary, as when one person enters another's house and takes something; larceny, as in slipping away with someone's purse in a public setting; and car theft. These distressing events affect far more older Americans than violent crime. Unfortunately, many of the states with relatively high affordability scores also have pretty high rates of property theft. A state's property crime rate (reported crimes per one thousand state residents) correlates positively with nonmetropolitan population and lower median sixty-five-or-older household income and negatively with lower median mortgage payment, FMAP, and lower cost of living, although most of these correlations are not statistically significant.

Figure 3.7 displays state variation on property crime rates.[28] Property crime is relatively low in the most northern states, and it tends to rise across progressively more southern states. So a retiree seeking affordability and safety has to choose carefully. Many of the states offering affordability lack safety from property crime (e.g., Alabama) or vice versa (e.g., Vermont).

Combining Affordability and Safety

Initially, we tried combining affordability and safety into one index by assigning states the number of their reverse ranking on affordability (see fig. 6.3 and table A.38) as well as the number of their reverse ranking on property crime (see table A.21) and dividing the sum of the two numbers by 2 for their overall scores. These results turned out to be difficult to interpret. We concluded that this schema likely violated both the priorities of most actual retirees as well as the thought processes of particularly savvy retirees who moved to achieve affordability. Save for a minority of older persons with costly and painful victimization experience, who might place an especially high priority on safety, we thought that the primary concern would be for affordability. For many individuals, getting their life in order at retirement first requires finding a location where their means are sufficient to support their needs and some particularly prominent wants. Then seniors might choose among the viable possibilities on

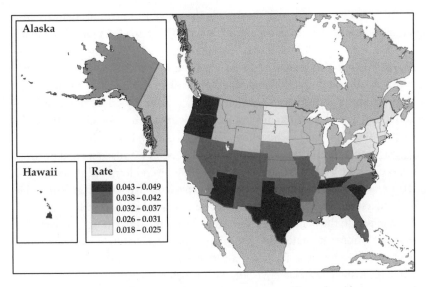

Figure 3.7: Property crime per 1,000 state residents (2005)

affordability based on safety concerns and perhaps other considerations such as the location of family or the climate.

Accordingly, we examined the states in the top third of the affordability ranking as shown in table 3.1. These states all scored above 2.0 on the affordability aspect of state senior friendliness (SSF) in table A.38. (In table 3.1, each state's affordability ranking is in parentheses behind its name.) Then we re-ranked these seventeen states according to their increasing property crime risk. We focus our discussion on the top ten states in table 3.1. These ten states all lie at or above the median score on property crime, meaning that they have *less* property crime than half the states. Somewhat surprisingly, these ten states offer considerable geographic diversity. In the northwestern and north-central regions they include Idaho, Montana, and Wyoming along with Iowa and the Dakotas. They also include Maine from the Northeast, West Virginia from the Mid-Atlantic, and Kentucky and Mississippi from the Southeast. These ten states, in our view, represent the best bets for retirees focused on affordability *and* safely.

Conclusions: Back to the Sanfords and the Tates

The Tates appear to be doing quite well, in spite of the reduction in Jim's bank pension just prior to their retirement. Although their retirement income is lower than they anticipated, they made the move from Connecticut to West Virginia (the fifth-ranked state in table 3.1). This afforded them three major benefits. First, they have cut their expenses sharply by moving to a much less expensive area. But second, they have moved to a state where living less expensively does not entail living dangerously or in the midst of squalor. West Virginia and Connecticut have identical state property crime rates, and they also found a neighborhood in West Virginia with much—not all—of the ambience of their former neighborhood in Connecticut. Third, they significantly increased their liquid assets by selling their house in Connecticut and purchasing their West Virginia house. They now have several hundred thousand dollars to use when necessary for various unexpected exigencies in later life. They are understandably quite satisfied with the outcomes of their move.

In contrast, the Sanfords in New Jersey (with the third most expensive cost of living among the states) are struggling. They received their expected retirement income, but it is far less than their income when they were working. Retiring in their familiar environment probably exacerbated their problems in cutting back on expenses. Carl could join a less expensive golf club, but then he would be separated from his golf buddies of many years. Jessica should probably give up the extravagant Saturday morning breakfast she shares with friends, but they would continue the practice while she sat lonely only a few

Table 3.1   Top seventeen states on the affordability aspect of SSF rank-ordered by property crime safety

Rank (scores)	States
1 (0.018)	South Dakota (8)
2 (0.020)	North Dakota (7)
3 (0.023)	Maine (12)
4 (0.025)	Kentucky (4)
5 (0.026)	West Virginia (2)
6 (0.027)	Idaho (15)
7 (0.028)	Iowa (16)
8 (0.031)	Montana (5), Wyoming (17)
10 (0.033)	Mississippi (1)
11 (0.037)	Louisiana (9)
12 (0.039)	Alabama (6), Oklahoma (10)
14 (0.041)	Arkansas (3)
15 (0.042)	New Mexico (11)
16 (0.042)	Tennessee (14)
17 (0.044)	South Carolina (13)

NOTE: These seventeen states score above 2.00 on the affordability aspect of SSF. A state's affordability ranking is in parentheses behind its name. Property crime scores represent property crimes per one thousand state residents.

blocks away. Yet the Sanfords know that something must change. They often spend a little more than their income each month, and they have less extensive liquid savings to fall back upon than the Tates. They realize that, across the next fifteen years, their medical or long-term care needs may well require significant payments from their savings, and they increasingly worry about ending up poor.

The Tates lived in a state even more expensive than New Jersey, and they suffered a serious setback when Jim's pension was taken over by the Pension Benefit Guaranty Corporation, yet they are doing fine now, while the Sanfords—facing an easier situation—are slowing going under. What do these two stories tell us? While they focus on financial viability rather than having fun in the sun, this situation reminds us of the contrast between Art and Karen Munro and Jerry and Arlene Senter in chapter 1. Art and Karen wanted to have fun in retirement, so they left their rather drab surroundings on the northern prairie and found what they wanted in the mountains of southeastern New Mexico. Jerry and Arlene Senter had imagined a retirement similar to the one the Munros have, but they could not generate the initiative to make it happen. So they are just hanging out at home on the prairie.

The Sanfords live more encouragingly than the Senters, but they exhibit a similar problem: through some combination of inadequate imagination and initiative they cannot live the life they wanted on their current income. In New Jersey, they live closer to West Virginia than the Tates did in Connecticut. A solution is right next door. Maybe the Sanfords would prefer Maine or Montana—both good bets on affordability and safety. Or maybe they should exert more discipline with regard to their spending in New Jersey. This third option would not provide them with a substantial nest egg by virtue of a house exchange, but maybe they prefer to stay close to family or friends.

In most regions of the United States people can find select states that offer affordability without sacrificing safety. Generally, if they explore (virtually then actually) these states, they will find neighborhoods that offer this combination of virtues and a range of ambience sufficient to please a wide swath of tastes as well. Numerous older Americans have already figured out at least the affordability part. Californians flock to the less expensive states of Arizona, Nevada, and Utah in retirement. Retirees in the Upper Midwest relocate across the southern tier from Arizona to Florida. And older Americans from the Northeast have been moving to Florida and other southeastern states for decades, but not all these destination states offer relatively safe environments. We hope the information in this chapter helps interested seniors identify affordable and safe relocation states that fit their preferences.

4

SUSTAINING HEALTH AND OBTAINING HIGH-QUALITY MEDICAL CARE

Here we examine two central issues for many seniors: where to live the healthiest lives and find the best medical care. We cannot control our genetic endowment, but to maintain our health we can avoid smoking and adhere to a sensible program of diet and exercise. Following desirable habits across a lifetime into retirement greatly improves the chances of remaining healthy as a senior. Yet even people who have lapsed in such practices at earlier stages of life can generally expect some salutary results from living more wisely in retirement. Seniors also need high-quality professional medical care for existing maladies and to help prevent developing additional health problems. Various states exhibit significantly different degrees of healthiness among both their general and their senior populations and sharply varying levels in the quality of the medical care they afford seniors. Once again, we consider a pair of contrasting examples.

Bob and Helen Wilson

Bob and Helen Wilson live in one of the suburban communities north of Dallas, Texas. He is seventy-two; she is seventy. Bob retired nine years ago, completely disenchanted with his job as a midlevel administrator in a pharmaceutical company; Helen has always centered her adult life on family and home. She actively works around the house and garden and shops for groceries and other things. She regularly visits a number of people, including her older daughter and her three teenage grandchildren, who live in nearby Fort Worth. She also chats and lunches with friends among her neighbors and members of her church. In many respects, she feels connected, happy, and healthy.

Bob fares less well. During the first couple of years after retiring, he puttered in his garage workshop and fixed things around the house, but his activity gradually declined. Now he does very little and has become increasingly overweight and lethargic. Apart from Helen, he talks to almost no one. He once played poker with a group of men on Friday evenings; he now stays home instead. He claims he is too tired. Helen knows that he will smoke and drink too much if he goes, so she does not encourage him to join them.

Over the past several years Bob has developed both emphysema and diabetes. For Helen, his declining condition came at a particularly unfortunate time. Her older brother, who never married, died recently, leaving her a modest inheritance. She would like to use it to travel. She and Bob did not get to travel while he was working and their daughters were growing up. Helen particularly wants to visit her younger daughter and two more grandchildren near Salt Lake City, Utah. But Bob feels hesitant about traveling and fears getting sick away from home. Unfortunately, Helen is afraid to go to Salt Lake City on her own and leave Bob alone to take care of himself.

In part, Bob exacerbates his own problems. He gets very little exercise. He eats too much. He eats foods that he should avoid. He still smokes a bit. He drinks too much. He sits around, becoming more socially isolated, self-absorbed, depressed, and irritable. Helen fears reminding him to check his blood glucose, and he monitors it only rarely. Bob is not getting much enjoyment out of life, and his predicament deprives Helen of opportunities she would explore if Bob were healthier, both physically and psychologically.

Despite their technical knowledge and skills, Bob's physicians do not address these problems. Bob sees a primary care physician, a pulmonologist for emphysema, and—occasionally—an endocrinologist about his diabetes. Yet these professionals do not coordinate their activities. The physician Bob sees for diabetes did not know about his emphysema until just a few weeks ago, when Bob's wheezing reached a level that was obvious. The physician he sees for emphysema still remains unaware of Bob's diabetes. Neither Bob nor his primary care physician has shared his complete medical profile with these specialists. The primary care physician thinks that he has done his job with respect to these illnesses by sending Bob to a specialist, and each specialist focuses on treatment within her or his own area of expertise.

Overall, no one—including Bob—ever takes overall responsibility; no one sits Bob down and explains the seriousness of his predicament, outlining how, in the absence of remedial action, his quality of life will go downhill sharply from here (through being tied to an oxygen tank or through disabling strokes or blindness). Specialists often experience difficulty receiving adequate Medicare payment for lengthy consultations with patients, but none of Bob's physicians has ever "prescribed" Bob—in anything other than the most casual terms— appropriate lifestyle changes, including joining one of several groups available in the Dallas area for learning more about better health habits and acquiring social support for practicing them. Does Bob and Helen's story remind you of people you know? All too many seniors fall into similar patterns.

Larry and Julie Crothers

Now consider Larry and Julie Crothers and why they recently moved back to Concord, New Hampshire, from Scottsdale, Arizona, a suburb of Phoenix. They initially relocated to Scottsdale from New Hampshire almost fifteen years ago to enjoy the sun and warmer winters. Last year, their daughter Caroline, a nurse in Concord, pressured them to move back to get better help with Larry's declining health. In broad outline Larry and Julie's tale resembles Bob and Helen's. But recently Larry and Julie, seventy-six and seventy-three, respectively, have chosen a different course, which has improved their quality of life. Larry's New Hampshire physicians proactively coordinate with one another and the family in fostering Larry's health, and they also apply the "best practices" standards disseminated by the Centers for Medicare and Medicaid Services more assiduously.

During Larry's initial appointment with his primary care physician in Concord, the geriatrician scheduled him an appointment with her nurse practitioner and a dietician to discuss his diabetes. They gave Larry a series of exercise and dietary guidelines and introduced him to the equipment required for monitoring his blood glucose levels. The nurse practitioner expressly invited Julie to be present, and she attended this session. When Larry's emphysema appeared a few months later, the primary care physician reacted with a similar process. In this second session, Julie expressed her fear that Larry was not taking the guidelines seriously enough. The physician then prescribed a series of professionally led sessions with a group of men and women his age having similar problems. At this juncture, Caroline, their daughter, began strenuously encouraging Larry to take these sessions—and his health and life generally—seriously.

As we can see, Larry's primary care internist carefully addressed Larry's overall situation. She acted to increase Larry's knowledge of healthier habits and helped provide him with social support for following them. While the internist served as Larry's physician for most matters, she referred Larry to a pulmonologist at one point shortly after Larry's emphysema developed. When she did so, she called the specialist, briefly outlining Larry's situation, and faxed him a copy of Larry's complete medical profile as well as the full gamut of Larry's prescribed remedies. Further, the primary care physician encouraged the pulmonologist, with some success, to join the "team" urging new lifestyle habits on Larry.

Larry now takes Ginger, his new golden retriever, on a lengthy daily walk, even during the winter months. He eats better, if not less, and his weight has dropped. With the help of the group sessions and nicotine gum, he has quit smoking. And he drinks less than he once did, partly because he is less lonely and depressed. His daughter and her family help to keep his spirits up. Larry's overall treatment program helps him feel better and get out more. In fact, he and Julie plan to join Martin, a friend Larry made through the group sessions, and Martin's wife, Janet, on a trip sponsored by the Smithsonian Institution to Native American cliff dwellings and related anthropological sites in the American Southwest early this coming April. Julie is thrilled at the prospect of the organized trip, and she and Larry will spend a few days afterward visiting their friends in Scottsdale. It will be spring—or nearly so—when they return to New Hampshire. Of course, they will both be delighted to retrieve Ginger from Caroline when they get back.

Acquiring and Maintaining Good Health

As we suggested in the introductory paragraph, three broad factors influence healthiness. Fortunate genetic endowment and related constitutional factors help some people become naturally more robust than others. For instance, Lance Armstrong, the seven-time winner of the Tour de France bicycle race, enjoys the capacity—at least partially genetically derived—to pump much more blood through his heart in a given stretch of time than most other people are able to do. Sound habits of exercising, eating a sensible diet, and avoiding or limiting risky behaviors such as smoking, drinking, and driving dangerously all contribute to good health. Finally, people need to get appropriate medical care when or even before illness or injury strike. Since none of us can alter our genetic endowment, the vignettes above and the sections below focus on the other two factors: healthy habits and appropriate medical care.

Larry now maintains better health habits than does Bob, and his health has actually improved with appropriate medical care that integrates his physicians, family members, and new friends, who all support his improving habits. Larry feels better, both physically and psychologically, than Bob does. And Bob's incapacities unfortunately impoverish Helen's life in various ways as well. At this juncture Larry and Julie can look forward to a more active and pleasant life than can Bob and Helen.

Assessing a State's Support of Healthy Aging and High-Quality Medical Care

The American states differ considerably on the healthiness of their senior populations and the quality of the medical care that Medicare patients receive. In contrast to their familiarity with the differences between Minnesota and Arizona winters, older Americans rarely recognize these cross-state divergences in retiree healthiness and medical care quality and are often surprised when they learn about them. Yet surely these latter differences can be just as important to senior well-being as those of winter climate. As the contrast between Bob and Larry suggests, people can benefit from factors such as careful coordination among their medical care providers and family members, and this coordination as well as other encouraging medical care features prevail more thoroughly in some states than in others.

Most of the medical care delivered to older Americans is at least partially paid for by the Medicare program. Medicare is, in part, an aspect of the national Social Security program, or Old-Age, Survivors, Disability and Hospital Insurance. Accordingly, its beneficiaries include the vast majority of Americans sixty-five or older, some younger disabled adults, and persons in end-state renal dialysis for kidney failure. These beneficiaries have contributed to Social Security's two trust funds: one for old age and disability, the other for hospital expenses. Two other aspects of Medicare insurance serve to pay physicians and some other medical care providers and to provide limited coverage for prescription drugs. Social Security beneficiaries have the option of signing up for these portions of Medicare (virtually all do) when they pick up hospital insurance. Monies to fund these latter two aspects of Medicare come from enrollees' insurance charges, user fees (in the form of deductibles and co-payments) and general federal revenues. Medicare also includes noninsurance components such as the Centers for Medicare and Medicaid Services's efforts to improve the quality of the medical care the program funds through the efforts of what are called *quality improvement organizations.*

Social Security pensions are "goods" (in both an economic and a philosophical sense), standardized payments for people with similar earnings histories, and do not vary on the basis of state of residence, but Medicare benefits take the form of "services" (economically—although still goods in a philosophical sense) delivered by private health care professionals and do vary in quality both within and across the states. These professionals differ in their training, efforts to remain up to date with regard to the flow of innovations in their rapidly changing fields of expertise, sense of responsibility to patients, integration with the medical community in the geographic area in which they practice, and numerous other matters that all contribute to variation in the quality of services they provide.[1] That medical professionals differ in the quality of their services is not surprising, but sharp cross-state variation in average quality is surprising. That physicians in New Hampshire and Texas, for instance, deliver, on average, medical services of quite different quality suggests that variation in other aspects of the American states—their social, economic, political, and medical professional institutions and environments—contribute to cross-state variation in the average quality of medical care delivered to Medicare patients.[2]

Healthy Aging

We first compare how states support the healthiness of their older residents, employing the Centers for Disease Control's (CDC's) *State-by-State Report Card on Healthy Aging* (hereafter the CDC healthy aging index) as our indicator.[3] The CDC determines the proportions of each state's sixty-five-or-older population that fall into fifteen encouraging (e.g., eating five or more servings of fruits and vegetables daily) or discouraging (e.g., currently smoking) categories and ranks the states on each of these criteria. Our measure averages these fifteen rankings, coordinated so that higher scores systematically indicate better outcomes (e.g., more elders eating substantial amounts of fruits and vegetables but fewer seniors smoking). Figure 4.1 shows the results.[4] With only a few exceptions, northern states dominate the higher ranks. In contrast, states in the lower ranks are predominantly southern, particularly southeastern.

The activities of health care professionals influence most of the fifteen criteria in the CDC's index either directly or indirectly. For instance, physicians may recommend that their older patients get vaccinated against pneumonia or have a mammogram. Or seniors may read an article or see a television program in which a medical authority encourages these practices. Cross-state variations

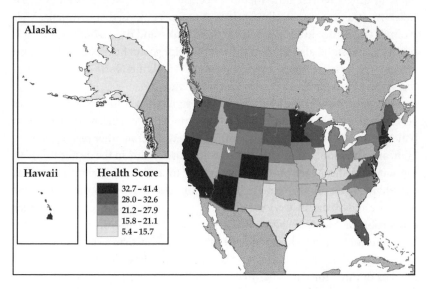

Figure 4.1: Healthiness of state residents sixty-five or older (2004)

on some of the CDC's criteria also likely reflect differences in general social practices or standards among the states (e.g., in smoking, acceptance of obesity, and social pressure for dental care). So differences in the activities of a state's medical care professionals and variation in more general social pressures (e.g., activities of senior advocacy groups, friends, or family to foster health consciousness) both help to explain the healthiness of a state's senior population. As table A.22 in the Appendix shows, seniors in states at the top of this ranking and those at the bottom differ substantially in health. Also, in chapter 6 we will explain how the egalitarian/moralistic culture that we discussed in chapter 2 facilitates social attitudes supporting healthiness, among both a state's general population and its older citizens.

Medical Care Quality: Best Practices

Seniors fall vulnerable to a greater range of health problems than do other adults, so persons over sixty-five need to get the best possible medical care. Figure 4.2 reveals states' overall rankings on the quality of a sample of twenty-four medical procedures delivered to Medicare patients as calculated by Jencks, Huff, and Cuerdon.[5] These procedures include hospital treatments for heart attack and stroke as well as ambulatory treatments for pneumonia, breast cancer, and diabetes. The states in the top ranks are, once again, predominantly northern. Geographically contiguous New Hampshire, Vermont, and Maine lead the ranking with others representing the north-central states as well as some western states. Another geographically contiguous group, composed of Louisiana, Mississippi, and Texas, holds the bottom three ranks, and other southeastern and south-central states also fall near the bottom, along with heavily populated and urban New Jersey, Illinois, and California. Overall, the North-South division that appeared in figure 4.1 carries over into figure 4.2.

Thus patients who use Medicare as the primary payer for medical expenses generally receive higher-quality care in a number of northern states than do patients throughout much of the South and a few states in other regions. Jencks, Huff, and Cuerdon measure a state's medical care quality in the degree to which the state's medical care professionals adhere to aspects of "best practices" as defined by quality improvement organizations associated with the Centers for Medicare and Medicaid Services (CMS). So, for instance, a state in which a larger proportion of Medicare heart attack patients receive aspirin within twenty-four hours of hospital admission will rank more highly than a state with a lower proportion on this criterion. CMS's best practices advisories, the practices defined as optimal for particular maladies, reflect ongoing research and change fairly often. Cross-state differences in medical care quality in Jencks, Huff, and

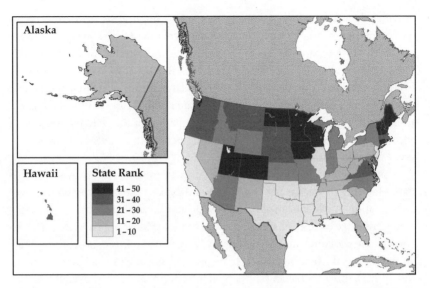

Figure 4.2: "Best practices" conception of medical care quality (2000–2001)

Cuerdon's ranking reveal the degree of attention that state public health and medical care professionals pay to these advisories, efforts to disseminate best-practices information to relevant personnel throughout the state, and the stringency of follow-up measures checking to see that CMS's best practices are actually employed. Jencks, Huff, and Cuerdon contend that even the performance of these activities by states at the top of their ranking leaves considerable room for improvement, but, as figure 4.2 suggests, these processes are performed far more successfully in New Hampshire than in Louisiana, and patients in the latter state pay for these differences in both quantity and quality of life.

While the best-practices conception of medical care quality holds widespread legitimacy, it acquires particular importance in instances in which patients have relatively rare maladies that are especially tricky to treat effectively. In these situations physicians who specialize and have treated a number of similar cases are apt to be up to date on, perhaps even to have contributed to defining, current best practices. In contrast, physicians who deal with an instance of a particular illness every few years or so tend to be less well informed.[6]

Medical Care Quality: Coordination of Care Elements

This third indicator comes at the issue of medical care quality from another, and perhaps unexpected, angle. Contrary to what might be anticipated from consumer experience generally, Baicker and Chandra argue that states that provide Medicare patients relatively *inexpensive* medical services are actually serving up better-quality care.[7] They contend that the relative inexpensiveness of care reflects greater reliance on treatment orchestrated by primary care physicians with less dependence on specialists. Baicker and Chandra's inexpensiveness criterion acquires credibility by correlating positively with Jencks, Huff, and Cuerdon's best-practices measure of state medical care quality at 0.64 and at 0.45 with the average life span of the population of the state in question—both statistically significant. This intriguing perspective holds particular relevance for older patients.

Growing evidence suggests that, for many common maladies, lower average state Medicare payments per beneficiary indicate (1) the relatively widespread orchestration of patients' medical care by primary care physicians, (2) relatively limited reliance on specialist consultations, and (3) more appropriate care—as portrayed in the contrasting vignettes involving Bob and Larry above. As we shall see below, this third point is likely to be particularly true for frail older patients with little chance of achieving substantial improvements in their overall physical condition.[8] In contrast, high-average state Medicare costs per beneficiary often come from patients being bounced from one specialist to another, as Jean's parents were in Florida (the fifth most expensive state in Baicker and Chandra's data). While specialist-intensive testing and treatment can, as acknowledged above, be technologically superior, it may also be uncoordinated and less helpful. Thus crucial elements of rather ordinary therapies may fall through the cracks between distinct specialties, and specialist-intensive treatment may end up being more inappropriate than less technologically sophisticated care.

For instance, in 2003 and with adjustments for relevant demographic factors such as age and sex, Medicare spending per patient in Miami was twice as high as in Minneapolis.[9] Yet Dartmouth investigators have found no evidence that higher medical expenses confer health benefits. Indeed, mortality rates rise in higher-spending regions, and functional outcomes are no better than in lower-spending regions. Further, in the higher-spending regions, the technical quality of care often falls, communication among providers suffers, continuity of care declines, and patients are generally less satisfied.[10] Older patients are particularly likely to need individual attention and coordination of care across physicians. Areas with many specialists often serve these needs poorly. Gawande illustrates these problems by comparing two counties in Texas, one with higher rates of specialist use, the other with lower. Quality of patient outcomes did not differ between the two, but per patient costs in the county with higher rates of specialist use were more than twice as great.[11]

Figure 4.3 reveals state ranks on the relative inexpensiveness of Medicare payments per beneficiary. The North-South distinctions so obvious in figures

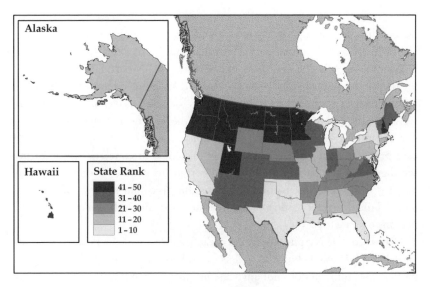

Figure 4.3: "Coordination of care elements" conception of medical care quality (2000–2001)

4.1 and 4.2 are more muted in figure 4.3. Instead of these being pronounced, states dominated (in terms of population) by large urban centers distinguish themselves from states in which a higher proportion of residents live in smaller cities and towns. (The percentage of a state's population living outside major metropolitan areas and the inexpensiveness of the medical care delivered to Medicare patients in the state correlate at 0.41—statistically significant.) This means that care is generally less expensive in nonmetropolitan areas. The top ranks of figure 4.3 still contain several northern, small-city states such as New Hampshire, South Dakota, Montana, North Dakota, and Idaho. The bottom ranks are less obviously southern than for figures 4.1 and 4.2, but virtually all these states (Louisiana, Texas, California, Maryland, Florida, New York, Massachusetts, New Jersey, Oklahoma, and Michigan) have a large city or cities that contribute heavily to the state's total population. Especially in the large urban centers of these states, medical care tends to draw extensively on a range of specialists with less coordination by primary care physicians.

Care Near the End of Life

Particularly near the end of life, older patients frequently benefit from coordination with their families and health professionals in choosing appropriate therapies during an evolving decline lasting months or even years. The best-practices conception of medical care quality discussed above may need redefinition for these older patients. Aggressive testing and treatment might not benefit a frail eighty-five-year-old patient with a terminal condition as clearly as they would a generally healthy fifty-five-year-old patient. This is particularly the case if the therapy in question involves a physically demanding operation with a long, painful recovery period. McCullough argues for a new model of caring for persons near the end of their lives: "slow medicine."[12] This model involves intensive communication among the patient, physicians and perhaps other health care providers, and the patient's family or "circle of concern," emphasizing the dignity of the patient and her or his right to choose among treatments based on extensive discussion of the possible risks and rewards of different levels of medical intervention. More treatment may not be better care for many persons over eighty.

Slow medicine is a philosophy and practice for care of elders based on individual and informed choice as well as careful coordination among concerned parties. McCullough does not advocate limiting care, but rather offering truly informed choice. He has developed this model of care over a number of years as a geriatrician in a continuing care retirement community (CCRC) where he found many residents wanting to avoid "death by intensive care." The older population near the end of life may benefit from a conception of best practices that stresses intensive communication with a primary care physician—hopefully a geriatrician—and slow, careful deliberation about appropriate care among all concerned, more than from immediate 911 calls and frequent trips to an emergency room. Some patients may opt to try to lengthen life at any cost in terms of pain and risk of losing functioning, but others may choose to avoid the most aggressive testing and treatment.[13] McCullough's point is that near the end of life in particular, each patient deserves a chance to hear the full range of options and to deliberate which to choose with whomever—family, lifelong friends, medical experts—she or he wants. McCullough practices this care with elders at the CCRC Kendal at Hanover. Kendal residents and their families report high satisfaction with their autonomy, compassionate care, and quality of life. Many also choose to forgo a range of heroic medical procedures near the end of life—particularly to avoid dying in hospital intensive care units (ICUs). A number of other programs in select communities across the country are picking up some or all slow medicine practices.

Our fourth indicator attempts to measure this approach. It involves the percentage of a state's Medicare patients, dying in 2005, who did *not* spend any time in an ICU or cardiac care unit (CCU) during their last six months of life. These patients avoided at least this particular intervention. There are of course many reasons why individuals would avoid entering these units during their final six months of life, and many Medicare patients might have had no need or opportunity to do so. But describing how a certain large group of patients die in different states lets us compare state orientations toward serious medical intervention late in life.[14]

Data presented by the *Dartmouth Atlas of Health Care* include the percentage of Medicare decedents admitted to an ICU or CCU during the last six months of their lives. To fit this indicator with the three previous ones, we reversed the measure so that it expresses the percentage who were not admitted. Figure 4.4 shows how states rank on this inversion of the *Dartmouth Atlas of Health Care* data.[15] As with figures 4.1 and 4.2, northern states from Maine to Montana dominate figure 4.4's top ranks. The bottom ranks in figure 4.4 distinguish states less in terms of a geographic region than in terms of high degrees of urbanization (e.g., Delaware), the presence of large cities (e.g., California, Florida, Illinois, New Jersey and Texas), or both.

Arguments could be made both for and against routinely using extraordinary therapies on patients near the end of life. But which approach fits best with other measures of medical care quality? The percentage of a state's Medicare decedents who avoid admission to an ICU or CCU during their last six months of life correlates positively and statistically significantly with the other three indicators of positive outcomes that we have introduced so far at 0.28 with the health of states' older residents, 0.70 with the best-practices conception of

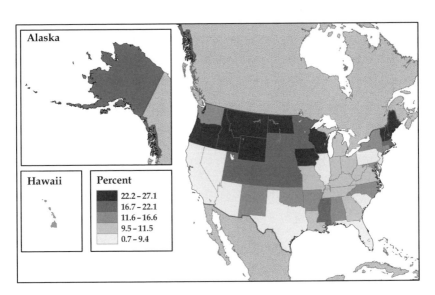

Figure 4.4: Medicare decedents not admitted to ICU/CCU during
last six months of life (2005)

medical care quality, and 0.59 with the coordination-of-care-elements concep-tion of medical care quality.[16] (The last two of these are statistically significant; the first just barely misses attaining statistical significance.) These correlations support the hypothesis that better care for elders near the end of life often means avoiding extreme medical interventions.

Overall

Variation among the states on these four indicators is associated with differ-ences in states' cultures. For instance, all four of these indicators of seniors' health and the quality of their medical care correlate positively and statistically significantly with the presence of a relatively egalitarian culture in a state. This means that when large cities dominate a state's population and social inequal-ity is greater, a large proportion of a state's older residents will have a harder time finding high-quality medical care. States with higher proportions of rural residents, for instance, rely much more sparingly on medical specialists. Spe-cific institutions in different states likely vary in how much they support the coordination-of-care-elements conception of medical care quality. For exam-ple, some state associations of primary care physicians may encourage and facilitate comprehensive medical care more thoroughly than others. Such dif-ferences would surely affect the health of older state residents.

Most of the states that entice seniors with outdoor activity and recreational lifestyles tend to do poorly in supporting healthy aging and high-quality med-ical care for seniors. In fact, only three states (Colorado, Hawaii, and Utah) appear among the top ten ranks on both of these aspects of state senior friend-liness (SSF), and two other states (Minnesota and North Dakota) that occupy top positions on healthy aging and high-quality medical care appear in the bottom-ten ranks on recreational lifestyle. (Compare tables A.36 and A.39 in the Appendix.) So while moving from Minnesota to Florida or one of the states in the Southwest may make sense early in retirement to enjoy milder climates and more outdoor recreational opportunities, returning to a state such as Min-nesota may also make sense when a retiree's need for high-quality medical care exceeds her or his capacity for engaging in outdoor recreation. It appears that many Minnesotans who migrated away early in retirement do return a couple of decades later. We do not have individual-level data to show that the people who enter Minnesota from another state in their mid-eighties are among those who left early in retirement, but limited case studies do suggest that this pattern of movement exists.[17] Across the United States, in-migration among retirees eighty-five or older correlates positively, but not statistically significantly, with all four of the measures introduced above. This suggests that some elders perceive the benefits in health and medical care quality that certain states offer and move to obtain them. More seniors could follow their example in the future.

Additional Indicators

We have compared how well different states support healthiness and high-quality medical care among seniors. Now we turn to the question of how these differences in quality relate to the quantity of life—our "so-what," or social outcome, indicator—and a couple of other indicators involving state healthiness and seniors access to physicians.

Quantity and Quality of Life

We expect that persons will live longer in states that support healthy lifestyles and high-quality medical care among seniors. We anticipate that retirees will live better (in the sense of being less afflicted by health problems that detract from quality of life) in these states too. Later, in chapter 6, we explore how a state's average life expectancy helps to validate the four indicators that we used in the previous section to predict a state's support of healthiness and high-quality medical care among seniors. For the moment, we limit ourselves to a discussion of figure 4.5,[18] which shows the life expectancy at birth for residents of different states.[19] States familiar from figures 4.1 through 4.4 appear in both the top and bottom ranks of figure 4.5, showing where people live the longest and shortest lives. All the states in the top ranks (longest lives) of figure 4.5 have appeared in the top ranks of figures 4.1 through 4.4 on at least one occasion. With the exception of Hawaii, states in the top ranks can reasonably be described as northern, representing contiguous groupings from New England, the north-central region, and the middle Rocky Mountain states. Remarkably, the ten states holding the bottom positions (shortest lives) form a contiguous group in the southeastern quadrant of the United States. Nine of these states also appeared in the bottom-ten ranks across figures 4.1 through 4.4, some on multiple occasions. The only newcomer to these bottom ranks in figure 4.5 is Tennessee.

Life expectancy at birth ranges slightly more than six years, from 73.7 (Mississippi) to 79.8 (Hawaii). Six years seems a short or a long time depending on the quality of life one experiences. Life expectancy indicates the quantity rather than the quality of life, and whether more is better hinges for some persons on quality. Quality of life assuredly springs from more than good health, but while not sufficient, good health clearly facilitates a better quality of life for most persons. Data from the CDC's healthy aging index that we introduced above

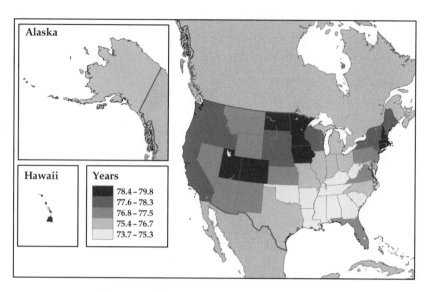

Figure 4.5: State life expectancy at birth (2000)

indicate that persons living in states with longer life expectancy also enjoy greater quality of life than those living in states with the lower life expectancy. Overall, quantity of life (life expectancy) correlates positively and statistically significantly at 0.79 with quality of life among seniors (as measured by the CDC's healthy aging index).

Just as quantity of life varies only slightly between states in adjacent ranks in figure 4.5, the quality of life of similarly ranked states also differs only modestly. But the quality of life enjoyed by seniors in states near the top of the life expectancy (quantity of life) ranking and the quality of life experienced by elders in states near the bottom of the life expectancy ranking differ quite substantially. Table 4.1 contrasts the top and bottom ten states in terms of life expectancy on the five factors that are arguably most indicative of quality of lived experience among the fifteen criteria included in the CDC's healthy aging index. The second and third columns in particular (unhealthy days and residents with frequent mental distress) indicate that where residents live longer, seniors enjoy better physical and mental health.

State Population Healthiness

Interstate migration has steadily increased across the past fifty years, but the vast majority of seniors in any particular state have lived in that state for some time. We recognize that people need to develop healthy habits and practices early in life, rather than in their fifties or sixties, for these habits and practices to help confer good health across the life course. So the health of a state's total population ought to predict the relative healthiness of its older residents. Figure 4.6 examines this question and shows the health rankings of overall state populations based on the United Health Foundation's *America's Health: State*

Table 4.1 Top and bottom ten life expectancy states on five measures of quality of life for sixty-five or older persons

Rank and State	Average number of days residents were physically unhealthy in the past month (rank) (2004)	Percent of residents with "frequent mental distress" (rank) (2003–2004)	Percent of residents with complete tooth loss (rank) (2004)	Percent "disabled" (rank) (2004)	Percent obese (rank) (2004)
Top ten states on life expectancy (2000)					
1 Hawaii	3.2 (1)	3.8 (1)	No data	20.6 (1)	10.2 (1)
2 Minnesota	5.2 (12)	4.2 (2)	14.3 (4)	38.5 (42)	22.6 (40)
3 North Dakota	5.4 (16)	5.4 (11)	25.0 (37)	34.0 (26)	23.6 (47)
4 Utah	5.7 (31)	6.2 (20)	13.6 (2)	39.9 (47)	20.3 (27)
5 Iowa	4.8 (3)	4.2 (2)	23.3 (33)	30.7 (8)	24.0 (49)
6 New Hampshire	5.7 (31)	5.8 (17)	21.1 (24)	32.5 (22)	19.2 (19)
7 Colorado	5.4 (16)	5.7 (15)	18.1 (15)	32.5 (22)	13.9 (2)
8 Connecticut	5.5 (24)	5.7 (15)	12.4 (1)	29.4 (3)	17.7 (6)
9 Massachusetts	4.9 (6)	6.2 (20)	16.5 (7)	31.2 (10)	17.2 (5)
10 California	5.4 (16)	8.5 (48)	13.6 (3)	32.4 (22)	18.6 (15)
Bottom ten states on life expectancy (2000)					
41 Georgia	6.8 (47)	6.3 (24)	28.3 (42)	41.2 (50)	21.1 (35)
42 Kentucky	6.6 (45)	10.3 (51)[a]	38.1 (49)	38.5 (42)	20.4 (28)
43 Oklahoma	6.0 (39)	7.3 (44)	31.2 (45)	39.6 (46)	18.1 (11)
44 Arkansas	6.0 (39)	6.4 (27)	24.7 (36)	34.4 (28)	19.1 (18)
45 Tennessee	5.9 (36)	6.8 (31)	32.3 (48)	31.6 (14)	20.4 (28)
46 West Virginia	5.9 (51)[a]	9.1 (49)	42.9 (50)	42.3 (51)[a]	22.6 (40)
47 South Carolina	6.6 (45)	7.1 (38)	26.1 (39)	34.5 (29)	22.5 (39)
48 Alabama	7.3 (49)	9.6 (50)	31.9 (47)	35.9 (36)	24.5 (50)
49 Louisiana	5.4 (16)	7.2 (41)	31.4 (46)	31.6 (14)	25.6 (51)[a]
50 Mississippi	7.3 (49)	7.0 (36)	29.6 (44)	39.5 (45)	22.6 (40)

[a] CDC's rankings includes the District of Columbia for a total of fifty-one ranks.

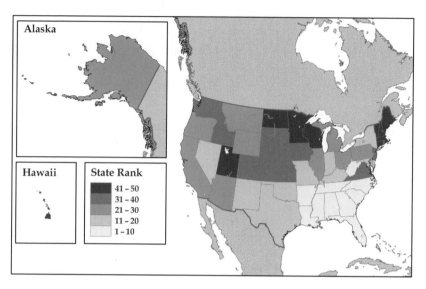

Figure 4.6: Healthiness of state population (2004)

Health Rankings—2004.[20] This eighteen-item index produces a rank-ordering of states that is remarkably similar to that generated by the CDC's healthy aging index in figure 4.1. The two rankings correlate at a statistically significant 0.71, which supports the hypothesis that adopting healthy lifestyles early in life leads to better quality of life as a senior. Figure 4.6 reveals the familiar North-South distinction once again. With the exceptions of Hawaii and Utah, northern states rank at the top. Further, southern—particularly southeastern—states occupy the bottom ranks. These results reinforce the idea that, in order to be a healthy senior, it helps considerably to follow healthy habits and seek appropriate preventive and therapeutic medical care throughout life, not just as a senior.

State Physician Availability

Overall, the primary factor that limits Americans' access to medical care is lack of medical care insurance, experienced by a relatively high percentage of citizens. But virtually all seniors have at least some insurance coverage through Medicare (which many supplement with a private group "Medigap" policy) or a combination of Medicare and Medicaid. So the degree of availability of physicians likely represents a more significant limitation on medical care access for older Americans. Figure 4.7 shows the distribution of physicians across the states. Massachusetts leads the pack with over two and one-half times the number of physicians (per one hundred thousand state residents) compared with

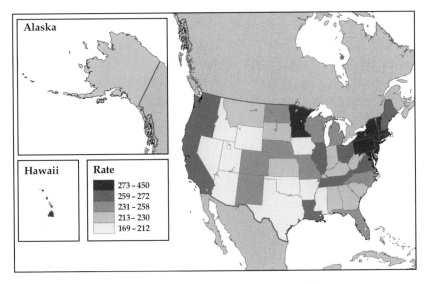

Figure 4.7: Physicians per 100,000 state residents

Idaho.[21] The states in the top ranks of figure 4.7 are again northeastern, with the exceptions of Hawaii and Minnesota. The Eastern Seaboard north of Washington, D.C., is awash in physicians by the standards of most of the rest of the United States.[22] This means that seniors can likely gain access to physicians more easily in the Northeast than in most other regions.

More generally, for both professional and perhaps personal reasons, physicians tend to congregate in urban areas, and physician availability in rural states such as Idaho inevitably suffers. Practitioners of medical specialties tend to distribute themselves among the states in ways that are even more disparate than for physicians overall. Once again, densely populated states with large cities attract far more and rural states substantially fewer specialists per one hundred thousand state residents. However, as we discussed above, access to specialists does not appear to translate into systematic health benefits for older Americans. States in the bottom ranks of figure 4.7 represent, with the exception of Iowa, a mixture of southern and western regions. For most of these states a substantial portion of the population lives outside metropolitan areas, but a majority of these states still have one or more major urban centers. A relatively low ratio of physicians to population may affect the health of older Americans adversely, for this ratio and the CDC healthy aging index correlate at a statistically significant 0.48. A higher number of physicians per one hundred thousand state residents appears to influence seniors to become better informed and to follow preventive measures and healthy habits more routinely.

Conclusions: Back to the Wilsons and the Crothers

All seven factors discussed above help us understand Larry and Julie's relative success, in contrast with Bob and Helen's growing frustrations arising from health-related issues. Their family situations reflect systematic state differences. Overall, most northern states have healthier general populations, and the practices of physicians and other medical professionals in these states help their populations to age in a healthier fashion. Additionally, a number of northern states provide higher-quality medical care to Medicare beneficiaries and offer less discouraging social environments for dying.

Accordingly, Larry Crothers acquired healthier habits through a combination of his own efforts in returning to New Hampshire from Arizona and the actions of others, including his medical care providers and family. Different state environments clearly influence the quality of medical and related services available to residents. New Hampshire, for instance, ranks among the top states in the CDC's healthy aging index on several items, including sixty-five-or-older residents having had a mammogram in the past two years (for women), having had a colorectal cancer screening, and being up to date on other selected preventive services (for men). This reflects the efforts of New Hampshire's relatively numerous physicians both directly, by fostering prevention among their patients, and indirectly, by encouraging television stations broadcasting to New Hampshire residents to include health segments in their news broadcasts and public service announcements. Various nonprofit groups and public-sector health bureaucracies advocate for these concerns as well. These efforts contribute to a relatively health-conscious social environment. Healthiness may be "contagious," particularly when physicians and communities emphasize prevention and best practices.

In contrast, seniors in a number of southern and a few other states appear less healthy and receive lower-quality medical care. For instance, seniors in Texas—where Bob Wilson lives—fall in or near the bottom ranks on a range of preventive measures. Medicare patients in Texas and many other southern states average lower-quality medical care, and Texas, along with most of its neighboring states, generally provides more discouraging social, medical, and legal environments for dying.[23] So, in fostering healthy patterns of life, the Wilsons in Texas have to rely far more thoroughly on their own initiative than do the Crothers in New Hampshire.

Thus, while the Wilsons' problems derive in part from their own shortsightedness and missteps, their social environment also constrains their efforts. The health habits of their friends and relatives are likely less encouraging than those of the Crothers', and their medical practitioners focus more on dispensing narrowly defined professional services rather than facilitating overall wellness. Poor health habits may also be contagious, especially where physicians and communities do not actively support healthiness.

So seniors differ in their personal situations, but our analyses suggest that they may benefit from a move—as the Crothers did—at the outset of retirement to states such as Arizona, Florida, or even the Wilson's home state of Texas for milder winters and more extensive recreational opportunities or to states such as Kentucky, Oklahoma, or West Virginia for affordable but relatively safe living conditions. But unless people make these moves considering medical care along with other factors (Colorado, Hawaii, or Utah in the mild climate and recreational opportunity instance or Maine, Montana, or North Dakota in the case of inexpensive, safe social environments), they may, as older retirees, need to plan for a second move—similar to the one that the Crothers made back to New Hampshire—to a state supporting senior health and high-quality medical care. (Compare tables A.36 and A.38 with tables A.39 in the Appendix.) Our vignettes also illustrate that the experience of moving early in retirement better prepares people for a second move later, whereas the Wilsons, who have lived all their lives in a particular locale, do not even think in terms of moving. As a consequence, their health may deteriorate more rapidly as they age.

5

As we Americans live increasing longer lives, and larger numbers of us will confront disabling health problems, particularly in extremely old age. The "old-old" do suffer from acute illnesses and injuries that require immediate medical attention, but in this chapter we focus on chronic physiological (e.g., severe arthritis) or cognitive (e.g., various forms of dementia) circumstances. Characteristically, help with these health problems means either palliation, easing physical pain or mental anguish, or maintenance, keeping elevated blood pressure under control through periodic monitoring and medication across the long term. Physicians do not generally cure arthritis, dementia, or elevated blood pressure. These patients increasingly need practical help with activities of daily living (ADLs) as well as assistance in monitoring a medical condition and sorting out appropriate medication. This chapter compares how well states provide these long-term care services to older persons.

According to the self-assessment reports in the Census Bureau's 2005 American Community Survey, 40 percent of Americans sixty-five or older exhibit at least one of five categories (cognitive, emotional, mobility, self-care, and sensory) of disability, and many experience two or more.[1] This amounts to nearly 14 million persons. Close to 60 percent of these (about 8 million) rely exclusively on family and friends for help. This assistance enables them to live in their own homes, or in the homes of family members or—less commonly— friends without turning to formal or professional assistance. Of the remaining 40 percent, or almost 6 million, roughly a quarter (1.5 million) reside in nursing facilities. State Medicaid programs pay for most or all of the care of nearly two-thirds of these individuals. Medicaid is a joint federal-state medical insurance program for members of selected groups (e.g., children, pregnant women and mothers of small children, older adults) who have extremely modest incomes and virtually no financial assets. The remaining three-quarters of those drawing on professional long-term care assistance (about 4.5 million) live either at home or other community venues, including adult day care; residential care homes; and what is now widely, but not universally, called assisted living. Many pay privately for professional long-term care services in these venues; others receive financial assistance through their state Medicaid Home and Community-Based

Services (HCBS) program.[2] We offer a brief introduction to these venues and means for paying for long-term care in the next section.

Introduction to Long-Term Care

Long-Term Care Venues

HOME

Most older Americans prefer to live in the familiarity of their own homes as long as possible. But those who depend on home-based professional long-term care may find it extremely expensive, sometimes more costly than nursing facility care. Many turn to public programs to pay for such care. State HCBS long-term care for older persons helps people acquire and pay for a range of support, from home renovations such as wider doors and entries without stairs to household (e.g., shopping and cooking), personal (e.g., bathing and dressing) and modest medical (e.g., sorting out daily medications and providing injections) services. But acquiring public-sector help with these matters can be a trial. As prerequisites, an older person must generally meet both the financial and assistance requirements for obtaining nursing facility care paid for by Medicaid in the state.

Financial requirements involve both assets and income; states vary within a federally prescribed range in the specifics, and these requirements routinely change each year. The Kaiser Family Foundation Web site (http://www.kff.org) provides up-to-date information on specific states. Generally, a person must have very limited assets apart from her or his home and its furnishings and a pretty low income—the upper income limit anywhere would likely be 300 percent of poverty ($31,200 for a single person in 2008) and is generally considerably lower. This income, minus various personal and possibly spousal allowances, would be applied toward payment of the services provided through Medicaid. Those with questions about these limits should contact their local Area Agency on Aging office.

A person's level of assistance rating depends on the number of ADLs she or he needs help with and also on the degree of assistance required. There are five basic ADLs: bathing, dressing, eating, toileting, and transferring (getting into or out of a bed or chair). States differ in their formal stated requirements, and within any state, individuals being assessed for Medicaid long-term care support often confront standards that vary with a number of factors, including the current condition of the state's finances.

COMMUNITY VENUES

Other individuals either choose to enter, or are forced by necessity out into, nonnursing home programs in their communities. Some spend their days in adult day care centers and return home in the evening. Others live in congregate settings that go by a variety of names and that we generically call residential care homes. These entities do not offer the level of care provided in nursing facilities and are thus generally less expensive, but residential care homes are not regulated anywhere near as thoroughly as nursing facilities. As we shall see later in this chapter, experts differ on how well even nursing facilities are regulated.

In the past couple of decades a new option has developed in community-based long-term care: "assisted living." Unfortunately, no standard definition exists across the states for what assisted living settings entail. In fact, in some states assisted living is not yet a legally recognized category of long-term care. In a few states (e.g., Kansas) the term denotes a private apartment that includes kitchenette, toilet, and bath; optional congregate meals; limited home health and personal care; social activities; and open access to the broader community at the individual resident's discretion. Thus, in contrast to nursing facilities, assisted living can offer relative privacy, freedom, and control over one's life. Accordingly, seniors who are more cognitively and physically healthy as well as financially secure widely prefer this form of congregate long-term care. Other states (e.g., North Carolina) do not distinguish as clearly between assisted living and residential care homes that offer less capacity for individual food preparation, widely shared toilets and baths, and limited access to the broader community.

Generally, these community-based options cost less than nursing facility care. However, the cost of particularly fancy assisted living in a state with a high cost of living may well exceed the cost of modest nursing facility care in a low-cost-of-living state.

INSTITUTIONALIZATION

Finally, some older people require nursing facilities, which residents can generally not leave of their own volition. In spite of a laboriously developed and imposing system of regulation, nursing facilities vary widely in actual quality. The design of nursing facilities allows them to cope with relatively high degrees of impairment. Thus people so cognitively impaired that they do not know where they are can be cared for more inexpensively and at far less stress to family members in a nursing facility than in other settings. But few people, whether residents or visitors, find nursing facilities congenial. Most would likely prefer a system in which individuals move through the three venues sequentially:

staying at home as long as possible, turning to something like the encouraging version of assisted living described above when staying at home becomes infeasible, and moving on to a nursing facility only when nothing else will suffice. Frequently, nursing facility care is the most expensive form of long-term care provided to older persons. Nursing facility residents find costs in excess of $6,000 per month ($200 per day) increasingly common, and, nationwide, average annual private-pay costs now exceed $75,000.

Paying for Long-Term Care

PAYING OUT OF POCKET

Paying for long-term care at home can run from as little as several hundred dollars a month to as much as $12,000 (or even more) a month, depending on the help required: from a little housework and periodic personal care to twenty-four-hour skilled nursing attendance. The kind of congregate community residential care that actually attracts many older people—top-of-the-line assisted living—varies in expense across and within the states. A reasonable range to consider would be from the high $4,000s to the low $7,000s per month, after significant "buy-in" costs in the instance of continuing care retirement communities (to be described below). Prospective residents have trouble finding nursing facilities charging below $5,000 a month. Many charge more than $7,000 a month. Annual private-pay nursing facility charges, then, usually run between $60,000 and $88,000.[3] Only a small portion of the current American population over sixty-five holds the combination of income and liquid assets to pay such bills for more than just a few months. Only a minuscule proportion of the population over eighty—the majority of people entering nursing homes—enjoys such income and assets. Within a few months, the vast majority of nursing facility residents exhaust their private assets and find themselves dependent on Medicaid to pay all or most of their nursing facility bills.

MEDICAID

The original Medicaid Act of 1965 required support for nursing facility services for older persons with sufficiently low income and financial asset levels who also met their states' nursing facility functional eligibility criteria. The federal government now allows the states to also use Medicaid funds to provide functionally eligible persons long-term care in their homes and the community-based venues described above if the expense does not exceed that of nursing facility care. And the Supreme Court's 1999 *Olmstead v. L.C.* decision encourages states to make greater use of these options. All states support home-based long-term care for these eligible persons. Most, but not all, states support congregate residential community-based care for these same individuals.

States' assistance comes in one or more of three distinct forms.[4] First, fourteen states support congregate residential community care through their basic state Medicaid plan. This means that any state resident who meets the criteria may receive the support. So for state budget officers, this option threatens unpredictable and potentially high costs.[5] Ten states employ state funds independent of Medicaid, allowing them to ignore Medicaid rules in the support financed in this manner. But most commonly, seniors acquire support for residential HCBS long-term care through waivers (generally 1915[c] waivers). These federal waivers allow states to offer long-term care services in different venues and in excess of those in their state plans so long as the costs per recipient do not exceed the average cost of nursing facility care. Waiver programs allow state officials to specify the total number, geographic scope, and participating groups of beneficiaries, as well as the specific services supported. Waivers also afford greater leniency with regard to beneficiaries' financial eligibility. Thus this form of support enables states to benefit from federal cost-sharing while also offering a way of limiting state costs. These waivers represent either the sole or primary means for providing Medicaid-supported HCBS long-term care for seniors in thirty-eight states, including eleven states that also provide this service through their basic state Medicaid plan or use independent state funds. Persons interested in specific states' policies can contact their Area Agency on Aging for information.[6]

COMMUNITY SPOUSE

If a Medicaid HCBS-supported resident of congregate residential care or a nursing facility resident whose costs are supported by Medicaid has a spouse who remains independent in the community, then the income and assets allowed to the couple exceed those suggested above. Basically, the community spouse may keep the couple's home, an automobile, and income deemed sufficient to allow her or him to live in the house and make use of the car. Once again, the Kaiser Family Foundation Web site (http://kff.org) provides up-to-date information on state variation and changes in the allowances of individual states.

ASSET TRANSFERS

In the past some people made themselves financially eligible for Medicaid support of long-term care by transferring assets to family members or others. Until recently, Medicaid generally used a "look-back" period of three years with regard to such transfers. (That is, the program ignored any asset transfer that occurred more than three years prior to the person's Medicaid application.)

Further, Medicaid used the date of the transfer as the start of any disqualification period. Transfers within the look-back period affected eligibility as follows. Suppose a woman transferred twenty-four thousand dollars to her son six months ago in a state in which the average monthly private-pay rate for nursing facilities was six thousand dollars. State Medicaid officials would divide the twenty-four-thousand-dollar gift by the six-thousand-dollar average monthly private-pay rate and determine that the woman would be ineligible for Medicaid payment of her nursing facility bills for four months after she transferred the funds. So the woman would be eligible immediately. If she had transferred ninety-six thousand dollars, she would have been ineligible for another ten months. Medicaid had employed this practice as standard operating procedure for a number of years.

However, the Deficit Reduction Act of 2005 significantly changed this practice. First, the look-back period now extends five years, not three. More important, the disqualification period now starts only after the woman has entered a nursing facility and has drawn her remaining assets down to a point at which she is otherwise (i.e., apart from the gift) eligible for Medicaid. At this point, she is completely dependent on the person to whom she transferred her assets to pay for her nursing facility bills until the end of her disqualification period. The beneficiary may have already spent the assets. The lesson to draw from this draconian bit of policy is, if an older person transfers assets, she or he should be sure to maintain assets sufficient to last for five years of nursing facility care. A reasonable estimate of what that would mean currently would be about $450,000. So a woman likely to need nursing facility care sometime in the next five years should not give away roughly her first half million dollars of savings that are not needed for other purposes.

Long-Term Care, Medical Care, and "American Exceptionalism"

Public policy affecting older adults in the United States distinguishes sharply between acute and long-term medical care. The federal government's Medicare program covers acute care. This national program standardizes eligibility requirements, although, as we demonstrated in chapter 4, it does not eliminate cross-state differences in quality of care. In contrast, the joint federal-state Medicaid program provides most public-sector support of long-term care.[7] Medicaid's structure fosters considerable cross-state variation in accessibility as well as quality of care. Moreover, Medicare is a social insurance program with benefits earned in part by recipients' prior contributions to the program's trust fund, whereas Medicaid, a public assistance program, distributes benefits on the basis of urgent need. So obtaining Medicaid support for long-term care routinely requires older-adult households to "spend down" their financial assets to poverty levels.

Distinguishing acute from long-term medical care in this fashion sets the United States apart from a number of other wealthy democracies, in which long-term care forms an integral aspect of medical care and acquires coverage from the societies' national medical care insurance programs. The absence of such a national medical care insurance program and the sharp distinction made between acute and long-term medical care in the United States are examples of what scholars often refer to as American exceptionalism.[8] Exceptional American practices such as these appear to arise from a combination of an unusually prominent ideology of individualistic self-reliance; a political system with numerous veto points; and a shifting kaleidoscope of relatively autonomous, powerful, private interests such as physicians, insurance companies, and—most recently—the pharmaceutical industry.[9] Whether the growth of older adults as a proportion of the American population over the next couple of decades will contribute to upgrading how the United States public sector deals with long-term care, bringing our society more into line with practices prevailing in Canada and Western Europe, or prompt a narrowing of existing practices (e.g., by further restricting asset transfers) as a means of containing expanding public-sector financial burdens, remains unclear.

LONG-TERM CARE INSURANCE

Most people find long-term care insurance more complicated and confusing than the other forms of insurance that contemporary Americans routinely buy. Insurance companies have offered these policies for only a quarter century or so, and neither providers nor consumers have extensive experience with them. Consequently, it pays to be careful.

For one thing, long-term care insurance is not for everyone. Those with liquid assets in excess of 1 million dollars can likely pay long-term care expenses if and when they arise. Those with virtually no liquid assets can probably rely on Medicaid. In any case, long-term care insurance remains sufficiently expensive so that people without extensive liquid assets usually cannot afford it. Thus long-term care insurance best serves persons in between these two extremes.

While relatively unusual instances occur in which individuals linger in long-term care for many years, most entering long-term care as elders will not need much of it. On average, people live about three years in a nursing facility. A policy with three or, if asset transfers are a consideration, five years of coverage is generally sufficient.

Perhaps most important, the primary focus should be on three points: the amount of the daily benefit, the level of inflation protection, and the length of the "elimination period." The daily benefit figure should be $250 or higher. Higher is better, but more expensive. Inflation protection is *absolutely essential*. Five percent compounding on the daily benefit with no cap on the total is likely insufficient but generally the best inflation protection offered. Purchasers should take the best inflation protection available, because long-term care costs currently inflate at more than 5 percent per year. The elimination period defines the length of time a policy holder has to spend in long-term care before the policy kicks in. Ninety days is pretty standard. This period is more viable if the policy allows that long-term care covered by another insurer (e.g., Medicare for recuperation from an illness or injury requiring hospitalization) counts toward the ninety days. Shorter periods are available, but are extremely expensive.

Superior policies cover the full range of contingencies we described above: home care, adult day care, and assisted living as well as nursing facility care. This type of coverage is frequently presented in ways that can be difficult to understand. Coverage that includes the HCBS options at 100 percent of charges up to a percentage—say 80—of the nursing facility daily rate represents a reasonable objective for potential customers.

Glossy insurance company brochures and price lists tend to downplay if not actually discourage options such as inflation protection, and many people end up buying less than optimal policies. For instance, they may cover more years than necessary but at a rate (and without inflation protection) that makes the policy of little value twenty or twenty-five years later, when care may be needed. Some purchasers may extend the elimination period to lower the policy premiums and then run themselves out of money before the policy kicks in after four or five months of paying whatever nursing facilities cost twenty or twenty-five years after they purchase the policy.

All sorts of tricky issues lie hidden in long-term care insurance, matters that no one would ever imagine prior to trying to purchase it. If a nursing facility resident's daily charge is less than the daily benefit, does the overage carry over and extend the benefit period? Are the policy's premiums waived when the policy holder is collecting benefits? Is there a "reasonable and customary" or "prevailing charge" provision associated with the daily benefit? Will the premium increase across time? (Possibly, but with most of the policies sold today pursuant to congressional standards, this happens only if the issuing company gains approval in a state to raise rates on an entire class of policy holders.) This list could go on and on. Purchasers of long-term care insurance need to proceed slowly and carefully. Finally, purchasers should try to choose a company with a long track record in the insurance business. Most people who turn out to need long-term care insurance will not need it until they reach their eighties. The leading edge of the baby-boom generation is composed of those barely in their sixties. Individuals need to purchase long-term care insurance from a company that will be around in twenty-five years. As in previous chapters, we illustrate a number of the points in this introduction through a pair of contrasting vignettes.

John and Marsha Garvey

By the time John and Marsha Garvey retired in 1989, they had become thoroughly fed up with the spiraling cost of living and the growing urban-suburban sprawl that transformed their once beloved small city of Santa Barbara on the central California coast. They followed the example of many other Californians and fled to Nevada, to the then relatively small, independent community of Henderson, southeast of Las Vegas. There they found modest property values and a much lower cost of living generally, and they initially enjoyed less heavy traffic than in increasingly clogged Santa Barbara, which had gradually morphed into a far-flung suburb of Los Angeles. They also found a mild and sunny climate not so different from that of Santa Barbara for much of the year. But from mid-May through mid-September they had to hide out in air conditioning to escape the dry summer heat. Henderson offered golf courses, and they made friends playing with other migrants. For more than a decade the Garveys enjoyed a leisurely existence among a large number of casual friends. They also began gambling, which—across time—increasingly occupied the summer months.

Then several years ago the Garveys' pleasant life began to slowly unravel. Initially, John's once amusing forgetfulness about the location of his keys blossomed into serious memory loss, and friends began to disappear. John also became a growing problem around the house for Marsha, who increasingly had to follow him around, turning off water faucets and the like. The crowning blow to their social life came when John had an unfortunate bowel movement at the table during a restaurant lunch with two other couples. That event prompted Marsha to withdraw into the house, dragging John along.

The growing stress on Marsha likely contributed to her small strokes. Marsha's health problems limited what she could accomplish on her own, and she found herself increasingly overwhelmed by John's needs. Her two sons were busy with their careers and families in Seattle and the San Francisco area. Sadly, Marsha learned that her golf friends quickly metamorphosed into bare acquaintances when she asked them for help. The receptionist in her physician's office suggested she call the local (Las Vegas) Area Agency on Aging (AAA) office.

She did and talked to a kind but discouraging man. He counseled that John needed professional long-term care. But getting him into such care required money, numerous decisions, and hours spent with complicated paperwork. He mentioned several nursing facilities in the Las Vegas area but indicated that Marsha would have to pay privately for a number of months before any of these facilities would be willing to continue with John on Medicaid, if that was even possible.

Marsha was shocked to think that they might need Medicaid. They had moved from California with several hundred thousand dollars. But they had lived well and had unexpectedly lost significant amounts gambling. Soon after Marsha started to manage their finances, she had suffered her strokes, and understanding their finances had simply receded beyond her grasp. When she explained about her strokes and her limited ability to deal with numbers, the man suggested that she hire a "case manager" and recommended two different women. The case manager would help with planning, decisions, acquiring services, and filling out paperwork.

The AAA representative also told Marsha that, even as a private-pay nursing facility applicant, she would confront multiple, complicated forms. Further, she learned that nursing facilities in the Las Vegas area enjoyed high demand, and individual facilities could often "cherry-pick" applicants who required less labor-intensive care. The AAA representative also warned her that, should she need it, Nevada's public-sector support of the entire range of long-term care options was limited and difficult to access.

Marsha tried repeatedly to reach each of the recommended case managers by phone. She has finally managed to get an appointment, the end of the next week, with one. In the meantime she has become alternatively increasingly frantic and depressed. Her house is a mess; she simply cannot keep up with John. Even the simplest tasks seem overwhelming to her. Further, she cannot leave John at home for even short trips to the supermarket or pharmacy, and driving with him in the suburban maze of Henderson—now engulfed by Las Vegas—scares her. She is fearful of having a traffic accident and making her problems worse. She does not want to bother her distant sons, in part because she feels ashamed about John's and her declining abilities. She lost much of her capacity with numbers through her strokes, leaving her largely in the dark about their finances, and she is terrified of turning their financial records over to a case manager whom she does not even know. Her life seems simply hopeless, and she currently sees no way to improve it.

Phil and Sandy Turner

The Garveys' scary situation mirrors the circumstances that confront ever larger numbers of increasingly disabled adults. But life in one's eighties need not go this badly. Consider the situation of Phil and Sandy Turner. They spent most of their working lives in a series of New England communities. When they retired in their mid-sixties more than fifteen years ago, they moved to the North Carolina shore near Topsail. Here they—similarly to the Garveys in Henderson, Nevada—initially found numerous benefits: less expensive property, a lower cost of living generally, reduced congestion, and a milder climate. They too made friends and played in the sun, but they also lived fairly frugally.

Early in their years in North Carolina, the Turners learned in the local weekly newspaper about an older couple nearby who faced problems similar to those we related above for the Garveys. Phil and Sandy had actually become involved in helping the couple for a brief time until the couple's children from Ohio showed up and moved them to Ohio. The experience of seeing the older couple's problems firsthand alerted Phil and Sandy to future possibilities. They enjoyed helping another older couple, but they also learned that their corner of North Carolina did not support highly vulnerable persons very well. They reevaluated their distance from their son and two daughters in New England. They vowed to make their own decisions about where and how they would live when they became less capable, rather than accepting the decisions of strangers or shifting responsibility for these decisions to their children.

It is one thing to make such vows, it is quite another to implement them in a timely fashion. In a sense, the Turners received a valuable, if initially painful, wakeup call about two years ago. Phil was on a ladder cleaning the exterior of some second-story windows when he caught his leg on the rope used for extending the ladder and fell. He broke his femur, among other more modest injuries. He and Sandy were surprised at the amount of time Phil took to recover even a small range of his normal activities around the house and town. They decided that they needed to relocate to a place with more support if—or more likely when—they once again found themselves unable to carry on their normal activities.

They talked with their children about the situation and eventually decided on a multistage senior community, or continuing care retirement community (CCRC), close to their younger daughter and near Durham, New Hampshire. They sold their house in North Carolina and bought into this CCRC, which we will call "the association." The association is a nondenominational nonprofit initiated by a group of local churches and run by a professional manager. It has about 250 resident households. A majority live independently in their own units on the property, but they can order personal, household, transportation, and modest medical services from the association staff as need arises. Some of the residents live in free-standing duplexes; others are in one wing of a multistory apartment building. The other wing of the building includes a number of assisted-living apartments, whose residents routinely receive some daily services as part of their contracts with the association. Some of the residents in this wing still drive their own cars and freely come and go as they choose. Others are less capable and remain in their rooms or the common areas, chatting with other residents, most of the time. The association offers a transportation service that will take these latter residents to physicians' appointments or shopping, with some advance notice. A separate building houses a nursing facility with a wing specializing in the care of persons with dementia.

At eighty-three and eighty-one, respectively, Phil and Sandy moved into one of the free-standing duplex units nearly a year ago. Although Phil experiences some modest memory lapses, they do not, at the moment, need any formal services from the association's staff, but after their experience with Phil's leg, they feel comfortable knowing that they can call for help if necessary. They do not know the woman in the other half of their duplex very well, but they have become friends with the couple on their side of the next duplex over. The two couples help each other with various problems as well as go out to lunch together in nearby Portsmouth and have one another over to socialize.

Phil and Sandy's younger daughter drops in from time to time on her way home to South Berwick from her job in Portsmouth. The Turners also have a son in Burlington, Vermont, and another daughter in Litchfield, Connecticut. Last summer, Phil and Sandy visited both these children and did some sightseeing in upper New England.

The Turners enjoy their current life. They have fairly regular contact with their children. They like their senior association and have made some new friends with common interests and concerns. Most of all, perhaps, they feel relieved. They know what the future likely holds. But they also know how to get help when needed—from a combination of family and association staff. They bought into the association with money from the sale of their North Carolina home; their Social Security, Phil's modest private pension, and their savings look to be sufficient to cover their likely association expenses for another decade. Their future life may not be pretty at times, but they have reduced the level of fear, uncertainty, chaos, and frenzy that Marsha Garvey is currently experiencing. Beyond the confines of their association, New Hampshire ranks sixth among the states on the accessible, high-quality long-term care dimension of state senior friendliness (SSF) that we consider in this chapter. It ranks first among the states on the sustaining health and medical care quality dimension that we addressed in the previous chapter. (See tables A.40 and A.39, respectively, in the Appendix.) So it appears that the Turners are well situated to manage the trials of aging that eventually confront us all.

Coping with the Dilemmas of Long-Term Care

Earlier in this chapter we discussed the full gamut of long-term care venues—one's own home; the local community, perhaps in an assisted living complex; and nursing facilities. Unfortunately, we lack comparable data for the first two of these options, which prevents rigorous comparisons of all options across states.[10] These limitations exist in spite of extensive efforts by a number of persons, particularly Bob Mollica and his associates at the National Academy of State Health Policy and Steve Eiken and his colleagues at Thomson Medstat, to provide new and better data for making these assessments.[11] Accordingly, our analyses here draw largely on the much more extensive data on nursing facilities, although problems exist with these data as well.[12]

We focus the four indicators in the next section, not just on state's nursing facilities, but more broadly on state Medicaid support of nursing facility long-term care. We do this because the vast majority of those who enter nursing facilities will soon become dependent on their state Medicaid programs to pay the bulk of their costs. So most nursing facility residents need both the quality of care that federal and state Medicaid programs strive to achieve and also the financial support that these programs provide. As we shall reinforce later, there seems to be an "economic substitution effect" between state Medicaid support for nursing facilities and for various forms of HCBS care. That is, states that support extensive, high-quality nursing facility long-term care do less well in supporting assisted living and other forms of congregate, residential, noninstitutional long-term care and vice versa.[13]

Assessing a State's Support of Accessible and High-Quality Long-Term Care

Older persons generally need Medicaid support to pay for nursing facility long-term care, and here we compare four aspects of different states' Medicaid nursing facility long-term care programs. The first indicator involves the number of beds in the program. This tells us how many persons can physically obtain one of the state's Medicaid-certified nursing facility beds. The next two indicators, in distinct but closely related ways, pertain to the program's financial resources. These resources heavily influence (1) the extent of the care that the state provides to the residents of its Medicaid-certified nursing facility beds and (2) the financial accessibility of these beds to the state's older residents. The fourth indicator examines the relative quality of a sample of the state's nursing facility processes. Taken together, these four indicators tell us a good deal about the accessibility and quality of a state's Medicaid-supported nursing facility long-term care program.

Medicaid-Certified Nursing Facility Beds per 1,000 Sixty-five-or-Older State Residents

The ratio of a state's certified nursing facility beds to the state's sixty-five-or-older population tells us about the physical accessibility of a state's Medicaid nursing facility long-term care program. Federal law requires inspections, called *surveys*, of Medicaid-certified nursing facility beds. These beds thus experience greater regulatory scrutiny than noncertified beds and they may promise better quality of care.[14] Further, a resident in a Medicaid-certified bed can generally remain there when her or his income and financial assets dwindle so that the resident becomes eligible for Medicaid. Medicaid will not pay for a nursing facility bed that it does not survey and certify. So a state with a higher number of Medicaid-certified nursing facility beds per one thousand older state residents supports more physical accessibility to nursing facility long-term care service than a state that supports fewer beds per one thousand older state residents. (The latter state *may* support a more ambitious Medicaid HCBS long-term care program. See fig. 5.7.)

Figure 5.1 compares states on numbers of Medicaid-certified nursing facility beds per one thousand state residents sixty-five or older.[15] Southern New England and, with the exception of Missouri, a band of states running from north (more states) to south (fewer states) through the central portion of the United States hold the upper positions in the ranking of states on this indicator. Most of the West; portions of the Southeast; and Maine, Michigan, and Missouri provide fewer Medicaid-certified beds per one thousand older residents. The sharply distinguished regional groupings of contiguous states that appear in figure 5.1 may arise from conscious emulation of neighboring states' policies in this regard or as a consequence of states in these different regions sharing particular orientations or demographics that help to foster regional similarities.

Percentage of State Medicaid Expenditures to Nursing Facilities

Next we examine financial accessibility by comparing states' financial support of their Medicaid nursing facility long-term care programs. One useful measure of financial support is the percentage of each state's Medicaid expenditures that are devoted to nursing facilities. Medicaid mandates that states cover certain

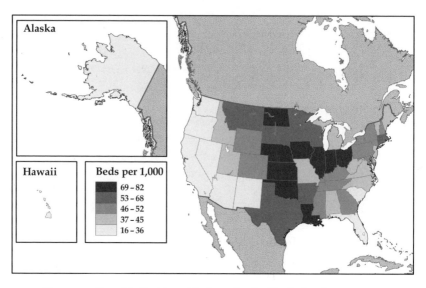

Figure 5.1: State Medicaid-certified nursing facility beds per 1,000 state
residents sixty-five or older (2003)

medical contingencies for particular groups of persons who fall below the program's income and financial asset thresholds. Generally, a substantial majority
of the Medicaid beneficiaries in each state are children in impoverished households and their mothers. But Medicaid also mandates long-term care for older
persons and people born with serious abnormalities or who experience disabling injuries as younger adults.[16] So while older long-term care beneficiaries
generally make up a relatively small proportion of a state's Medicaid recipients, the total amount spent on these individuals persistently (i.e., month after
month) runs far higher than the total spent on youngsters and their mothers,
who have more periodic and usually more modest expenses.

The proportion of a state's Medicaid expenditures going to nursing facilities characteristically indicates something about both the state's demographics
and its commitment to using its Medicaid program to help older persons attain
nursing facility long-term care. States have some leeway in deciding how generous their basic Medicaid plans are in helping members of these various
groups, and states can add—often maintaining federal cost sharing in the process—services (e.g., via the waivers we discussed in the section "Introduction
to Long-Term Care" above) to particular groups that are not mandated by the
Medicaid law.

Figure 5.2 compares the proportion of each state's Medicaid expenditures devoted to nursing facilities.[17] The pattern resembles the one in figure 5.1

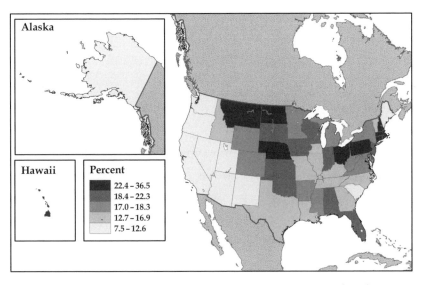

Figure 5.2: State Medicaid expenditures to nursing facilities (2003)

for the number of Medicaid-certified beds per one thousand older state residents. The north-central and northeastern regions dominate the top ranks on this indicator. The proportion of states' Medicaid expenditures devoted to nursing facilities correlates (statistically significantly) at 0.55 with the number of Medicaid-certified nursing facility beds. This means that states with more Medicaid-certified nursing facility beds spend, as we should expect, more to maintain the residents who occupy the beds. Once again, states in the West and Maine and South Carolina appear near the bottom of the ranks on this indicator.

Medicaid Nursing-Facility Expenditures per 1,000 Sixty-five-or-Older State Residents

Cromwell, Hurdle, and Schurman argue that the best measures of a public social program's support consider the degree of financial support across the total number in the potential beneficiary pool.[18] Accordingly, another indicator of states' generosity toward older residents financially obtaining access to nursing facility long-term care focuses on a state's nursing facility expenditures per 1,000 sixty-five-or-older state residents. This indicator measures resources per potential beneficiary that the previous indicator lacked.

Figure 5.3 portrays state variation on this indicator.[19] The strong pattern of figure 5.1 is much weaker here, but northeastern and north-central states spend more heavily per older state resident than others, and western and southeastern

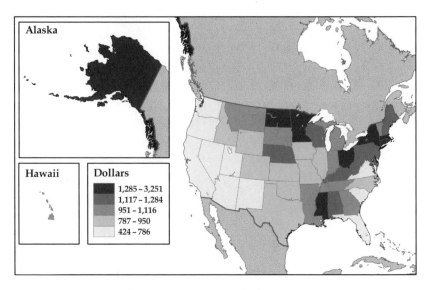

Figure 5.3: State Medicaid nursing facility expenditures per
1,000 sixty-five or older state residents (2003)

states tend to be the skimpiest spenders. This indicator correlates reasonably
well with our measure of physical accessibility (Medicaid-certified beds per
1,000 sixty-five-or-older states residents)—0.36, statistically significant—and
quite closely with our indicator of program financial support (percentage of
state Medicaid expenditures devoted to nursing facilities)—0.69, statistically
significant. This indicates that seniors in states with more physically accessible
Medicaid nursing facility long-term care programs also receive more financial
support (per potential resident), making these programs more financially accessible as well.

Quality of State Nursing Facility Processes Scale

When the physical and particularly financial accessibility of states' Medicaid
nursing facility long-term care programs increase, we might expect greater quality in the resulting nursing facility services. However, this prediction ignores
competing incentives for the providers of long-term care services. Nationwide, nearly two-thirds of Medicaid-certified nursing facilities operate on a
for-profit basis, and more than half are owned and operated by large corporate
chains.[20] So investor demands for profits compete for resources with quality of
care. Thus, we need to examine whether increased resources actually produce
better quality.

Still other uncertainties complicate this inquiry. The federal government has developed processes for inspecting or surveying the quality of nursing facility services associated with the Medicare (generally only for short-term recuperation and rehabilitation) and Medicaid programs.[21] These efforts have produced the Online Survey, Certification and Reporting (OSCAR) system and the related Minimum Data Set (MDS; both available through http://cms.hhs.gov). But experts disagree on the reliability and validity of these data.[22] In addition, consumer-oriented quality indicators are available to seniors and their families through Nursing Home Compare at http://medicare.gov. So while we use the best data currently available for cross-state comparisons of nursing facility quality, experts disagree about the accuracy of these data.

We construct our quality of state nursing facility processes scale from OSCAR data. Our scale includes data on the percentages of a state's nursing facilities *without* deficiencies with respect to preserving resident dignity and food sanitation, as well as maintaining an accident-free environment and satisfactory facility housekeeping.[23] Figure 5.4 compares the quality of states' nursing facility processes (darker shades indicate higher quality). With a few exceptions, states in the Upper Midwest and the Northeast show fewer deficiencies in care. States with more deficiencies are scattered geographically, and a few states in generally high-quality regions (i.e., Maine, Michigan, Minnesota, Washington, and Wyoming) exhibit greater deficiencies. This processes scale correlates positively with our indicators for the physical accessibility of a state Medicaid program's

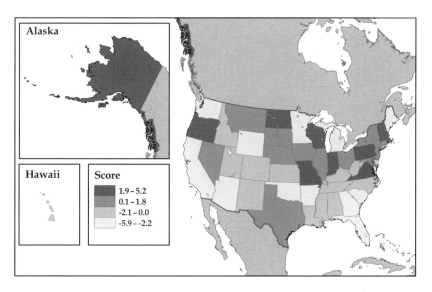

Figure 5.4: Quality of state nursing facility processes scale (2003)

support of nursing facility long-term care for older persons (0.12), the program's financial support (0.37), and combined financial support and accessibility (0.37), although only the last two correlations coefficients are statistically significant. This indicates that as the number of beds and particularly the financial support of state Medicaid nursing facility long-term care programs for older persons increase, so too does the quality of state Medicaid-certified nursing facility services. Some evidence suggests that a state with better nursing facility care also requires more training time for HCBS long-term care staff.[24] These patterns suggest significant differences between states in political attention to and social support for seniors' long-term care.

Overall

With some exceptions, north-central and northeastern states tend to provide proportionately more beds and greater financial support for their state Medicaid nursing facility long-term care programs for older residents than do other states. States in the Southeast and particularly the West tend to skimp by comparison in terms of both numbers of beds and financial support. The quality of nursing facility processes follows a similar but somewhat less clearly defined pattern.

We should reinforce a couple of caveats with regard to these results. First, the process quality data, drawn from OSCAR, remain controversial among specialists who disagree about the extent and severity of their reliability and validity limitations. Second, all four of the indicators presented so far focus on nursing facility long-term care for older persons. Whatever the shortcomings of these data on nursing facilities, they afford more extensive cross-state comparisons than do the existing data on HCBS care. State-level data on HCBS services afford only a few broad comparisons with nursing facility long-term care. For one, state Medicaid nursing facility and HCBS congregate residential expenditures appear to be inversely related, so that if a state does relatively well on one, it tends to do rather poorly on the other. For another, as the quality of a state's nursing facility processes improves, the training time that the state requires for HCBS caregivers increases.

Additional Indicators

As in previous chapters, we use the four indicators above to assess state senior friendliness (SSF) in terms of the accessibility and quality of long-term care. We now examine three additional indicators to help place these four in a broader context. The first of these additional indicators is, once again, our "so-what," or social outcome, indicator.

State Nursing Facility Residents' Quality-of-Life Outcomes Scale

When a state Medicaid program provides generous physical accessibility and financial support for nursing facility long-term care for older persons as well as greater quality of nursing facility processes, we expect that the state's nursing facility residents will enjoy better quality-of-life outcomes compared to states offering less accessibility, financial support, and process quality. We designed our state nursing facility residents' quality-of-life outcomes scale to test this hypothesis. Unfortunately, no large, independent surveys of nursing facility residents' views on their quality of life exist, so our scale draws again on Centers for Medicare and Medicaid Services data. We measure residents' quality-of-life outcomes with the percentages of a state's nursing facility residents who *avoid* certain undesirable conditions: having pressure sores, being restrained, being bedridden, and receiving nourishment through a feeding tube. These four conditions represent physically painful and emotionally distressing experiences. Nursing facility residents who avoid them likely enjoy a higher quality of life than those who endure them. We construct this scale through added z-scores of the four elements as we explained for our quality of state nursing facility processes scale above. (See also note 23.)

Figure 5.5 compares states on our state nursing facility residents' quality-of-life outcomes scale.[25] A large block of states centered in the north-central region but extending south to include Arizona and New Mexico and a much smaller group of states in New England rank highest on the quality-of-life outcomes for their nursing facility residents. In sharp contrast, residents' quality of life in states of the Southeast, the Pacific West, and Maine ranks much lower. With some variation, all five figures presented so far in this chapter share this pattern of states in the north-central and northeastern regions tending to rank near the top and states in the Southeast and West ranking near the bottom. So, unsurprisingly, this quality-of-life outcomes scale correlates positively with each of the four previous program indicators at 0.37 (physical accessibility), 0.36 (financial support), 0.17 (financial support and accessibility), and 0.35 (quality of nursing facility processes). Only the 0.17 correlation coefficient fails to achieve a level of statistical significance. This indicates that as the physical and financial accessibility and the quality-of-care processes of a state's Medicaid nursing facility long-term care program improve, the residents' quality-of-life outcomes rises.

Previous analyses including several control variables produced results allowing us to impute causation to the correlations in the previous paragraph.[26] In

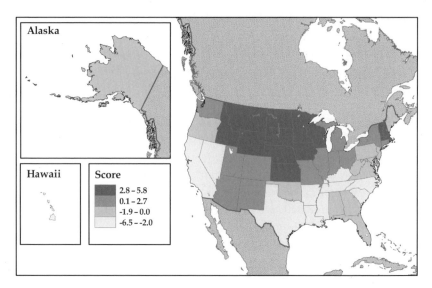

Figure 5.5: State nursing facility residents quality-of-life outcomes scale (2003)

other words, the greater senior friendliness—in terms of physical and financial accessibility as well as process and outcome quality—that the states with the darker shades in figure 5.5 achieve is not inadvertent. Rather, it is the result of conscious efforts that state officials and attentive publics undertake to attain these ends.

Average State Medicaid Nursing Facility Reimbursement Rate

We also expect that the average state Medicaid nursing facility reimbursement rate (per resident day) will influence the quality of nursing facility processes and nursing facility residents' quality-of-life outcomes in a state. Seniors in states that provide higher reimbursements are more likely to suffer fewer problems in their care.

In any state, only a few nursing facilities serve an entirely private-pay resident population. These nursing facilities generally serve the high end of the market with fancy accommodations and prices. A few "nursing facilities" try to scrape by on the low end without Medicaid certification, but these tend to resemble residential care homes more than nursing facilities. The vast majority of nursing facilities in any state will serve a mixture of private-pay and Medicaid residents. Many older people enter nursing facilities as private-pay residents, but the vast majority become Medicaid-supported residents fairly quickly. Medicaid reimbursement rates are considerably lower than the rates charged private-pay residents, and at any given time Medicaid supports most of the residents in most nursing facilities. So we expected nursing facilities in states with fairly high Medicaid reimbursement rates to provide higher-quality care to and possibly better quality-of-life outcomes for their residents than nursing facilities in states with lower Medicaid reimbursement rates.

But once again competing incentives such as investor profits also seem to influence the relationship between reimbursement rate and quality of care. Figure 5.6 compares average state Medicaid nursing facility reimbursement rates, adjusted for each state's cost of living.[27] Although a number of states in the Northeast rank fairly high in figure 5.6, this pattern differs from analyses of the preceding five factors in this chapter. Indeed, although state Medicaid nursing facility reimbursement rates do correlate positively and statistically significantly with state Medicaid nursing facility expenditures per one thousand state residents (our financial support and accessibility indicator), these reimbursement rates have little effect on process quality or resident quality of life. Process quality correlates positively and modestly at 0.12 with reimbursement rate, and resident quality of life negatively and modestly at −0.11. This means that state-level reimbursement rates bear little relation to the average quality of nursing facility care in a state or the state's nursing facility residents' average quality of life. The state level of analysis offers only limited assessment of the effects of reimbursement rate on the quality of processes and resident outcomes at the

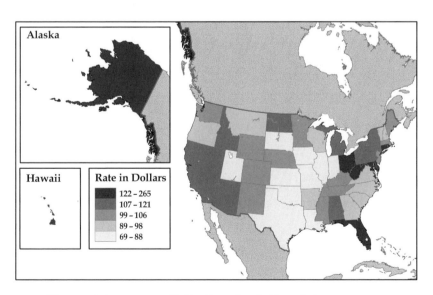

Figure 5.6: Average state Medicaid nursing facility reimbursement rate
(adjusted for state cost of living) (2003)

facility level, and our correlations do not control for "case-mix" or how the nursing facility populations in various states might differ in terms of the difficulty of the care they require. Nonetheless, it is intriguing that state average Medicaid nursing facility reimbursement per resident day correlates negatively with three of the five indicators of nursing facility care accessibility and quality. These analyses raise the fear that higher facility-level Medicaid revenues are siphoned off to ends other than resident care.[28]

HCBS Aged/Disabled Waiver Expenditures per 1,000 Sixty-five-or-Older State Residents

We use Medicaid HCBS aged/disabled waiver expenditures per one thousand older state residents as a rough HCBS counterpart for Medicaid nursing facility expenditures per 1,000 sixty-five-or-older state residents in the previous section.[29] This allows us to compare cross-state expenditure patterns of Medicaid nursing facility long-term care and HCBS long-term care for older persons. This is one of the few aspects of Medicaid-supported HCBS care for which cross-state data reasonably comparable to those which we have provided above for Medicaid-supported nursing facilities are available.[30]

Figure 5.7 shows how the states vary on this HCBS indicator.[31] No clear geographic pattern emerges in figure 5.7, and we can conjure no parsimonious

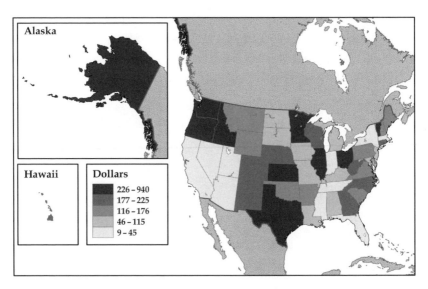

Figure 5.7: State HCBS aged/disabled waiver expenditures per 1,000 sixty-five or older state residents (2004)

explanation for the rank-ordering of states on this indicator. This seeming randomness appears in other HCBS indicators as well, and suggests that state-level HCBS aged/disabled public policy remains in an early, virtually ad hoc stage. The pattern in figure 5.7 does replicate, very modestly, the economic substitution effect that we mentioned above. That is, state Medicaid nursing facility expenditures and state Medicaid HCBS expenditures (each per one thousand older state residents) correlate negatively but modestly (−0.02). This suggests that these two categories of spending represent portions of a relatively fixed "pie," so that as one increases the other declines.

Back to the Garveys and the Turners

Marsha Garvey and her husband, John, although he is less conscious of it, find themselves in a difficult situation partly because of too little knowledge, foresight, and planning. When they retired, they moved to an area of the country that does not support the needs of vulnerable citizens well. They neglected to maintain, foster, or rekindle relations with their distant children. They accepted a broad range of fairly shallow recreation-based relationships among other newcomers to Henderson, and they failed to build more meaningful friendships that would afford them some support in time of need. They also overlooked their prospective limitations and the eventual need for accessible, high-quality long-term care options in the Las Vegas region.

Yet their problems are exacerbated by the Nevada social environment's neglect of the vulnerabilities of the "old-old." Nevada ranks forty-ninth among the states in terms of Medicaid nursing facility expenditures and forty-fourth in terms of Medicaid HCBS aged/disabled waiver expenditures (both per one thousand state residents sixty-five or older). It averages thirty-eighth among the states in its rank on the seven indicators in this chapter and an additional, summary indicator we introduce later, in chapter 6. It provides a limited supply of long-term care facilities of varying sorts. Nevada does better at supporting the limited facilities it has, ranking eighteenth on Medicaid nursing facility reimbursement and twentieth on the quality of nursing facility processes scale. But overall, Nevada residents needing long-term care tend to confront a sellers' market and limited public support. Nevada also ranks first—far ahead of the second-place state—in suicides among persons sixty-five or older (and the population generally), a position that likely reflects the difficulties of finding solutions to the problems of old age.

In contrast, the Turners found more supportive circumstances in New Hampshire. To some degree the Turners worked to achieve their own good fortune in comparison with the Garveys. They always maintained close relations with their children and have moved back near them in their old age. They seek deeper friendships that transcend playfulness. Perhaps, most important, they became aware fairly early on in their retirement of the vulnerabilities of old age and figured out how to attain assistance before becoming physically frail or cognitively deficient. Nonetheless, they have faced less difficult circumstances than those of the Garveys. They have enjoyed more help from their children. And services available in New Hampshire have facilitated their efforts as well. Across the seven indicators introduced in this chapter and one remaining in chapter 6, New Hampshire averages a ranking of fourteenth. It is second among the states on the quality of state nursing facility processes scale, and it falls among the lower half of the states only on nursing facility reimbursement (thirty-sixth).

New Hampshire offers a more supportive social environment to those suffering the vulnerabilities of old age by providing supportive communities (chapter 2) on which it ranks eighth among the states (Nevada is thirty-eighth) and its first-place ranking with regard to sustaining health and obtaining high-quality medical care (Nevada is thirty-sixth). (See tables A.37 [for supportive communities] and A.39 [for health and medical care quality] in the Appendix.) Large numbers of older people tend to be unaware of or ignore these state differences. Nevada ranks first among the states in terms of net in-migration for persons eighty-five or older. Some of these individuals will have the cleverness, insight, and material resources to do well by themselves. But Nevada offers a social environment that is unquestionably less friendly toward the vulnerabilities of old age than the Turners have found in New Hampshire. All the analyses in this chapter emphasize that seniors benefit from striving to anticipate their future needs and planning accordingly.

6

Jerry and Arlene Senter are idling away their days in Iowa and dreaming enviously about Art and Karen Munro's adventurous new experiences and friends in the scenic mountains of southeastern New Mexico. Arnie and Muriel Hestir feel trapped and live without clear positive purpose in their changing neighborhood near Atlanta, whereas Nancy Currier has carved out a meaningful and supportive life in Minneapolis. Carl and Jessica Sanford's financial situation gradually deteriorates while they persist in an unaffordable lifestyle in New Jersey; by contrast, while Jim and Sonia Tate cannot match the Sanfords' financial resources, their move from Connecticut to West Virginia leaves them in a better financial position to enjoy a similar life. Bob and Helen Wilson, near Dallas, find health limitations needlessly narrowing their lives, but after Larry and Julie Crother's move back to New Hampshire, , the Crothers, with similar medical problems to the Wilsons', are expanding their horizons. John and Marsha Garvey's dreams of fun in the mild winters of southern Nevada have withered with increasing physical and cognitive infirmities, yet in the face of similar difficulties Phil and Sandy Turner live an interesting and well-supported life in New Hampshire.

These stories of contrasting disappointment and success at different stages of aging illustrate troubling dilemmas. All these individuals struggled over difficult decisions involving retirement and further aging. Two different challenges contribute to the divergent results for them and for seniors generally. First, some seniors lack appropriate information about choices and their likely outcomes. In the absence of adequate information, retirees and their families often run into unanticipated problems. Second, the distinctive physical, socioeconomic, and public policy characteristics of each state influence seniors' chances of finding suitable recreational opportunities, supportive and engaging communities, affordable and safe places to live, or high-quality medical or long-term care.

So how can retirees make better choices? We do not advise on individual decisions, but this chapter presents older Americans with the best composite picture available of how each state ranks in its support of these five basic, distinct needs. Different portions of older Americans express different priorities. Some concentrate on having fun outdoors in a mild climate, while others struggle with a serious illness. Still others engage in a frustrating search for suitable long-term care. But for individual older people these priorities tend to occur sequentially rather than simultaneously. Barring a premature death, those who are aging usually pass through consecutive stages in which they experience three or perhaps more of five different central needs successively. No state supports all these needs well, and this contributes to the difficulty for older Americans in their making decisions. We believe that information is empowering, and the more older citizens understand how the capacities of different states match their own shifting needs and distinct priorities, the more likely they are to make good choices.

Does each community within a state offer the same opportunities and problems that define the state overall? Certainly not. Within each state, certain towns and cities exhibit much better weather, more vitalizing community organizations, greater affordability and safety, or superior forms of medical or long-term care than do others. There are numerous sources—books, periodicals, and Web sites—that rank individual communities on their desirability as retirement havens.[1] Once retirees identify certain states, these sources can be useful at the virtual-search stage in selecting particular regions of states for closer attention. However, most of these guides focus more on the recreational concerns of the relatively young, active, and financially secure retirees whom we discussed in chapter 1 than on the other prominent aging issues that we have dealt with in chapters 2 through 5 above. We think that this narrower orientation is short-sighted and may contribute to serious problems for seniors across later stages of aging. It is the orientation that fostered the grave current situation of John and Marsha Garvey in Nevada. We have provided the information on acquiring more meaning and social support, greater affordability and safety, and better health and high-quality medical and long-term care in the hope of encouraging retirees to face the reality of their probable needs and best options across the stages of aging.

Why do states matter? States' social and political characteristics exert considerable influence on how well or poorly older citizens can meet particular needs. State legislatures routinely make policy decisions that affect a state's older residents, and these outcomes generally hold across a state's towns and cities. For instance, Iowa chooses to license considerably more Medicaid-certified nursing facility beds per 1,000 sixty-five-or-older residents than Nevada, where the Garveys live. Retirees thinking of moving to a state benefit from knowing how well the state supports, not only recreational opportunities, but also supportive and engaging communities, affordable and safe places to live, health and high-quality medical care, and the accessibility and quality of long-term care.

Why do states differ so much in supporting older citizens? The Garveys' personal choices do not completely explain their desperate and seemingly hopeless situation. In this chapter we explain how and why certain states better support seniors on some issues rather than others. We explain these cross-state differences by drawing on basic state characteristics as well as patterns of emulation among states. People may ignore these factors and the variations in state senior friendliness (SSF) associated with them because they seem vague, complex, or irrelevant, but they do so at their peril. Basic social, political, and economic differences among states directly affect the lives of older residents. We explain how various state characteristics influence the lives of older citizens, creating— for instance—a situation in which nursing facility care is simply much more financially accessible to frail older residents of Iowa than to their counterparts in Nevada. Many seniors remain blissfully unaware of how these state characteristics affect their lives.

As older citizens develop greater awareness of these differences, they may prompt states, particularly those currently offering lackluster-quality medical or long-term care, to support better services. But serious obstacles persist. States generally try to attract young-old retirees. States receiving such migrants gain tax revenue—through income, sales, and possibly property and other taxes. The migrants typically gain either improved recreational opportunities or a reduced cost of living, often accompanied by less social congestion. This "win-win" strategy resembles state efforts to attract businesses through tax rebates and other financial inducements, which generally operate through a quid pro quo. States drawing new businesses from elsewhere gain tax base and employment opportunities (thus minimally reducing unemployment benefits and in many states increasing income tax revenues), while the businesses acquire lower production costs than they would experience in other states.

For migrant retirees, the early win-win situation declines as they age. States continue to reap benefits for a time with respect to most migrant medical costs, which are paid primarily by Medicare (incoming federal dollars, from the states' perspective) and migrants' private Medigap insurance and out-of-pocket payments. However, the income and assets of some migrants dwindle over time, leaving them poor enough to use the states' Medicaid programs as their Medigap policies, thus becoming public-sector liabilities. But migrants suffer when the quality of medical care delivered through Medicare is lower (as it often is) than it is in their states of origin.

As aging migrants require Medicaid for long-term care or other state-level public assistance, the situation deteriorates further, becoming clearly "lose-lose." Many states to which retirees migrate for recreation or lower cost of living have more limited Medicaid long-term care accessibility and quality than the states from which the migrants move. So the migrating retirees often receive poorer care than they would have in their states of origin. In addition, the receiving states will be burdened with the cost of the migrants' long-term care. The annual per recipient cost of this burden to the states rivals those of educating a child at a private university or maintaining a criminal in a highly secure prison. We may reasonably question the morality of states encouraging the young-old to relocate within their borders if they are unwilling to pay for the eventual consequences, but it is easy to understand that state officials do not relish taking up this financial burden for recent migrants.

Creating a Multidimensional Measure of State Senior Friendliness

First, we provide a picture of differing state support for older residents, drawing on the data of chapters 1 through 5 to compare five distinctive dimensions—recreational lifestyle, meaningful contributions and supportive communities, affordability and safety, health and high-quality medical care, and accessible, high-quality long-term care—of state senior friendliness (SSF). In developing this picture, we build on previous work in related areas.[2]

To create state scores on each of these five dimensions, we do the following. We transform the four variables that we used as our primary indicators for each dimension by converting them into units of "standard deviation" known as *z-scores*. This places them on a standard metric so that we are comparing apples to apples rather than to oranges.[3] Then for each dimension we add the four z-scores to create a dimensional score for each state. This gives us a standard way of comparing each state's senior friendliness on each of the five dimensions. These composite dimensional scales allow readers to compare states' positions on any one dimension of SSF with their positions on the other dimensions. When people make decisions about moving early in retirement, they often focus on priorities related to one or maybe two dimensions. As they age, their needs change, and frequently so too do the states that support these later priorities. (Figs. 6.1 through 6.5, introduced below, display these results, which are based on the rank-orderings in tables A.36 through A.40, respectively, in the Appendix.)

Recreational Lifestyle

In assessing each state's senior friendliness with regard to recreational lifestyle, we combine the following four indicators introduced in chapter 1 into a scale. These indicators are (1) state climate, (2) the percentage of a state's sixty-five-or-older population that does *not* live alone, (3) the proportion of a state's sixty-five-or-older residents who are *not* disabled, and (4) the proportion of gross state product derived from a certain type of tourism. These four indicators, or variables, pick up different aspects of what we mean by the term *recreational lifestyle*. So, collectively, the four reflect the recreational lifestyle dimension of SSF in a more complete and satisfactory way than any of them do individually. Variables 2 and 3 focus specifically on older state residents. Variables 1 and 4 relate to anyone living in or visiting a state, but particularly to the young-old with more leisure time and flexibility to travel or move than persons in other age cohorts. Rankings of the states on these four variables appear in tables A.1 through A.4 in the Appendix. Combined, the four variables produce a scale of the recreational lifestyle SSF dimension on which the states vary as shown in figure 6.1. This scale has a Cronbach's alpha, an indicator of index quality, of 0.66. This is lower than the alpha for any of our other scales, which usually are close to or exceed the generally accepted standard of 0.80 for a high-quality scale.[4]

Meaningful Contributions and Supportive Communities

We merge another four variables—introduced in chapter 2—to construct a composite scale that shows the relative opportunities afforded by various states for meaningful contributions and supportive communities. The variables are (1) a state's score on Putnam's Social Capital Index II,[5] (2) the proportion of a state's sixty-five-or-older population voting in the 2004 presidential election,

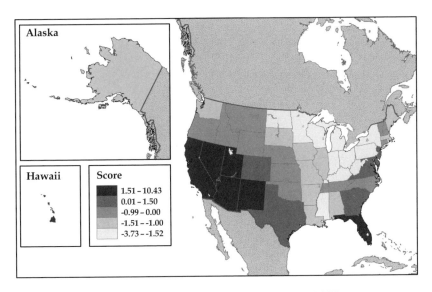

Figure 6.1: Recreational lifestyle dimension of SSF

(3) a state's Gini index, reversed so as to represent a measure of income *equality,* and (4) the percentage of a state's sixty-five-or-older population living above the federal poverty line. Variable 2 measures senior civic involvement, while variable 4 indicates the degree to which a state's socioeconomic environment supports or encourages activism among seniors. Variables 1 and 3 relate to a state's entire population, the former as a measure of civic involvement, the latter as an indicator of how thoroughly the state's social environment fosters citizen activism. Rankings of the states on these four variables appear in tables A.8 through A.11. The alpha for these index elements is 0.80, indicating that all these elements are closely correlated with one another. Figure 6.2 displays cross-state variation on this SSF dimension.

Affordability

As we indicated in chapter 3, affordability and safety do not co-vary in a way allowing them to be indexed together. Unfortunately, highly affordable states tend to be somewhat less safe than highly expensive ones. So we focus throughout most of this chapter—as in chapter 3—on affordability. We address safety at a later point in this chapter. We assess the affordability dimension of SSF by amalgamating the following four variables introduced in chapter 3: (1) the percentage of a state's population that lives outside of metropolitan areas, (2) a state's median mortgage payment (reversed), (3) a state's federal medical

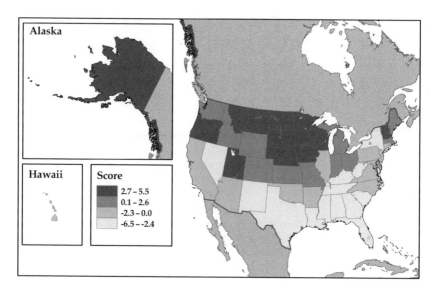

Figure 6.2: Meaningful contributions and supportive communities dimension of SSF

assistance percentage, and (4) a state's sixty-five-or-older median household income (reversed). Variables 1 through 3 do not focus on older state residents in particular. Rather, they describe aspects of the social and economic environment affecting people of all ages. Variable 4 does focus on how older state residents' income levels mesh with this environment. Rank-orderings of the states on these four variables appear in tables A.15 through A.18. The alpha of 0.90 indicates quite strong correlations among these scale elements. Figure 6.3 shows how states vary on this dimension of SSF.

Health and High-Quality Medical Care

To assess the health and high-quality medical care dimension of SSF, we combine four variables that we introduced in chapter 4: (1) the CDC's healthy aging index,[6] (2) the "best practices" conception of the quality of medical care delivered to Medicare patients,[7] (3) the "coordination of care elements" conception of the quality of medical care delivered to Medicare patients,[8] and (4) the percentage of Medicare decedents in a state who were *not* admitted to an intensive care unit or cardiac care unit during the last six months of their lives. All four of these variables are focused on older individuals. Rank-orderings of the states on these four variables appear in tables A.22 through A.25. The alpha for this index is 0.82, another strong reading. Figure 6.4 portrays cross-state variation on this dimension of SSF.

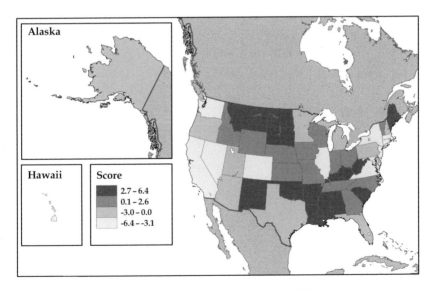

Figure 6.3: Affordability dimension of SSF

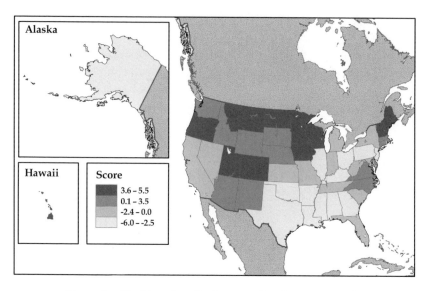

Figure 6.4: Health and medical care quality dimension of SSF

Obtaining High-Quality Long-Term Care

We assess the dimension of SSF dealing with the accessibility and quality of long-term care by merging four variables introduced in chapter 5: (1) Medicaid-certified nursing facility beds per one thousand state residents sixty-five or older, (2) the percentage of a state's Medicaid expenditures going to nursing facilities, (3) state Medicaid nursing facility expenditures per one thousand state residents sixty-five or older, and (4) our quality of state nursing facility processes scale. Once again, all four of these variables are focused on older persons or issues that relate virtually exclusively to them. Rank-orderings of the states on these four variables appear in tables A.29 through A.32. The alpha for this index is 0.74, below optimal, but certainly adequate. Figure 6.5 shows how the states vary on this SSF dimension.

Relations Among the SSF Dimensions

When people learn that we study relative SSF, they invariably ask us which state is the most senior friendly. We answer that it depends on one's preeminent needs or priorities. Table 6.1 shows that correlations among the five dimensional scales are often weak, negative, or both. The recreational lifestyle

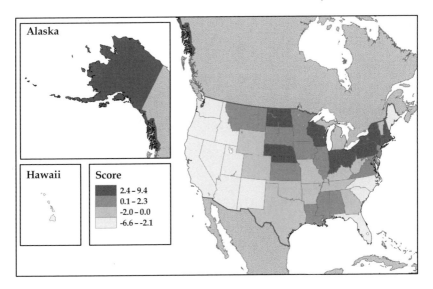

Figure 6.5: Accessible and high-quality long-term care dimension of SSF

dimension correlates at −0.11 with the meaningful contributions and supportive communities dimension; −0.42 with the affordability dimension; −0.02 with the health and high-quality medical care dimension; and −0.55 with the accessible, high-quality long-term care dimension. These correlations indicate that states with mild climates and many recreational opportunities often do not foster meaningful contributions and supportive communities (−0.11) or support senior health and high-quality medical care (−0.02). Further, states that are senior friendly on recreational lifestyle generally do poorly on affordability (−0.42) and particularly on providing accessible, high-quality long-term care (−0.55). Arizona, for instance, ranks third among the states on our recreational lifestyle dimension, but thirty-second on the meaningful contributions and supportive communities dimension, eighteenth on the health and high-quality medical care dimension, thirty-first on affordability, and fiftieth on accessible, high-quality long-term care. The states highly supportive of recreational lifestyles generally do not display strengths on the other four dimensions of SSF.

The meaningful contributions and supportive communities dimension correlates at −0.11 with recreational lifestyle (as we described above); −0.07 with affordability; 0.79 with health and high-quality medical care; and 0.20 with accessible, high-quality long-term care. This means that states that are senior friendly in fostering meaningful contributions and supportive communities generally offer lackluster support for recreational lifestyles; affordability; and

Table 6.1   Relations (correlations) among the five dimensions of SSF

	1 Recreational lifestyle	2 Contributions/ community	3 Affordability	4 Health and high-quality medical care	5 Accessible high-quality long-term care
1 Recreational lifestyle	1.00				
2 Contributions/ community	−.11	1.00			
3 Affordability	−.42**	−.07	1.00		
4 Health and high-quality medical care	−.02	0.79***	−.07	1.00	
5 Accessible, high-quality long-term care	−.55***	0.20	−.10	0.16	1.00

NOTE: Significant at < 0.05 = *; at < 0.01 = **; at < 0.001 = ***.

accessible, high-quality long-term care. But they are states that also are routinely senior friendly on the health and high-quality medical care dimension. This strong association between the meaningful contributions and supportive communities and the health and high-quality medical care SSF dimensions suggests some common thread, which we discuss below.

The affordability dimension correlates at −0.42 with the recreational lifestyle dimension and −0.07 with the meaningful contributions and supportive communities dimension (both covered above) and at −0.07 with the health and high-quality medical care and −0.10 with the accessible, high-quality long-term care dimension. This means that most states that are senior friendly on affordability are not supportive of meaningful contributions and supportive communities, health and high-quality medical care and accessible, high-quality long-term care dimensions of SSF. Further, states that perform well with respect to affordability tend to be pretty senior *unfriendly* on the recreational lifestyle dimension of SSF. So similarly to states ranking highly on the recreational lifestyle SSF dimension, states ranking highly on affordability generally lack strengths on the other four SSF dimensions. Thus young retirees who are looking primarily for affordable states need to be particularly aware of the downsides of these states and realize that they may well need to move again later in order to find strong support for needs that will grow more prominent as they age.

States' rankings on the health and high-quality medical care dimension correlate at –0.02 with the recreational lifestyle, 0.79 with the meaningful contributions and supportive communities, and –0.07 with the affordability dimensions (all introduced above) as well as at 0.16 with the accessible, high-quality long-term care dimension. We note again the high positive correlation between the health and high-quality medical care and the meaningful contributions and supportive communities dimensions. Yet, somewhat surprisingly, states that strongly support seniors' health and medical care quality are not particularly likely to provide accessible, high-quality long-term care.

We have already discussed each correlation with the accessible, high-quality long-term care dimension, but we note again its –0.55 correlation with the recreational lifestyle dimension. This tells us that the seniors in the states most supportive of outdoor recreational activities generally will not find the most accessible and highest-quality long-term care.

An Addendum on Safety

In chapter 3 we compared the seventeen (top third) affordability states on their safety (property crime rates) rankings.[9] People who need affordability presumably also want safety. Table 6.2 shows how the top seventeen affordability states rank on safety as well as the other four dimensions of SSF. The correlations, across all fifty states, between safety, affordability, and the other four SSF dimensions appear in the bottom row of table 6.2.

Property crime rates and affordability appear in the first two columns of table 6.2. (Property crime rate is reversed, so high rankings [e.g., second place for South Dakota] mean low rates.) No clear relationship emerges between this safety index and affordability across all fifty states (correlation of 0.02 in the bottom row). But a couple of other, significant relationships emerge when all fifty states are considered. States that are senior friendly on the recreational lifestyle dimension tend to also have higher property crime rates, and those that score highly on the accessible, high-quality long-term care dimension of SSF tend to have lower property crime rates. Once again, these findings indicate that seniors should consider their priorities (current and future) carefully before making decisions about living in various states.

Summary of Composite State Rankings on the Five Dimensions

As figure 6.1 and table A.36 show, western—particularly southwestern—and southeastern states essentially monopolize the top ranks of the recreational

Table 6.2 Rankings of the top seventeen states on the SSF affordability dimension, on property crime and the other SSF dimensions

State	Property crime rate (reversed)[a]	Affordability	Recreational lifestyle	Contributions/ communities	Health and high-quality medical care	Accessible high-quality long-term care
South Dakota	2	8	30	5	17	13
North Dakota	3	7	48	4	6	3
Maine	5	12	34	17	7	43
Kentucky	10	4	49	48	44	29
West Virginia	13	2	50	45	33	32
Idaho	15	15	15	18	19	39
Iowa	17	16	31	9	10	14
Montana	22	5	16	1	8	15
Wyoming	23	17	18	16	23	35
Mississippi	25	1	42	50	50	23
Louisiana	31	9	32	42	49	21
Alabama	33	6	36	43	41	22
Oklahoma	35	10	25	31	46	27
Arkansas	38	3	29	36	43	30
New Mexico	43	11	7	39	22	45
Tennessee	45	14	23	46	37	33
South Carolina	47	13	11	41	28	44
Correlations[b]	1.00	0.02	−0.50***	0.25	0.29*	0.60***

NOTE: Significant at < 0.05 = *; at < 0.001 = ***.
[a] The property crime rate (per one thousand state residents) index is reversed so that high rankings (e.g., second place for South Dakota) mean low rates.
[b] Correlations between property crime rate (reversed) and the five SSF dimensions for all fifty states.

lifestyle dimension scale. These states include the western Sunbelt states as well as a few, more northern states of the West. The bottom ranks are drawn mostly from the Northeast and the Upper Plains. But a couple of southeastern states—Kentucky and Mississippi—appear in this group as well.

Top-ranked states on the meaningful contributions and supportive communities dimension lie in the North from Alaska to New Hampshire, but predominantly in the northwestern and north-central regions. (See fig. 6.2 and table A.37.) States at the bottom of the meaningful contributions and supportive communities dimension are, with the exception of Nevada and New York, in the southeastern or south-central regions. So the leading and laggard states on these first two dimensions largely flip-flop around an East-West axis dividing North from South.

On the affordability dimension of SSF the top states tend to form a diagonal along an axis from the Southeast to the Northwest/north-central region. States low on affordability do not group themselves in a clear geographic pattern. They are mostly coastal in the Northeast or Pacific West, although Colorado and Illinois are members of this group as well. (See fig. 6.3 and table A.38.)

Unsurprisingly, given the high (0.79) correlation between the health and high-quality medical care dimension and the meaningful contributions and supportive communities dimension, the identities of high- and low-ranking states on the former nearly mirror those for the latter. Top states are generally northern and include states from New England, the Upper Midwest, and the mountain West. With several, mostly contiguous exceptions (Illinois, New Jersey, Pennsylvania, and Ohio), the states ranked in the bottom positions are south-central and southeastern. (See fig. 6.4 and table A.39.)

As figure 6.5 and table A.40 show, states ranking near the top of the accessible, high-quality long-term care dimension of SSF generally represent the Northeast and Upper Midwest. The states holding the bottom ranks on this dimension form a scattered lot that includes representatives of the West and Southeast.

In summary and with some exceptions, different southern regions lead on the recreational lifestyle dimension of SSF. Various northern regions tend to lead on the meaningful contributions and supportive communities; the health and high-quality medical care; and the accessible, high-quality long-term care dimensions. Northwestern/north-central and south-central/southeastern regions provide greater affordability. Generally, the laggard states lie in the regions obverse from the leaders. In a couple of instances, these laggards are narrowly and clearly geographically focused. For instance, a group of south central states hold a near monopoly on the bottom ranks of the health and high-quality medical care dimension.

Consequences of These Rankings

What difference does it make for older Americans to live in a state that ranks near the top or the bottom on any of these dimensions of SSF? To offer answers to this question we developed a "so-what" variable for each dimension. These variables might also be called *social outcome measures*. That is, they measure distinct social outcomes for older persons associated with states' positions on particular composite indicators. We introduced these social outcome variables as the first variable in the "Additional Indicators" sections of chapters 1 through 5.

We show here how a state's recreational lifestyle score influences the state's net in-migration among persons sixty-five to seventy-four as a percentage of the state's sixty-five-to-seventy-four population, revealing in the process how younger retirees "vote with their feet" in terms of interstate migration. For the meaningful contributions and supportive communities dimension, we examine the effect of patterns of civic involvement, income equality, and relative affluence on the broad orientations among a state's population toward citizen activism and the inclusiveness of participation in social life associated with Elazar's egalitarian/moralistic political culture. For the affordability dimension we demonstrate how our four central indexes relate to a state's cost-of-living index (reversed), displaying how inexpensively, overall, individuals can live in the state. For the health and high-quality medical care dimension we chose the state's average life expectancy as our social outcome variable. This measures the average quantity, rather than quality, of life. But a state's life expectancy correlates strongly and positively with each of the four measures that constitute our health and high-quality medical care dimensional scale. We expect the composite scale formed from these four quality-of-life indexes (e.g., the healthiness of a state's older residents) to influence the quantity of life positively. Next, we examine the influence a state's score on the accessible, high-quality long-term care dimension has on our scale for the state's nursing facility residents' quality-of-life outcomes. This variable enables us to examine the degree to which accessible, high-quality long-term care contributes to positive life outcomes for a state's nursing facility residents.

Each of these five social outcome variables correlates positively and statistically significantly with the associated dimension of SSF: recreational lifestyle and a state's net sixty-five-to-seventy-four net in-migration (0.61); meaningful contributions and supportive communities and a state's political culture (0.76); affordability and a state's cost of living (reversed) (0.69); health and high-quality medical care and a state's life expectancy (0.73); and accessible, high-quality long-term care and the quality-of-life outcomes for a state's nursing facility residents (0.41).

To show how a state's standing on various dimensional scales affects these social outcome variables, we control for the effects of some other influences. In the regression analysis depicted in table 6.3, the effects of the various SSF dimensions (the independent variables) on each of the social outcome indicators (the dependent variables) appear in the various columns. But in contrast to the correlation coefficients that we have dealt with previously, the regression coefficients in each row of the table measure the effect of the SSF dimension in that row on each specific social outcome variable, *controlling for the effects of the other four dimensions.* So, for instance, as we move from states in lower to those in higher ranks on the recreational lifestyle dimension, the rate of the states' sixty-five-to-seventy-four net in-migration increases sharply (the bold 9.10) in the upper-left-hand corner of the table), controlling for the effects of the other four SSF dimensions. The strength of the effect of an independent variable on a dependent variable is indicated by the ratio between the regression coefficient and the standardized error (in parentheses beneath it) or t-score. The asterisks indicate levels of strength of effect that are strong enough to have occurred by chance 5 percent of the time (*), 1 percent of the time (**), and 1/10 of 1 percent of the time (***).[10]

We ideally expect that each of the five dimensions of SSF would have both (1) a stronger positive effect on the social outcome associated with it than on the other four social outcome indicators and (2) a stronger positive effect on the social outcome associated with it than do any of the other SSF dimensions. This would mean that the five bold regression coefficients running from the

Table 6.3   Regression coefficients on the social outcome, or "so-what," variables for the scales of the five SSF dimensions

Dependent variables Independent variables	Net 65-to-74 in-migration	Index of Elazar's state political culture	State cost of living (reversed)[a]	Life expectancy at birth	State nursing facility residents' quality of life outcomes
Recreational lifestyle	**9.10***** (1.81)	−0.37 (0.20)	0.006 (0.004)	0.08 (0.05)	−0.05 (0.14)
Contributions/ communities	−1.27 (1.79)	**0.72***** (0.20)	0.002 (0.003)	0.05 0.05	0.45** (0.14)
Affordability	4.51** (1.21)	−.39** (0.14)	**.018***** (0.002)	−.14*** (0.03)	0.04 (0.09)
Health and high-quality medical care	0.07 (1.75)	0.38 (0.20)	−0.010* (0.003)	**0.26***** (0.05)	0.23 (0.13)
Accessible, high-quality long-term care	−1.56 (1.53)	−0.16 (0.17)	−0.007* (0.003)	0.03 (0.04)	**0.24*** (0.12)
Adjusted R square	0.56	0.63	0.71	0.78	0.61

NOTE: Significant at < 0.05 = *; at < 0.01 = **; at < 0.001 = ***. Standard errors are in parentheses beneath the regression coefficients.
[a] More decimal places are necessary to reveal the values in this column because we are predicting a small number with considerably larger numbers.

upper left to the lower right would each represent the strongest positive effect in its row and column. We achieve this goal on nine of these ten comparisons but not on the second count with the accessible, high-quality long-term care dimension and its social outcome indicator, state nursing facility residents' quality-of-life outcomes. The effect that this dimension has on this social outcome is statistically significant but weaker than the effect exerted by the meaningful contributions and supportive communities dimension. As states' political cultures move from hierarchical/traditionalistic through individualistic to egalitarian/moralistic, the residents of the states nursing facilities enjoy better life outcomes.

These results support our view that SSF is a multidimensional concept. Different stages of aging prompt distinct life priorities. Portions of the older American population find themselves focusing on one or possibly two of these priorities at any given time. The states, in turn, tend to specialize in supporting different priorities. Virtually all states support one priority at least reasonably well, a number of states sustain two priorities pretty well, and a small fraction of the states are among the leaders in supporting three priorities (see figs. 6.1 through 6.5). Table 6.1 shows that states that are highly supportive of a particular priority often offer lackluster or even very poor support of some other priorities. Further, table 6.3 gives us an indication of the practical effects of matches and disparities in these intersections of senior priorities and state support. For instance, some states that offer a relatively low cost of living, thus allowing retirees with modest incomes to stretch their resources further, also attract a relatively large number of sixty-five- to seventy-four-year-old migrants. But they also tend to have unhealthy older populations and to provide rather poor medical care to Medicare patients. Combinations of need-service matches and disparities such as these have prompted our suggestions that older Americans consider two interstate moves, rather than just one, as they mature through successive stages of aging.

Why States Are Supportive (or Not) of Various Dimensions of SSF

Why do the states support forms of SSF differently? We draw on research explaining cross-state public policy differences to help answer this question. The political, economic, and social factors that are important in elucidating many cross-state differences in public policy cannot fully explain the ranks of states across the distinct dimensions of SSF. Most noticeably, a state's ranking on the recreational lifestyle dimension rests significantly on temperature, sunshine, and humidity levels, which state policy makers cannot control.

Karch's review of this literature points to four broad factors explaining cross-state policy differences.[11] One of these is a state's predisposition or inclination to support extensive, state-level public programs that benefit vulnerable citizens, including many seniors. Common measures for such an inclination include political culture and the political ideology of public officials or ordinary citizens. At least some of the programs and orientations that varying cultures and ideologies foster influence several dimensions of SSF. In table 6.4 we measure this factor with an index for Elazar-Douglas-Wildavsky's conception of state political culture.[12] A second factor is the degree to which a state's political parties compete with each other. Intense competition between the two major parties for voters' support generally fosters more extensive public programs.[13] Karch's third explanatory factor is the material capacity of a state to support extensive public programs. Common indicators for this factor include state tax capacity (total state taxable resources per capita), a state's fiscal situation in terms of the relationship between its revenues and expenditures, and different measures of private sector affluence. In table 6.4 we use public-sector tax capacity and the median income for a state's sixty-five-or-older households as indicators.[14] The fourth factor in Karch's model involves the severity of the need that target populations of citizens have for public-program assistance. This factor is frequently measured by demographic data, including the percentage of state population sixty-five or older in table 6.4.[15]

Karch's model does not exhaust all the factors frequently employed by social scientists who study cross-state differences in programs or orientations. Schneider and Ingram, for instance, contend that the images, which political elites and ordinary citizens hold about a public program's target population, affect the generosity of program benefits and the user friendliness of its administration.[16] They argue that political elites and citizens generally perceive older adults favorably, but often hold negative images of minorities.[17] Numerous studies find evidence that, as the prevalence of minority beneficiaries rises, program generosity declines and program administration becomes less friendly.[18] We use the percentage of a state's sixty-five-or-older population that is minority in order to measure this selective perception effect.[19]

Further, Walker maintains that states' geographic proximity to certain trend-setting states influences the timing of program adoption and the precise nature of what is adopted.[20] We operationalize a related concept of regional patterns with the average degree of generosity with which a state's contiguous neighbors apply a public program of broad interest to seniors. Several factors suggest that differences in state residential property tax abatement for seniors make a reasonably broad indicator of SSF, although this very breadth also means that it will not be strongly and positively associated with all five of our

SSF dimensions.[21] First, nationwide, 80 percent of people sixty-five or older own their residences. But, second, the median income for households of those who are sixty-five or over stands at about half that for the general U.S. population. So a fairly broad spectrum of the sixty-five-or-older population is likely quite interested in reducing their taxes. Yet, third, most people sixty-five or older pay relatively modest income and Social Security taxes, and state property taxes represent a fairly large portion of their overall tax bill.[22] Accordingly, we average a state's contiguous neighbors' abatement of senior residential property taxes to represent regional levels of general SSF and examine its influence on the five specific dimensions of the concept.[23]

Putnam and his colleagues (with reference to Italian regions) as well as Amenta, Carens, and Olasky (in a study of the American states) find that certain social structures in the distant past depress or elevate citizen activism in support of particular public social programs in the present.[24] For instance, states with a history of narrowly hierarchical institutions such as slavery continue to experience lower levels of citizen activism in the present in comparison with states that have more egalitarian and inclusive histories. So current support through citizen activism for vulnerable groups in society likely suffers in states with a history of narrowly hierarchical institutions.

Unfortunately, Amenta, Carens, and Olasky's historical-depressive-effects factor correlates closely with other, arguably more central or immediate explanatory factors and thus creates multicollinearity problems. So we eliminate it from our analysis below, but related work indicates that a state history including significant experience with slavery exerts an independent effect on public-policy differences.[25] Further, our scale for the meaningful contributions and supportive communities SSF dimension represents our best prospect for measuring Amenta, Carens, and Olasky's concept of citizen activism. But we cannot reasonably employ it in table 6.4 as an independent variable, since it is an essential dependent variable in the analysis. Consequently, we set both activism-depressing historical effects such as slavery and elevating effects such as citizen involvement aside in table 6.4 and use seven variables representing six of the seven categories of factors introduced above.

Recreational Lifestyle

Regression of the seven independent variables in table 6.4 offers a partial explanation for a state's position on the recreational lifestyle dimension of SSF, explaining just less than half (0.46) of the variation among the states. The only statistically significant effects are positive ones for the median income of sixty-five-or-older state households and the percentage of a state's sixty-five-or-older

Table 6.4 Regression coefficients on the five SSF dimensions of seven prominent explanatory factors

Dependent variables / Independent variables	Recreational lifestyle	Contributions/ communities	Affordability	Health and high-quality medical care	Accessible, high-quality long-term care
Elazar-Douglas-Wildavsky state political culture	0.01 (0.10)	0.46*** (0.09)	−0.20** (0.07)	0.40** (0.11)	−.05 (0.12)
Ranney's index of state political party competition	−2.29 (4.19)	−1.81 (3.87)	−1.92 (3.06)	−2.75 (4.61)	−9.08* (5.06)
State tax capacity	−.80 (1.92)	−1.86 (1.77)	−13.47*** (1.40)	−1.06 (2.11)	8.80*** (2.32)
Median income of a state's 65-or-older households[a]	0.00044** (0.00012)	0.00037** (0.00011)	−0.00031** (0.00009)	0.00009 (0.00013)	−.00044** (0.00015)
Proportion of a state's population that is 65 or older	0.22 (0.19)	0.15 (0.18)	−0.33* (0.14)	0.20 (0.21)	0.11 (0.23)
Proportion of a state's 65-or-older population that is minority	0.09** (0.03)	−0.07* (0.03)	−0.09** (0.02)	−0.01 (0.04)	−.02 (0.04)
Average senior residential property tax abatement of contiguous states	0.28 (0.16)	0.11 (0.15)	0.05 (0.12)	0.43* (0.17)	0.14 (0.19)
Adjusted R square	0.46	0.64	0.81	0.50	0.32

NOTE: Significant at < 0.05 = *; at < 0.01 + **, at < 0.001 = ***. Standard errors are in parentheses beneath the regression coefficients.

[a] This variable is corrected for state cost of living. Additionally, more decimal places are necessary in this row because we are using relatively large numbers to predict small numbers.

population composed of minorities. The first effect is consistent with the widespread perception that moving in retirement to support a penchant for outdoor recreational activity is positively associated with income. The second would seem to be a largely historical artifact of slavery and more recent Hispanic and Asian immigration patterns coincidentally overlapping with states that offer mild winter climates.

Meaningful Contributions and Supportive Communities

Our seven independent variables account for nearly two-thirds (0.64) of the variation in states' support of the meaningful contributions and supportive communities SSF dimension. The largest (statistically significant and positive) contribution comes from state political culture. In chapter 2 we portrayed a state's political culture as the result of a state's position on this SSF dimension. Now we are doing the reverse. Is this unreasonable? Many, likely most, scholars who study culture would argue that this relationship is symbiotic. They understand the relations between culture and social structures such as income distributions and voting patterns as involving reciprocal causation.

Once again, the median household income of older state residents and the proportion of minorities among a state's seniors exert statistically significant effects. The positive effect of income is consistent with the widely recognized tendency for various forms of constructive social participation to be positively associated with income, education, and job status, or what sociologists refer to as socioeconomic status (SES). The negative effect for social diversity suggests that greater diversity depresses supportive community feelings.[26] So seniors will find meaningful contributions and supportive communities more easily in states with greater elder ethnic homogeneity and higher incomes among their sixty-five-or-older residents

Affordability

Our seven independent variables initially appear to do a terrific job of explaining more than 80 percent (0.81) of the cross-state variation on the affordability dimension of SSF. But one of the four elements of the scale for the SSF affordability dimension is a state's sixty-five-or-older median household income (reversed), so using sixty-five-or-older median household income as an independent variable artificially enhances this variable's statistically significant negative effect. Nonetheless, there are four other statistically significant negative effects, including Elazar-Douglas-Wildavsky state political culture, state tax capacity, the proportion of a state's population that is sixty-five or older, and the percentage of this older population that is minority. We expected four of these five influences on affordability. States with relatively low-income popula-tions and relatively modest public-sector financial resources generate relatively inexpensive social environments. Further, relatively low-income populations tend to be more conservative, especially socially conservative (hierarchical), rather than egalitarian and are not necessarily enthusiastic about public pro-grams that support seniors. The negative effect of the proportion of a state's population that is sixty-five or older may arise in part from the lower poverty levels among older persons that Social Security fosters. However, the negative effect of the percentage that minorities constitute of this older population sur-prises us.

Health and High-Quality Medical Care

Our seven independent variables account for 50 percent of the cross-state variation on the health and high-quality medical care SSF dimension. The statistically significant effects are unsurprising. The effect of Elazar-Douglas-Wildavsky state political culture closely resembles the situation with respect to the meaningful contributions and supportive communities dimension of SSF. We think that this cultural variable provides the common thread mentioned above with respect to table 6.1 that explains the close association between these two dimensions of SSF.[27] In addition, the generosity of neighboring states' sen-ior residential property tax abatements influences states' support of the health and high-quality medical care SSF dimension positively. This effect is indica-tive of the pronounced regional groupings that appear in figure 6.4 and table A.39 with respect to this dimension of SSF. Relative generosity of states' senior residential property tax abatements may also have roots in the distinctive state cultures described by Elazar, Douglas, and Wildavsky.[28]

These seven variables collectively explain only 50 percent of the cross-state variation in the health and high-quality medical care SSF dimension. Why this proportion is so modest is less clear than in the instance of the recreational life-style dimension, for which state climate was an obvious exogenous explanatory factor. In the instance of the health and high-quality medical care dimension, we think that adding (currently nonexistent) measures for the professional cul-tures of relevant medical care providers (e.g., registered nurses, primary care physicians, and geriatricians and other specialists) would help us to explain more variance.

Accessible, High-Quality Long-Term Care

Our seven independent variables explain just under one-third (0.32) of the cross-state variation in the accessible, high-quality long-term care dimension of SSF. This relatively low proportion of variance explained surprises us, given that this dimension is arguably the one most closely linked to aspects of public policy. The statistically significant effects on the accessibility and quality of long-term care include a positive influence for state tax capacity and negative effects for state political party competition and the median household income of older state residents. We expected each of these. First, we have found in other work that using Medicaid funds for older state residents' long-term care has more bipartisan support than do state-level public social programs focused on other target populations, so a negative effect for party competition seems reasonable.[29] Second, Medicaid-supported nursing facility long-term care is an expensive service requiring extensive public resources. Third, lower-income older persons draw more heavily on Medicaid to finance their long-term care expenses.

Overall

Each of the seven independent variables, which we have drawn from political science and sociological studies of cross-state policy differences, produces at least one statistically significant effect across the five SSF dimensions. But three variables exert particularly powerful or systematic effects. One of these is cultural inclination. Elazar-Douglas-Wildavsky state political culture exerts three powerful, expected effects: positive for the meaningful contributions and supportive communities as well as the health and high-quality medical care dimensions and negative in the instance of the affordability dimension.

The other two variables producing powerful and expected effects represent public and private material capacity, respectively. State tax capacity affects the affordability dimension negatively and the accessible, high-quality long-term care dimension positively. The median income of states' sixty-five-or-older households has the most systematically powerful and expected effects: positive on the recreational lifestyle and meaningful contributions and supportive communities dimensions and negative on the affordability and accessible, high-quality long-term care dimensions. Collectively, then, a cultural orientation toward using public policy to improve the lives of as large a proportion of the population as possible coupled with the material capacity to support this inclination explain a good deal of the variation in SSF across the American states.

The proportion of minorities in a state's sixty-five-or-older population exerts three statistically significant effects across our five SSF dimensions. The positive effect on the recreational lifestyle dimension essentially reflects historical and geographical accidents. The other two statistically significant effects are negative. The negative effect on the meaningful contributions and supportive communities dimension unfortunately indicates that, at least at the state level, community solidarity often suffers as ethnic diversity increases. We have no clear explanation for the negative effect on the affordability dimension.

Three other independent variables each produce a single statistically significant effect. Increasing political party competition affects the accessible, high-quality long-term care dimension negatively, suggesting that bipartisan concern for older citizens can overcome at least some economic and social conservatives' aversion to expensive public programs. The negative effect of the proportion of a state's population that is sixty-five or older on the affordability dimension may arise in part because Social Security places floors under the household incomes of older citizens. Finally, the average senior residential property tax abatement of a state's contiguous neighbors produces a statistically significant (positive) effect only on the health and high-quality medical care dimension. That this variable, representing a senior-friendly public policy of broad appeal, reveals only a single statistically significant effect across our five SSF dimensions reinforces our view that SSF is a multidimensional concept.

These analyses show that basic state features and patterns of cross-state emulation matter to the lives of their older residents. Differences in state cultural orientations and in states' material capacity to support generous orientations toward vulnerable groups can enrich or limit opportunities for older Americans.

Imagine, for a few moments, the retirement party that Art and Karen Munro's friends threw for them a few years ago. The party occurred in late September, before most of their "snowbird" friends took off for winter locales in southern states, and a couple of friends who had previously moved to southern locations attended while on trips north to enjoy early autumn in the Upper Midwest. An extensive group of friends and acquaintances surrounded Art and Karen, and they both really enjoyed the affair. They left the party with unusually warm feelings about their lives and friends in Iowa, feelings that might have led them to hesitate about moving if they had not been so far along in their plans for relocating.

Art and Karen looked forward to their move to New Mexico and had prepared well. By the time of their retirement party they had already lined up a buyer for their Iowa home and had located a house in New Mexico on which they were currently negotiating. Indeed, within just a few weeks of the party, they had packed up and moved. They have never regretted the move. They love the gorgeous scenery of southeastern New Mexico. They have found a number of interesting acquaintances among other new arrivals and a couple of increasingly good new friends. They spend their ample leisure in activities—fishing and pottery—that have intrigued them for years. Compared with Jerry and Arlene Senter, who are shuffling idly around their house in Iowa, Art and Karen clearly made a wise and successful move. So far, so good.

New Mexico serves their current purposes quite well. The state ranks seventh on the recreational lifestyle SSF dimension. It ranks eleventh on the affordability dimension, higher than any of the six states above it on recreational lifestyle, and this is important because the Munros live on a modest income.[1] Art and Karen are in relatively good health, and they may well enjoy a decade or more in the New Mexico sun before experiencing serious problems. But eventually, such problems are likely to appear. Rural southeastern New Mexico does not offer extensive support for health care among older residents. New Mexico ranks twenty-second on the health and high-quality medical care SSF dimension. So the Munros would have to drive two to three hours to the University of New Mexico Medical Center in Albuquerque, partly on hazardous mountain roads, to get top-notch medical care for serious health problems. New Mexico ranks forty-fifth on the accessible, high-quality long-term care SSF dimension, just above Nevada, where the Garveys experienced their difficulties. Further, New Mexico offers few prospects for improvement in these rankings across the next decade or so. For instance, it ranks thirty-ninth on the meaningful contributions and supportive communities dimension of SSF. This is right above Florida, where Jean's parents found themselves pretty much on their own. (See tables A.36 through A.40 in the Appendix for the rankings referred to in this paragraph.)

So, sooner or later, the Munros, who have handled basic retirement issues well so far, will likely confront new, different, serious challenges that their current location supports far less well than it does their present life. What are they going to do? We have described a rough sequence of basic aging issues and how they match or are at odds with the capacities of the various states to provide supportive responses to specific needs.

Our central message suggests a multistage approach to aging. Young retirees seeking excellent outdoor recreational opportunities, more meaningful opportunities for contributing to their communities, or a reduced cost of living can find states that offer exceptional support for these specific objectives. But they may need to consider another move later on to a state that offers high-quality medical or long-term care. The Web sites listed in table E.1 may facilitate this process. However, we mention in closing, once again, some caveats with respect to this "two-step" suggestion.

Making Big Decisions Carefully

States famous for delightfully mild climates may have high-elevation areas with bitter winters or, as a result of prevailing winds, regions with distressingly sticky summers. States generally offering good affordability also have expensive neighborhoods, sometimes expensive whole regions. States with high overall levels of constructive citizen activism will have pockets riddled with crime, drug abuse, and other social ills, making them unsuitable for vulnerable older persons. States whose physicians generally earn high marks for the quality of care they deliver also have some bad apples among them. And there will also be some discouraging examples among the nursing facilities in states whose facilities generally achieve high-quality care. Retirees should examine a range of aspects of a new location before they move. They can start by using any computer connected to the Internet; however, getting thoroughly acquainted with a new locale requires an on-site visit or visits—the longer, the better.

We recognize that the location of and relationships with adult children may make permanent moves from one state to another undesirable or impractical.

For this reason some people spend particular seasons in a state other than that of their primary residence. The snowbirds of the Upper Midwest, for instance, travel to Arizona and the Rio Grande Valley of New Mexico or Texas to enjoy milder winters. Some rent houses seasonally; others have recreational vehicles or time-share arrangements. This solution allows retirees to spend winters in different states in successive years. These seasonal moves, however, work out less well for those with other priorities. Making meaningful contributions and finding supportive communities generally require a more permanent base in a location than snowbirding affords.

Table E.1   Helpful Web sites

Organization/Program	Web site
AARP Public Policy Institute	http://www.aarp.org/ppi
Age-Friendly States	http://www.agefriendlystates.com
Bowling Alone	http://bowlingalone.com
Brookings Institution	http://www.brookings.edu
Bureau of Justice Statistics	http://www.bjsdata.ojp.usdoj.gov
Bureau of Labor Statistics	http://www.bls.gov
Census Bureau	http://www.census.gov
Centers for Disease Control	http://www.cdc.gov
Centers for Medicare and Medicaid	http://cms.hhs.gov
Corporation for National and Community Service (Senior Corps)	http://www.nationalservice.org
Dartmouth University	http://dartmouthatlas.org
Disaster Center	http://www.disastercenter.com
Elder Economic Security Standard	http://www.wowonline.org/ourprograms/eesi
Forbes	http://www.forbes.com
Home and Community-Based Services	http://www.hcbs.org/moreInfo-php
Inter-University Consortium for Social and Political Research	http://www.icpsr.umich.edu
Kaiser Family Foundation	http://www.kff.org
National Association of Area Agencies on Aging	http://www.n4a.org
National Center for State Higher Education and Policy Making Analysis	http://www.higheredinfo.org
National Climate Data Center	http://www.ncdc.noaa.gov
Nursing Home Compare	http://www.medicare.gov
United Health Foundation	http://www.unitedhealthfoundation.org

NOTE: More specific locations for particular information are provided in the notes to the text.

Investing in Others

Developing and maintaining positive relations with others enhance retirement as much as they do any other stage of life. Older people benefit enormously from good relations with their children, even if achieving this goal requires considerable effort. Retirees should recognize that their children may become their caregivers. Jean's parents, for instance, were essentially rescued by their children. This occurred initially when her parents' strokes and other problems temporarily incapacitated either her father or mother in Florida. Jean and a sister-in-law who lived in Florida rushed to the scene, provided immediate help themselves, and hired more long-term assistance of various sorts. Across her parents' gradual decline these trips became an overwhelming burden, and Jean moved her mother and father to Maine, where family members could provide more routine assistance beyond that available from her parents' retirement community, then their assisted living center, and finally their nursing facility. Historically, women have provided most family care, but several decades of relatively high divorce rates and growing numbers of middle-aged women who are employed full-time will likely increase the care from middle-aged men—as in the example of Jean's brothers and their families helping with their parents.

Given this, retirees should certainly take the location of their adult children into account when considering moving from state to state, particularly when the former do so for the purposes of obtaining better medical or long-term care. Usually adult children are concerned for their parents' welfare, and they can play a crucial role in improving the care their parents receive as hospital patients or nursing facility residents. The upside possibilities with one's children are more positive than with long-term friends, who, understandably, feel reluctant to get involved in health or caregiving issues or with paid caregivers. Moreover, the side benefits to involving a child may include having quarrels of the past dissipate in favor of previously unimagined meaningful relationships.

Maintaining and building relationships in the broader community also help preserve the welfare of older persons. Many relationships that arise from recreational activities such as playing golf will not withstand the demands of caregiving, but investing time and effort in community causes, as Nancy Currier has done, is more apt to build a supportive community that will respond when needed. For instance, the father of one of the authors (Charles), not generally a warm person, actually enjoyed and felt good about making deliveries for Meals on Wheels to a group of shut-in elders. He found a sense of companionship he valued with several of them, and he helped with some of their other needs as a result of his preexisting relationship. It is still the case that such friends, even when armed with legal authority, may feel tentative or uncomfortable about exercising it without the consent of the recipient's living children.

Planning, Following Up, and Reassessing

As with most other aspects of life, people need to apply imagination and planning, show some initiative, and—inevitably—have some luck to create circumstances that support their priorities. The probability of developing these circumstances improves when older people plan for retirement well in advance, test the comfort of various scenarios in their imagination, and discuss with others the viability of their plans. Across large numbers of persons, those who consider the future and examine various possibilities enjoy better outcomes than those who make spur-of-the-moment decisions or—perhaps even worse— like Jerry and Arlene Senter in Iowa never get around to creating any new directions at all. At a minimum, planning greatly reduces the uncertainty and stress that often afflicts those who neglect it.

Some individuals plan but never convert their plans into actions. Taking a big step—such as moving to another state—in retirement becomes easier the more relevant experience a person has. The experience that counts for cross-state retirement moves is on-the-ground familiarity with the new location. Minimally, people should spend several days in a location before they reach a decision to relocate. We advise those who are thinking of moving to use vacations during the years prior to retirement—as Art and Karen Munro did—to become more familiar with several possible locations. Comparing multiple locations generally helps one to recognize the strengths and weaknesses of each.

Imagination, planning, and initiative do not guarantee success in locating a suitable spot in a new retirement state. Success in retirement, as in other stages of life, generally requires an irreducible element of good luck. But luck arises in part from preparation and effort, so imagination, planning, and initiative may foster good luck.

However good retirees' initial plans turn out to be, older persons should periodically reassess their plans on the basis of new experience. This is exactly what Carl and Jessica Sanford are *not* doing in New Jersey. Surviving changing economic circumstances often requires that people reassess and adjust their previous decisions.[2] As retirements lengthen to multiple decades, financial resources that seemed more than ample at the outset often dwindle to inadequacy or even disappear—as Jean's parents' resources did—as a result of inflation a quarter century later. Taking time to reassess, upgrading savings when possible, and becoming more aggressive about downsizing in the process helps to avoid outliving one's financial resources.

Art and Karen Munro's situation illustrates that other aspects of retirement call for periodic reassessment. The Munros will almost surely grow increasingly dependent on high-quality medical care, long-term care, or both. Phil and Sandy Turner's move from North Carolina to New Hampshire, taken prior to the onset of severe health limitations, shows how periodic reassessment can reduce anxiety in the present and ensure greater security and comfort in the future. Larry and Julie Crothers' reassessment, prompted by their daughter, led to their move from Arizona to New Hampshire after serious health difficulties had appeared. Yet it has also yielded benefits. Based on the tenets of "slow medicine," we recommend that retirees write out their medical care preferences around age sixty-five and review this document they've created every few years as their circumstances change.[3] We advise that older persons make a geriatrician their primary physician—as Larry Crothers has done—as opposed to relying chiefly on a series of specialists for different maladies. A geriatrician generally provides more coordinated care and will often employ invasive tests and seriously painful treatments less routinely.

Across the stages of aging, seniors' priorities shift, and different American states vary considerably in support for different priorities. Taking these two facts into consideration helps older people cope more successfully with the growing challenges of contemporary aging. We hope that the information in this book helps to "nudge" older Americans to decisions that reduce stress and increase security in aging.[4] After all, the problems of older citizens in the United States will become the problems of everyone who grows old.

APPENDIX

Table A.1   State ranking and scores on climate index (1961–1990)

Rank (Score)	State(s)
1 (20.5)	Arizona
2 (18)	California
3 (17.5)	Nevada, New Mexico
5 (16.5)	Oklahoma, Texas
7 (14.5)	Kansas, Utah
9 (14)	Hawaii, South Carolina
11 (13)	Arkansas, Colorado, Georgia
14 (12.5)	Mississippi, Nebraska
16 (11.5)	Alabama, Florida, Louisiana
19 (11)	North Carolina
20 (10.5)	Missouri
21 (10)	Delaware, Tennessee, Virginia
24 (9.5)	Maryland, South Dakota
26 (9)	Kentucky
27 (8.5)	Illinois, Iowa, New Jersey, Wyoming
31 (8)	Connecticut, Idaho, Oregon, Rhode Island
35 (7.5)	Indiana, Massachusetts
37 (7)	Montana
38 (6.5)	Ohio, Pennsylvania, Washington
41 (6)	West Virginia
42 (5.5)	North Dakota
43 (5)	New York
44 (4.5)	Michigan, Vermont
46 (4)	Maine, Minnesota, Wisconsin
49 (3)	New Hampshire
50 (0)	Alaska

Table A.2 State ranking and percentages on sixty-five-and-older residents who do not live alone (2005)

Rank (Percentage)	State(s)	Rank (Percentage)	State(s)
1 (81.6)	Hawaii	44 (68.3)	Massachusetts
2 (77.8)	Utah	45 (68.2)	South Dakota
3 (76.1)	Alaska	46 (68.0)	Indiana, Wisconsin
4 (75.1)	Arizona	48 (67.9)	West Virginia
5 (74.4)	California	49 (67.6)	Nebraska
6 (74.3)	Florida	50 (66.8)	North Dakota
7 (74.1)	Texas		
8 (73.1)	Delaware, Nevada		
10 (72.9)	Idaho		
11 (71.9)	Georgia, Maryland		
13 (71.8)	Washington		
14 (71.6)	New Mexico		
15 (71.4)	Oregon		
16 (71.3)	New Hampshire, South Carolina		
18 (71.0)	Arkansas, Colorado, Montana, New Jersey, Tennessee, Virginia		
24 (70.9)	North Carolina		
25 (70.7)	Vermont		
26 (70.0)	Mississippi, Missouri		
28 (69.7)	Wyoming		
29 (69.6)	Michigan		
30 (69.4)	Alabama, Connecticut, Oklahoma		
33 (69.3)	Kansas, Rhode Island		
35 (69.0)	Louisiana, Minnesota, New York		
38 (68.9)	Illinois		
39 (68.8)	Maine		
40 (68.6)	Iowa		
41 (68.5)	Kentucky, Ohio, Pennsylvania		

Table A.3 State ranking and scores on sixty-five-and-older residents who are not disabled (2005)

Rank (Score)	State(s)	Rank (Score)	State(s)
1 (80.3)	Nevada	42 (72.1)	Kansas
2 (79.7)	Arizona	43 (71.7)	Missouri
3 (79.4)	Hawaii	44 (71.6)	Alabama
4 (78.4)	Florida	45 (71.0)	Louisiana
5 (78.1)	Utah, Delaware	46 (70.4)	West Virginia
7 (77.6)	New Jersey	47 (70.1)	Oklahoma
8 (77.4)	Maryland	48 (69.6)	Kentucky
9 (77.0)	California	49 (69.3)	Arkansas
10 (76.7)	Maine	50 (66.7)	Mississippi
11 (76.3)	New Hampshire		
12 (76.2)	Colorado		
13 (76.1)	Michigan, Virginia, Wisconsin		
16 (75.9)	Pennsylvania		
17 (75.7)	New York		
18 (75.6)	Massachusetts		
19 (75.5)	Connecticut		
20 (75.3)	Minnesota, Vermont		
22 (75.1)	New Mexico		
23 (74.4)	Iowa, North Carolina, Wyoming		
26 (74.2)	Illinois		
27 (74.1)	Indiana, Montana, South Carolina, Washington		
31 (73.9)	Nebraska		
32 (73.7)	South Dakota		
33 (73.6)	Ohio, Oregon		
35 (73.4)	Idaho		
36 (73.3)	Georgia		
37 (73.2)	North Dakota		
38 (73.1)	Rhode Island		
39 (72.5)	Alaska, Tennessee		
41 (72.3)	Texas		

Table A.4 State ranking and percentages on recreational opportunities (2004)

Rank (Percentage)	State(s)	Rank (Percentage)	State(s)
1 (26.6)	Nevada	46 (3.4)	New York, Washington
2 (16.0)	Hawaii	48 (3.1)	Indiana, Ohio
3 (7.9)	Montana	50 (2.3)	Delaware
4 (7.7)	Florida		
5 (7.5)	Wyoming	NOTE: Recreational opportunities equals domestic tourism as a percentage of gross state product.	
6 (7.4)	Mississippi		
7 (6.9)	New Mexico		
8 (6.8)	Vermont		
9 (5.9)	Louisiana, South Carolina		
11 (5.7)	South Dakota		
12 (5.6)	New Hampshire, North Dakota		
14 (5.5)	Idaho		
15 (5.2)	Arizona, Arkansas, Tennessee		
18 (5.0)	Colorado		
19 (4.9)	Maine		
20 (4.8)	Utah		
21 (4.6)	Iowa, Missouri, Virginia		
24 (4.5)	Georgia		
25 (4.4)	Kentucky, Nebraska		
27 (4.3)	California, Illinois, Oregon		
30 (4.2)	Alabama, Alaska, Kansas, Maryland		
34 (4.1)	North Carolina		
35 (4.0)	Oklahoma, West Virginia		
37 (3.9)	Connecticut, New Jersey		
39 (3.8)	Minnesota		
40 (3.7)	Texas, Wisconsin		
42 (3.6)	Rhode Island		
43 (3.5)	Massachusetts, Michigan, Pennsylvania		

Table A.5 State ranking and rates on sixty-five-to-seventy-four net in-migration (1995–2000)

Rank (Rate)	State	Rank (Score)	State
1 (132.7)	Nevada	33 (−11.2)	Wisconsin
2 (125.5)	Arizona	34 (−11.3)	Pennsylvania
3 (97.8)	Florida	35 (−12.6)	Nebraska
4 (45.6)	South Carolina	36 (−13.4)	North Dakota
5 (39.4)	Delaware	37 (−13.8)	Rhode Island
6 (25.7)	North Carolina	38 (−15.2)	California
7 (23.1)	Idaho	39 (−16.0)	Iowa
8 (22.5)	Arkansas	40 (−16.3)	Indiana
9 (18.6)	New Mexico	41 (−18.9	Ohio
10 (18.3)	Mississippi	42 (−20.2)	Minnesota
11 (16.4)	Tennessee	43 (−24.0)	Maryland
12 (15.2)	Georgia	44 (−25.2)	Massachusetts
13 (11.6)	Alabama	45 (−25.3)	Michigan
14 (9.2)	Utah	46 (−30.0)	New Jersey
15 (7.2)	Texas	47 (−36.9)	Illinois
16 (6.3)	Oklahoma	48 (−38.4)	Connecticut
17 (5.0)	Montana	49 (−53.6)	New York
18 (4.2)	Virginia	50 (−59.3)	Alaska
19 (2.7)	Oregon		
20 (2.0)	Maine		
21 (1.6)	West Virginia		
22 (1.5)	Missouri		
23 (0.9)	Kentucky		
24 (0.8)	New Hampshire		
25 (−4.3)	South Dakota		
26 (−4.8)	Colorado		
27 (−5.1)	Louisiana		
28 (−5.5)	Wyoming		
29 (−5.6)	Vermont		
30 (−6.8)	Washington		
31 (−7.1)	Hawaii		
32 (−9.0)	Kansas		

Table A.6 State ranking and rates on eighty-five-or-older net in-migration (1995–2000)

Rank (Rate)	State	Rank (Rate)	State
1 (88.0)	Nevada	33 (−3.2)	Ohio
2 (62.5)	Alaska	34 (−3.6)	Florida
3 (40.0)	Colorado	35 (−3.7)	Oklahoma
4 (31.9)	Maine	36 (−4.2)	Nebraska
5 (30.5)	Maryland	37 (−5.4)	Louisiana
6 (29.8)	Virginia	38 (−5.5)	New Jersey
7 (27.7)	Washington	39 (−6.1)	Michigan
8 (27.4)	Wyoming	40 (−6.3)	Missouri
9 (27.1)	New Hampshire	41 (−7.0)	Massachusetts
10 (26.3)	Georgia	42 (−8.4)	Alabama
11 (26.0)	North Carolina	43 (−13.3)	Hawaii
12 (23.2)	South Carolina	44 (−15.4)	Mississippi
13 (22.6)	Vermont	45 (−15.6)	Kentucky
14 (22.2)	Arizona	46 (−16.3)	Arkansas
15 (21.9)	Delaware	47 (−18.8)	Illinois
16 (17.3)	Utah	48 (−21.2)	West Virginia
17 (15.4)	Tennessee	49 (−22.5)	North Dakota
18 (14.8)	Idaho	50 (−40.5)	New York
19 (14.4)	Rhode Island		
20 (13.6)	Oregon		
21 (13.3)	Texas		
22 (13.1)	Montana		
23 (11.1)	New Mexico		
24 (10.7)	Connecticut		
25 (9.4)	Minnesota		
26 (8.7)	Kansas		
27 (5.4)	Wisconsin		
28 (0.6)	Iowa		
29 (0.3)	Indiana		
30 (0.0)	South Dakota		
31 (−0.2)	California		
32 (−2.7)	Pennsylvania		

Table A.7 State ranking and rates on sixty-five-or-older suicides per 1,000 sixty-five-or-older residents (average 2000–2002)

Rank (Rate)	State	Rank (Rate)	State
1 (32.12)	Nevada	33 (14.14)	South Dakota
2 (26.15)	Idaho	34 (13.56)	Wisconsin
3 (25.87)	Montana	35 (13.35)	Nebraska
4 (24.31)	New Mexico	36 (13.23)	Hawaii
5 (23.71)	Oregon	37 (13.13)	Kansas
6 (23.28)	Colorado	38 (12.93)	Mississippi
7 (23.09)	Arizona	39 (12.88)	New Hampshire
8 (22.79)	Wyoming	40 (12.65)	Maryland
9 (20.90)	Washington	41 (12.33)	Illinois
10 (20.84)	Vermont	42 (11.41)	Iowa
11(19.52)	West Virginia	43 (11.28)	Delaware
12 (19.37)	Florida	44 (11.16)	Pennsylvania
13 (18.72)	Virginia	45 (11.01)	Minnesota
14 (17.96)	North Carolina	46 (9.71)	Connecticut
15 (17.94)	Tennessee	47 (9.25)	New Jersey
16 (17.93)	Georgia	48 (8.30)	New York
17 (17.80)	Utah	49 (7.25)	Rhode Island
18 (17.65)	California	50 (6.48)	Massachusetts
19 (17.63)	Alabama		
20 (17.51)	Arkansas		
21 (17.12)	Oklahoma		
22 (16.43)	Kentucky		
23 (16.06)	Louisiana		
24 (15.94)	Missouri		
25 (15.73)	Texas		
26 (15.21)	North Dakota		
27 (15.15)	Alaska		
28 (15.17)	Ohio		
29 (14.95)	Maine		
30 (14.94)	Indiana		
31 (14.90)	South Carolina		
32 (14.20)	Michigan		

Table A.8 State ranking and scores on Putnam's Comprehensive Social Capital Index II (2000)

Rank (Score)	State(s)	Rank (Score)	State(s)
1 (1.71)	North Dakota	35 (−0.32)	Virginia
2 (1.69)	South Dakota	36 (−0.35)	New Mexico
3 (1.42)	Vermont	37 (−0.36)	New York
4 (1.32)	Minnesota	38 (−0.47)	Florida
5 (1.29)	Montana	39 (−0.50)	Arkansas
6 (1.15)	Nebraska	40 (−0.55)	Texas
7 (0.98)	Iowa	41 (−0.79)	Kentucky
8 (0.77)	New Hampshire	42 (−0.82)	North Carolina
9 (0.67)	Alaska, Wyoming	43 (−0.83)	West Virginia
11 (0.65)	Washington	44 (−0.88)	South Carolina
12 (0.59)	Wisconsin	45 (−0.96)	Tennessee
13 (0.57)	Oregon	46 (−0.99)	Louisiana
14 (0.53)	Maine	47 (−1.07)	Alabama
15 (0.50)	Utah	48 (−1.15)	Georgia
16 (0.41)	Colorado	49 (−1.17)	Mississippi
17 (0.38)	Kansas	50 (−1.43)	Nevada
18 (0.35)	Hawaii		
19 (0.27)	Connecticut		
20 (0.22)	Massachusetts		
21 (0.10)	Missouri		
22 (0.07)	Idaho		
23 (0.06)	Arizona		
24 (0.00)	Michigan		
25 (−0.01)	Delaware		
26 (−0.04)	New Jersey		
27 (−0.06)	Rhode Island		
28 (−0.08)	Indiana		
29 (−0.16)	Oklahoma		
30 (−0.18)	California, Ohio		
32 (−0.19)	Pennsylvania		
33 (−0.22)	Illinois		
34 (−0.26)	Maryland		

Table A.9 State rankings and percentages on sixty-five-or-older presidential voting (2004)

Rank (Percentage)	State(s)	Rank (Percentage)	State(s)
1 (87.2)	South Dakota	37 (70.1)	Illinois
2 (86.9)	Montana	38 (69.8)	New Jersey
3 (86.5)	Utah	39 (69.4)	Georgia
4 (82.5)	Minnesota	40 (68.6)	Florida, West Virginia
5 (82.2)	Oregon	42 (67.9)	Maryland
6 (81.8)	North Dakota	43 (67.4)	Virginia
7 (81.2)	Wisconsin	44 (66.9)	California
8 (80.5)	New Hampshire	45 (65.8)	Arizona
9 (79.4)	Alabama	46 (65.6)	Texas
10 (78.7)	Kansas	47 (64.8)	Tennessee
11 (77.9)	Louisiana	48 (64.6)	Hawaii, Nevada
12 (77.5)	Washington	50 (62.9)	New York
13 (77.3)	Maine		
14 (77.2)	Massachusetts, Oklahoma		
16 (76.6)	Nebraska		
17 (76.4)	New Mexico		
18 (75.7)	Colorado, Missouri		
20 (75.4)	Delaware		
21 (75.3)	Iowa		
22 (75.0)	Wyoming		
23 (73.3)	Alaska		
24 (73.1)	North Carolina		
25 (73.0)	Ohio		
26 (72.8)	Kentucky		
27 (72.7)	Indiana, Rhode Island		
29 (72.6)	South Carolina		
30 (72.5)	Michigan		
31 (71.7)	Vermont		
32 (71.6)	Idaho		
33 (70.8)	Arkansas, Pennsylvania		
35 (70.4)	Connecticut		
36 (70.2)	Mississippi		

Table A.10 State ranking and scores on income equality (Gini reversed) (1999)

Rank (Score)	State(s)	Rank (Score)	State(s)
1 (0.598)	Alaska	43 (0.530)	Florida
2 (0.590)	North Dakota, Utah	44 (0.525)	Alabama, California
4 (0.587)	Wisconsin	46 (0.523)	Connecticut, Texas
5 (0.586)	New Hampshire	48 (0.522)	Mississippi
6 (0.582)	Iowa	49 (0.517)	Louisiana
7 (0.577)	Vermont	50 (0.501)	New York
8 (0.576)	Indiana, Nebraska		
10 (0.574)	Minnesota		
11 (0.573)	Idaho		
12 (0.572)	Wyoming		
13 (0.571)	Delaware		
14 (0.566)	Hawaii, Maine, Maryland, South Dakota		
18 (0.565)	Kansas		
19 (0.564)	Montana, Nevada		
21 (0.563)	Washington		
22 (0.562)	Oregon, Colorado		
24 (0.560)	Michigan		
25 (0.559)	Ohio		
26 (0.551)	Missouri, Virginia		
28 (0.550)	Arizona		
29 (0.548)	North Carolina, Pennsylvania		
31 (0.546)	South Carolina		
32 (0.545)	Oklahoma		
33 (0.544)	Illinois		
34 (0.543)	Rhode Island		
35 (0.542)	Arkansas		
36 (0.540)	New Jersey, New Mexico		
38 (0.539)	Georgia		
39 (0.537)	Massachusetts		
40 (0.535)	Tennessee		
41 (0.532)	Kentucky, West Virginia		

Table A.11 State ranking and percentages on sixty-five-and-older state residents above the federal poverty level (2005)

Rank (Percentage)	State(s)	Rank (Percentage)	State(s)
1 (95.0)	Oregon	39 (87.1)	North Carolina
2 (94.1)	Minnesota	40 (87.0)	Arkansas
3 (93.4)	Delaware, Montana	41 (86.5)	West Virginia
5 (93.2)	Alaska	42 (85.8)	Louisiana
6 (93.1)	Ohio	43 (85.7)	Texas
7 (92.7)	Utah	44 (85.4)	Oklahoma
8 (92.6)	Connecticut	45 (85.2)	New York
9 (92.4)	New Jersey	46 (83.9)	South Carolina
10 (92.2)	Iowa	47 (83.5)	Alabama
11 (92.0)	Massachusetts	48 (82.2)	New Mexico
12 (91.9)	Kansas	49 (81.5)	Kentucky
13 (91.7)	Vermont	50 (79.3)	Mississippi
14 (91.3)	Idaho		
15 (90.9)	Nevada		
16 (90.7)	Washington		
17 (90.6)	Missouri		
18 (90.4)	Pennsylvania		
19 (90.3)	California		
20 (90.2)	Nebraska		
21 (90.0)	Arizona, Virginia		
23 (89.8)	New Hampshire, Michigan, Rhode Island		
26 (89.2)	Illinois, Wyoming		
28 (89.1)	Maryland		
29 (89.0)	Hawaii, Maine		
31 (88.3)	Florida		
32 (88.2)	Indiana, Tennessee		
34 (88.1)	North Dakota		
34 (88.0)	Wisconsin		
36 (87.8)	Colorado		
37 (87.5)	South Dakota		
38 (87.3)	Georgia		

Table A.12 State political culture per
Elazar-Douglas-Wildavsky (mid-1960s)

Rank (Score)	State(s)
1 (15)	Minnesota, Utah, Vermont
4 (14)	Colorado, Maine, Michigan, North Dakota, Oregon, Wisconsin
10 (13)	California, Kansas, New Hampshire, Washington
14 (12)	Idaho, Montana, South Dakota
17 (11)	Connecticut, Iowa, Nebraska, Wyoming
21 (10)	Illinois, Massachusetts, New York, Ohio, Rhode Island
26 (9)	Alaska, Indiana, Nevada, New Jersey, Pennsylvania
31 (7)	Arizona, North Carolina
33 (6)	Delaware, Maryland
35 (5)	Hawaii, Missouri
37 (4)	Florida, Kentucky, Oklahoma, Texas, West Virginia
42 (3)	Alabama, Arkansas, Georgia, Louisiana, New Mexico
47 (2)	Mississippi, South Carolina, Virginia
50 (1)	Tennessee

NOTE: Cultures are assigned numbers from
15 (relatively thorough egalitarian/moralistic)
through individualistic to 1 (relatively
thorough hierarchical/traditionalistic).

Table A.13 State ranking and scores on Berry, Ringquist, Fording, and Hanson's citizen liberalism (2004)

Rank (Score)	State	Rank (Score)	State
1 (81.63)	Massachusetts	33 (43.76)	Montana
2 (71.18)	New York	34 (42.74)	Texas
3 (68.30)	Connecticut	35 (41.48)	Florida
4 (67.85)	Rhode Island	36 (41.14)	South Carolina
5 (67.62)	Maine	37 (41.03)	Louisiana
6 (66.88)	West Virginia	38 (40.25)	Iowa
7 (66.53)	Vermont	39 (40.17)	Tennessee
8 (65.16)	Delaware	40 (39.19)	Alabama
9 (62.81)	Hawaii	41 (36.22)	Georgia
10 (61.62)	North Dakota	42 (35.41)	Kansas
11 (60.41)	Illinois	43 (34.53)	Mississippi
12 (60.06)	Maryland	44 (34.37)	Alaska
13 (59.80)	New Jersey	45 (34.32)	Kentucky
14 (58.31)	California	46 (31.40)	Nebraska
15 (57.11)	Washington	47 (30.38)	Utah
16 (56.99)	Oregon	48 (28.29)	Oklahoma
17 (55.13)	New Mexico	49 (26.77)	Wyoming
18 (54.41)	Colorado	50 (16.89)	Idaho
19 (53.86)	Pennsylvania		
20 (52.09)	Nevada		
21 (51.96)	Arkansas		
22 (51.83)	Michigan		
23 (51.66)	Ohio		
24 (51.63)	Wisconsin		
25 (48.68)	South Dakota		
26 (48.03)	Minnesota		
27 (47.42)	Virginia		
28 (46.88)	Missouri		
29 (46.15)	Arizona		
30 (45.76)	Indiana		
31 (45.62)	North Carolina		
32 (44.20)	New Hampshire		

Table A.14 State district electoral competition X Democratic government control (1980s)

Rank (Score)	State(s)	Rank (Score)	State(s)
1 (31.85)	Vermont	33 (14.33)	Nebraska
2 (30.98)	West Virginia	34 (13.86)	North Dakota
3 (28.30)	Minnesota	35 (13.13)	Utah
4 (27.17)	Rhode Island	36 (13.06)	Pennsylvania, South Carolina
5 (25.89)	Hawaii	38 (12.95)	Ohio
6 (25.67)	Connecticut	39 (11.25)	South Dakota
7 (25.59)	Nevada	40 (11.13)	Texas
8 (25.16)	California	41 (11.03)	Georgia
9 (23.68)	Washington	42 (10.81)	Louisiana
10 (22.69)	Delaware	43 (10.30)	Mississippi
11 (22.41)	Oregon	44 (10.10)	Arizona
12 (22.32)	Maryland	45 (9.75)	Montana
13 (21.98)	New York	46 (9.45)	Kansas
14 (21.82)	Virginia	47 (8.82)	New Hampshire
15 (21.44)	New Mexico	48 (7.37)	Wyoming
16 (21.30)	Maine	49 (7.15)	Arkansas
17 (19.98)	Indiana	50 (7.08)	Idaho
18 (19.27)	Massachusetts		
19 (18.78)	North Carolina		
20 (18.69)	Kentucky		
21 (18.30)	Michigan		
22 (10.03)	Missouri		
23 (18.01)	Iowa		
24 (17.88)	Wisconsin		
25 (17.32)	Alaska		
26 (17.15)	Alabama		
27 (17.08)	Colorado		
28 (15.91)	New Jersey		
29 (15.16)	Florida		
30 (15.12)	Tennessee		
31 (15.10)	Illinois		
32 (14.73)	Oklahoma		

Table A.15 State ranking and percentages on nonmetropolitan population (2000)

Rank (Percentage)	State(s)	Rank (Percentage)	State(s)
1 (82.7)	Vermont	35 (31.0)	Hawaii
2 (76.1)	Mississippi	36 (29.0)	Texas
3 (75.4)	Maine	37 (27.0)	Washington
4 (74.5)	Wyoming	38 (25.3)	Colorado
5 (74.2)	South Dakota	39 (23.8)	Arizona
6 (74.0)	Montana	40 (21.7)	Utah
7 (71.7)	West Virginia	41 (21.6)	Illinois
8 (76.8)	Arkansas	42 (19.8)	Maryland
9 (64.1)	North Dakota	43 (18.3)	New York
10 (61.9)	Iowa	44 (16.4)	Connecticut
11 (61.2)	Kentucky	45 (16.1)	Nevada
12 (57.0)	Oklahoma	46 (15.7)	Florida
13 (55.7)	Alaska	47 (11.6)	California
14 (55.5)	Alabama	48 (11.5)	Rhode Island
15 (55.4)	New Hampshire	49 (11.2)	Massachusetts
16 (55.1)	Kansas	50 (7.9)	New Jersey
17 (53.3)	Idaho, North Carolina, South Carolina		

NOTE: Nonmetropolitan means clusters of less than fifty thousand people.

Rank (Percentage)	State(s)
20 (52.9)	Nebraska
21 (52.6)	New Mexico
22 (47.9)	Tennessee
23 (47.0)	Wisconsin
24 (44.9)	Minnesota
25 (44.8)	Missouri
26 (43.9)	Indiana
27 (43.3)	Louisiana
28 (42.2)	Oregon
29 (38.7)	Georgia
30 (35.6)	Ohio
31 (33.8)	Michigan
32 (33.4)	Virginia
33 (33.1)	Pennsylvania
34 (32.2)	Delaware

Table A.16 State ranking and amounts on median mortgage payment (reversed) (2005)

Rank (Amount)	State(s)	Rank (Amount)	State(s)
1 (1,203)	West Virginia	34 (704)	Oregon
2 (1,158)	Arkansas	35 (649)	Minnesota
3 (1,130)	Mississippi	36 (609)	Hawaii
4 (1,087)	Alabama, Oklahoma	37 (589)	Virginia
6 (1,065)	Kentucky	38 (557)	Colorado
7 (1,054)	Louisiana	39 (548)	Nevada
8 (1,028)	North Dakota	40 (546)	Washington
9 (1,014)	South Dakota	41 (545)	Illinois
10 (1,012)	Wyoming	42 (523)	Alaska
11 (1,010)	Tennessee	43 (439)	Maryland
12 (1,009)	South Carolina	44 (434)	New Hampshire
13 (1,004)	Idaho	45 (415)	Rhode Island
14 (996)	New Mexico	46 (348)	New York
15 (992)	Iowa	47 (282)	Connecticut
16 (974)	Montana	48 (219)	Massachusetts
17 (971)	Missouri	49 (88)	California
18 (969)	Indiana	50 (62)	New Jersey
19 (932)	Kansas		
20 (911)	North Carolina		
21 (907)	Maine		
22 (893)	Nebraska		
23 (859)	Ohio		
24 (806)	Arizona		
25 (804)	Pennsylvania		
26 (800)	Vermont		
27 (794)	Georgia		
28 (787)	Michigan		
29 (780)	Texas		
30 (758)	Utah		
31 (754)	Delaware		
32 (753)	Florida		
33 (742)	Wisconsin		

Table A.17 State ranking and percentages on federal medical assistance (2005)

Rank (Percentage)	State(s)	Rank (Percentage)	State(s)
1 (77.08)	Mississippi	33 (57.58)	Alaska
2 (74.75)	Arkansas	34 (56.71)	Michigan
3 (74.65)	West Virginia	35 (55.90)	Nevada
4 (74.30)	New Mexico	36 (55.38)	Rhode Island
5 (72.14)	Utah	37 (53.84)	Pennsylvania
6 (71.90)	Montana	38 (50.38)	Delaware
7 (71.04)	Louisiana	39 (50)	California, Colorado, Connecticut, Illinois, Maryland, Massachusetts, Minnesota, New Hampshire, New Jersey, New York, Virginia, Washington
8 (70.83)	Alabama		
9 (70.82)	Idaho		
10 (70.18)	Oklahoma		
11 (69.89)	South Carolina		
12 (69.60)	Kentucky		
13 (67.49)	North Dakota		
14 (67.45)	Arizona		
15 (66.03)	South Dakota		
16 (64.89)	Maine		
17 (64.81)	Tennessee		
18 (63.63)	North Carolina		
19 (63.55)	Iowa		
20 (62.78)	Indiana		
21 (61.15)	Missouri		
22 (61.12)	Oregon		
23 (61.01)	Kansas		
24 (60.87)	Texas		
25 (60.44)	Georgia		
26 (60.11)	Vermont		
27 (59.68)	Ohio		
28 (59.64)	Nebraska		
29 (58.90)	Florida		
30 (58.47)	Hawaii		
31 (58.32)	Wisconsin		
32 (57.90)	Wyoming		

Table A.18 State ranking and amounts on median sixty-five-and-older household income (reversed) (2005)

Rank (Amount)	State	Rank (Amount)	State
1 (23,092)	Mississippi	33 (15,560)	Illinois
2 (22,242)	West Virginia	34 (15,441)	Massachusetts
3 (22,208)	Louisiana	35 (15,365)	Oregon
4 (21,738)	Kentucky	36 (14,921)	Florida
5 (21,492)	Arkansas	37 (13,849)	Colorado
6 (21,112)	North Dakota	38 (13,294)	New Hampshire
7 (20,714)	Alabama	39 (13,284)	Arizona
8 (20,279)	Tennessee	40 (12,760)	Virginia
9 (19,213)	South Dakota	41 (12,653)	Washington
10 (19,063)	Oklahoma	42 (12,274)	Utah
11 (19,023)	Pennsylvania	43 (12,269)	New Jersey
12 (18,852)	South Carolina	44 (12,249)	Connecticut
13 (18,844)	North Carolina	45 (11,218)	California
14 (18,489)	Maine	46 (11,162)	Delaware
15 (18,273)	Georgia	47 (10,946)	Nevada
16 (18,162)	Nebraska	48 (8,212)	Alaska
17 (18,161)	Montana	49 (7,749)	Maryland
18 (17,957)	Ohio	50 (609)	Hawaii
19 (17,878)	Missouri		
20 (17,760)	Wisconsin		
21 (17,639)	Iowa		
22 (17,592)	Rhode Island		
23 (17,528)	New Mexico		
24 (17,431)	Wyoming		
25 (17,117)	Indiana		
26 (17,003)	Kansas		
27 (16,800)	Michigan		
28 (16,785)	New York		
29 (16,669)	Vermont		
30 (16,211)	Idaho		
31 (16,115)	Texas		
32 (15,699)	Minnesota		

Table A.19 State ranking and scores on cost of living (reversed) (2003)

Rank (Score)	State(s)	Rank (Score)	State(s)
1 (0.617)	Mississippi	35 (0.455)	Washington
2 (0.614)	Oklahoma	36 (0.452)	Colorado
3 (0.614)	Texas	37 (0.449)	Alaska, Hawaii, Illinois, Minnesota
4 (0.613)	Arkansas		
5 (0.608)	West Virginia	41 (0.432)	Rhode Island
6 (0.599)	Louisiana	42 (0.410)	California
7 (0.598)	Alabama	43 (0.409)	Maine
8 (0.595)	Kentucky	44 (0.388)	Vermont
9 (0.585)	South Carolina	45 (0.354)	New York
10 (0.583)	Tennessee	46 (0.351)	Pennsylvania
11 (0.579)	Florida	47 (0.348)	New Hampshire
12 (0.571)	North Carolina	48 (0.307)	New Jersey
13 (0.565)	Georgia	49 (0.298)	Connecticut
14 (0.549)	Montana	50 (0.282)	Massachusetts
15 (0.545)	New Mexico		
16 (0.543)	Idaho		
17 (0.538)	Virginia		
18 (0.536)	Arizona		
19 (0.534)	Wyoming		
20 (0.507)	Delaware		
21 (0.505)	Iowa		
22 (0.503)	Missouri		
23 (0.501)	Kansas, Maryland		
25 (0.499)	Indiana		
26 (0.498)	North Dakota		
27 (0.493)	South Dakota		
28 (0.492)	Utah		
29 (0.491)	Ohio		
30 (0.489)	Nebraska		
31 (0.486)	Nevada		
32 (0.480)	Oregon		
33 (0.473)	Michigan, Wisconsin		

Table A.20 State ranking and rates on sixty-five-and-older homicides per 1,000 sixty-five-and-older state residents (2004)

Rank (Rate)	State(s)	Rank (Rate)	State(s)
1 (0)	Delaware, Iowa, Wyoming	47 (0.049)	Vermont
4 (0.002)	Minnesota	48 (0.051)	Arkansas, Utah
5 (0.005)	Massachusetts	50 (0.063)	New Mexico
6 (0.006)	Hawaii, Idaho, Rhode Island, Wisconsin		
10 (0.007)	Connecticut, Washington		
12 (0.009)	New Hampshire		
13 (0.010)	Illinois		
14 (0.012)	Montana, North Dakota, West Virginia		
17 (0.013)	Nebraska, New York, Oregon, Pennsylvania		
21 (0.015)	Ohio		
22 (0.017)	Maine		
23 (0.018)	Indiana, Maryland		
25 (0.019)	Alabama		
26 (0.020)	South Carolina		
27 (0.022)	Colorado		
28 (0.023)	Alaska, California		
30 (0.024)	Michigan		
31 (0.026)	Missouri, New Jersey, Oklahoma, Texas		
35 (0.027)	Tennessee, Virginia		
37 (0.028)	Florida		
38 (0.031)	Louisiana, South Dakota		
40 (0.032)	North Carolina		
41 (0.033)	Kentucky		
42 (0.035)	Arizona		
43 (0.036)	Mississippi, Nevada		
45 (0.037)	Georgia, Kansas		

Table A.21 State ranking and rates on property crimes per one thousand state residents (2005)

Ranking (Rate)	State(s)
1 (0.018)	New Hampshire, South Dakota
3 (0.020)	North Dakota
4 (0.021)	New York
5 (0.023)	Maine, New Jersey, Vermont
8 (0.024)	Massachusetts, Pennsylvania
10 (0.025)	Kentucky
11 (0.026)	Connecticut, Virginia, West Virginia, Wisconsin
15 (0.027)	Idaho, Rhode Island
17 (0.028)	Iowa
18 (0.031)	Delaware, Illinois, Michigan, Minnesota, Montana, Wyoming
24 (0.033)	California, Mississippi
26 (0.034)	Nebraska
27 (0.035)	Indiana
28 (0.036)	Alaska, Maryland
30 (0.037)	Kansas, Louisiana, Ohio
33 (0.039)	Alabama, Missouri, Oklahoma, Utah
37 (0.040)	Florida
38 (0.041)	Arkansas, Colorado, North Carolina
41 (0.042)	Georgia, Nevada, New Mexico
44 (0.043)	Oregon, Tennessee, Texas
47 (0.044)	South Carolina
48 (0.048)	Arizona, Hawaii
50 (0.049)	Washington

NOTE: Property crimes include burglary, larceny theft, and auto theft.

Table A.22 State ranking and scores on CDC's healthy aging index (2004)

Rank (Score)	State(s)	Rank (Score)	State(s)
1 (41.4)	Connecticut	34 (19.3)	South Carolina
2 (37.9)	Minnesota	35 (19.1)	Nevada
3 (36.8)	Massachusetts	36 (18.6)	Tennessee
4 (36.7)	Rhode Island	37 (16.4)	Arkansas, Idaho
5 (35.7)	Arizona	39 (16.3)	Missouri
6 (35.5)	California	40 (16.0)	Oklahoma
7 (35.4)	Colorado	41 (15.7)	Indiana
8 (34.7)	Delaware	42 (15.5)	Louisiana
9 (33.6)	Hawaii	43 (15.0)	Illinois, Texas
10 (32.7)	New Hampshire	45 (12.2)	Alaska
11 (32.6)	Wisconsin	46 (11.1)	West Virginia
12 (32.5)	Maine	47 (9.9)	Georgia
13 (32.4)	Montana	48 (7.7)	Alabama
14 (31.7)	South Dakota	49 (6.3)	Mississippi
15 (31.2)	Oregon	50 (5.4)	Kentucky
16 (30.9)	Florida		
17 (30.7)	Washington		
18 (29.5)	Vermont		
19 (29.0)	Maryland		
20 (28.3)	Virginia		
21 (27.9)	Iowa		
22 (27.4)	North Dakota, Utah		
24 (26.5)	New Jersey		
25 (26.3)	Wyoming		
26 (24.4)	Nebraska		
27 (23.9)	New York		
28 (23.7)	Michigan		
29 (22.7)	Ohio		
30 (21.5)	North Carolina		
31 (21.1)	New Mexico		
32 (20.7)	Pennsylvania		
33 (20.4)	Kansas		

NOTE: Score is rank (reversed) averaged across fifteen criteria.

Table A.23 State ranking on "best practices" conception of medical care quality (2000–2001)

Rank	State	Rank	State
1	New Hampshire	33	Alaska
2	Vermont	34	West Virginia
3	Maine	35	Nevada
4	North Dakota	36	New Mexico
5	Utah	37	Ohio
6	Iowa	38	Tennessee
7	Colorado	39	Kentucky
8	Wisconsin	40	Florida
9	Connecticut	41	Alabama
10	Minnesota	42	New Jersey
11	Oregon	43	California
12	Nebraska	44	Oklahoma
13	Montana	45	Illinois
14	Delaware	46	Georgia
15	Massachusetts	47	Arkansas
16	Hawaii	48	Texas
17	Rhode Island	49	Mississippi
18	Virginia	50	Louisiana
19	Washington		
20	South Dakota		
21	Wyoming		
22	Idaho		
23	North Carolina		
24	New York		
25	Maryland		
26	Michigan		
27	Indiana		
28	Missouri		
29	Arizona		
30	Kansas		
31	Pennsylvania		
32	South Carolina		

NOTE: Ranking is average rank across twenty-four criteria.

Table A.24 State ranking on "coordination of care elements" conception of medical care quality (2000–2001)

Rank	State	Rank	State
1	Hawaii	33	Georgia
2	Utah	34	Connecticut
3	New Hampshire	35	Missouri
4	Oregon	36	Nevada
5	South Dakota	37	Pennsylvania
6	Montana	38	Alaska
7	North Dakota	39	Mississippi
8	Idaho	40	Rhode Island
9	Minnesota	41	Michigan
10	Washington	42	Oklahoma
11	Iowa	43	New Jersey
12	New Mexico	44	Massachusetts
13	Wisconsin	45	New York
14	Maine	46	Florida
15	Arizona	47	Maryland
16	Virginia	48	California
17	Indiana	49	Texas
18	Vermont	50	Louisiana
19	Kansas		
20	Colorado		
21	North Carolina		
22	Nebraska		
23	South Carolina		
24	Ohio		
25	Delaware		
26	Arkansas		
27	West Virginia		
28	Kentucky		
29	Wyoming		
30	Tennessee		
31	Alabama		
32	Illinois		

Table A.25 State ranking and percentages on Medicare decedents not admitted to an ICU/CCU during the last six months of life (2005)

Rank (Percentage)	State	Rank (Percentage)	State
1 (27.1)	Vermont	37 (10.6)	Kentucky
2 (26.9)	North Dakota	38 (10.5)	Missouri
3 (25.1)	Idaho	39 (10.4)	Michigan, Ohio
4 (24.4)	New Hampshire	41 (9.4)	Delaware
5 (23.7)	Iowa, Oregon	42 (9.3)	South Carolina
7 (23.0)	Maine	43 (7.8)	Arizona
8 (22.6)	Wisconsin	44 (7.5)	Pennsylvania
9 (22.5)	Montana	45 (6.2)	Nevada, Texas
10 (22.2)	Wyoming	47 (5.4)	Illinois
11 (22.1)	South Dakota	48 (4.9)	California
12 (21.6)	Utah	49 (1.1)	Florida
13 (21.3)	Rhode Island	50 (0.7)	New Jersey
14 (20.3)	Alaska		
15 (20.0)	Minnesota		
16 (19.1)	Kansas, Massachusetts		
18 (18.3)	Colorado		
19 (17.9)	Nebraska		
20 (17.2)	Mississippi		
21 (16.6)	Connecticut		
22 (16.5)	New Mexico		
23 (16.4)	New York		
24 (16.3)	Oklahoma, Washington		
26 (14.8)	Arkansas		
27 (14.4)	Hawaii		
28 (12.1)	Alabama		
29 (11.9)	North Carolina		
30 (11.6)	Maryland		
31 (11.5)	West Virginia		
32 (11.4)	Georgia		
33 (11.3)	Indiana, Virginia		
35 (11.1)	Louisiana		
36 (10.9)	Tennessee		

Table A.26 State ranking and years on
life expectancy at birth (2000)

Rank (Score)	State(s)
1 (79.8)	Hawaii
2 (79.1)	Minnesota
3 (78.7)	North Dakota, Utah
5 (78.5)	Iowa, New Hampshire
7 (78.4)	Colorado, Connecticut, Massachusetts
10 (78.3)	California, Nebraska
12 (78.2)	Rhode Island, Vermont, Washington
15 (78.1)	Wisconsin
16 (78.0)	Idaho, South Dakota
18 (77.9)	New York, Oregon
20 (77.6)	Maine
21 (77.5)	Arizona, Florida, Kansas, New Jersey
25 (77.3)	Montana, New Mexico
27 (77.1)	Wyoming
28 (76.9)	Virginia
29 (76.8)	Pennsylvania
30 (76.7)	Alaska, Illinois, Texas
33 (76.6)	Delaware
34 (76.5)	Michigan
35 (76.4)	Ohio
36 (76.3)	Maryland
37 (76.2)	Indiana, Missouri
39 (75.9)	Nevada
40 (75.8)	North Carolina
41 (75.3)	Georgia, Kentucky, Oklahoma
44 (75.1)	Arkansas
45 (75.0)	Tennessee, West Virginia
47 (74.9)	South Carolina
48 (74.6)	Alabama
49 (74.4)	Louisiana
50 (73.7)	Mississippi

Table A.27 State health ranking and scores (2004)

Rank (Score)	State(s)	Rank (Score)	State(s)
1 (25.0)	Minnesota	36 (−4.2)	Missouri
2 (23.9)	New Hampshire	37 (−5.8)	Nevada
3 (22.8)	Vermont	38 (−6.6)	New Mexico
4 (17.7)	Hawaii	39 (−7.1)	Kentucky
5 (17.6)	Utah	40 (−7.2)	Oklahoma
6 (17.3)	Massachusetts	41 (−7.5)	North Carolina
7 (15.8)	North Dakota	42 (−8.4)	Florida
8 (15.0)	Connecticut	43 (−10.4)	Alabama, West Virginia
9 (14.4)	Wisconsin	45 (−11.1)	Georgia
10 (13.7)	Maine	46 (−12.2)	Arkansas
11 (13.2)	Iowa	47 (−12.9)	South Carolina
12 (11.7)	Nebraska	48 (−13.1)	Tennessee
13 (11.6)	Colorado	49 (−20.2)	Mississippi
14 (10.9)	Rhode Island	50 (−21.3)	Louisiana
15 (9.1)	Washington		
16 (7.3)	Kansas		
17 (7.2)	New Jersey		
18 (6.4)	Idaho		
19 (6.3)	South Dakota		
20 (5.9)	Virginia		
21 (5.2)	Oregon		
22 (3.6)	California		
23 (3.0)	Arizona		
24 (2.9)	Alaska		
25 (2.8)	Pennsylvania		
26 (2.1)	Montana, Ohio		
28 (2.0)	Wyoming		
29 (0.3)	Illinois, Michigan		
31 (0.1)	New York		
32 (−0.1)	Delaware, Indiana		
34 (−2.0)	Maryland		
35 (−2.7)	Texas		

Table A.28 State ranking and number of physicians per one hundred thousand state residents (2004)

Rank (Number)	State(s)	Rank (Number)	State(s)
1 (450)	Massachusetts	38 (219)	South Dakota
2 (411)	Maryland	39 (213)	Alabama, Indiana
3 (389)	New York	41 (212)	Texas
4 (363)	Connecticut	42 (209)	Utah
5 (362)	Vermont	43 (208)	Arizona
6 (351)	Rhode Island	44 (203)	Arkansas
7 (310)	Hawaii	45 (188)	Wyoming
8 (306)	New Jersey	46 (187)	Iowa
9 (294)	Pennsylvania	47 (186)	Nevada
10 (281)	Minnesota	48 (181)	Mississippi
11 (272)	Illinois	49 (171)	Oklahoma
12 (270)	Virginia	50 (169)	Idaho
13 (267)	Maine		
14 (265)	Washington		
15 (264)	Louisiana		
16 (263)	Oregon		
17 (261)	Ohio, Tennessee		
19 (260)	New Hampshire		
20 (259)	California		
21 (258)	Colorado		
22 (254)	Wisconsin		
23 (248)	Delaware		
24 (253)	North Carolina		
25 (245)	Florida		
26 (242)	North Dakota		
27 (240)	Michigan, New Mexico		
29 (239)	Missouri, Nebraska		
31 (230)	Kentucky, South Carolina		
33 (229)	West Virginia		
34 (222)	Alaska		
35 (221)	Montana		
36 (220)	Georgia, Kansas		

Table A.29 State ranking and numbers on Medicaid-certified nursing facility beds per 1,000 sixty-five-or-older state residents (2003)

Rank (Number)	State(s)	Rank (Number)	State(s)
1 (82)	Iowa	48 (21)	Nevada
2 (76)	Kansas	49 (17)	Alaska
3 (73)	Indiana, Louisiana	50 (16)	Hawaii
5 (71)	Illinois, Nebraska, Oklahoma		
8 (70)	North Dakota, Ohio		
10 (68)	South Dakota		
11 (66)	Arkansas, Connecticut		
13 (65)	Minnesota		
14 (62)	Rhode Island		
15 (61)	Massachusetts		
16 (60)	Montana, Wisconsin		
18 (56)	Texas		
19 (52)	Mississippi, Tennessee		
21 (51)	New Hampshire, Wyoming		
23 (50)	Kentucky		
24 (49)	New York		
25 (48)	Georgia, Pennsylvania		
27 (47)	Maryland		
28 (46)	Colorado		
29 (45)	Alabama, New Jersey, Vermont		
32 (44)	Delaware		
33 (42)	Missouri, North Carolina		
35 (40)	Idaho, Maine, Michigan, West Virginia		
39 (38)	Virginia		
40 (37)	Utah		
41 (36)	South Carolina		
42 (34)	California, Washington		
44 (33)	New Mexico		
45 (28)	Florida, Oregon		
47 (23)	Arizona		

Table A.30 Ranking and percentages on state Medicaid expenditures to nursing facilities (2003)

Rank (Percentage)	State(s)	Rank (Percentage)	State(s)
1 (36.5)	Rhode Island	38 (13.6)	Tennessee, Vermont
2 (33.0)	North Dakota	40 (13.3)	North Carolina
3 (31.6)	Connecticut	41 (12.6)	Nevada
4 (26.9)	Massachusetts	42 (11.3)	California
5 (25.9)	Pennsylvania	43 (11.0)	South Carolina, Washington
6 (25.3)	Ohio		
7 (24.9)	New Hampshire	45 (10.6)	Maine
8 (23.6)	Hawaii	46 (9.1)	Oregon, Utah
9 (23.3)	Montana	48 (8.1)	New Mexico
10 (22.5)	Nebraska	49 (8.0)	Arizona
11 (22.3)	New Jersey	50 (7.5)	Alaska
12 (21.6)	South Dakota		
13 (21.4)	Wisconsin		
14 (20.5)	Alabama, Oklahoma		
16 (20.3)	Delaware		
17 (20.0)	Indiana, Iowa		
19 (19.9)	Kansas		
20 (19.3)	Florida		
21 (18.3)	Arkansas, Michigan		
23 (18.2)	Mississippi		
24 (18.0)	Colorado		
25 (17.9)	Maryland, Virginia		
27 (17.7)	Minnesota, West Virginia		
29 (17.6)	New York		
30 (17.2)	Wyoming		
31 (16.9)	Kentucky		
32 (16.2)	Louisiana		
33 (16.1)	Missouri		
34 (15.4)	Georgia		
35 (15.0)	Illinois		
36 (14.5)	Texas		
37 (14.4)	Idaho		

Table A.31 State ranking and amounts on Medicaid nursing facility expenditures per 1,000 sixty-five-or-older state residents (2003)

Rank (Expenditure)	State(s)	Rank (Expenditure)	State(s)
1 ($3,251)	Rhode Island	34 (933)	Illinois
2 (2,485)	New York	35 (925)	Colorado
3 (2,260)	Connecticut	36 (924)	Iowa
4 (2,002)	Massachusetts	37 (897)	Kansas
5 (1,710)	Ohio	38 (856)	North Carolina
6 (1,564)	North Dakota	39 (837)	Texas
7 (1,563)	Alaska	40 (806)	Idaho
8 (1,430)	Delaware	41 (786)	South Carolina
9 (1,370)	Minnesota	42 (776)	California
10 (1,340)	Mississippi	43 (739)	Florida
11 (1,284)	Pennsylvania	44 (719)	Washington
12 (1,266)	New Hampshire	45 (683)	Virginia
13 (1,257)	Maryland	46 (599)	New Mexico
14 (1,245)	Nebraska	47 (535)	Utah
15 (1,201)	Alabama	48 (458)	Arizona
16 (1,197)	New Jersey	49 (444)	Nevada
17 (1,180)	Wisconsin	50 (424)	Oregon
18 (1,174)	Kentucky		
19 (1,170)	Maine, West Virginia		
21 (1,116)	Louisiana		
22 (1,089)	Vermont		
23 (1,087)	South Dakota		
24 (1,072)	Arkansas		
25 (1,053)	Hawaii		
26 (1,034)	Indiana		
27 (1,021)	Tennessee		
28 (1,000)	Georgia		
29 (996)	Montana		
30 (960)	Michigan		
31 (950)	Wyoming		
32 (946)	Oklahoma		
33 (935)	Missouri		

Table A.32 State ranking and scores on the quality of state nursing facility processes scale (2003)

Rank (Score)	State(s)	Rank (Score)	State(s)
1 (5.223)	Alaska	33 (−1.536)	West Virginia
2 (4.837)	New Hampshire	34 (−1.538)	Kansas
3 (4.577)	Virginia	35 (−1.623)	Kentucky
4 (4.311)	Massachusetts	36 (−1.842)	Louisiana
5 (4.288)	Rhode Island	37 (−2.174)	Utah
6 (3.748)	Wisconsin	38 (−2.194)	Minnesota
7 (3.124)	Indiana	39 (−2.217)	South Carolina
8 (2.815)	Oregon	40 (−2.279)	Florida
9 (2.679)	Pennsylvania	41 (−2.791)	Wyoming
10 (2.576)	North Dakota	42 (−2.987)	California
11 (2.313)	Vermont	43 (−3.325)	Michigan, Washington
12 (2.149)	Missouri	45 (−3.405)	Georgia
13 (1.791)	New Jersey	46 (−4.124)	Maine
14 (1.750)	South Dakota	47 (−4.966)	Oklahoma
15 (1.699)	New York	48 (−5.024)	Arkansas
16 (1.284)	Maryland	49 (−5.234)	Delaware
17 (1.158)	Connecticut	50 (−5.891)	Arizona
18 (1.152)	Illinois		
19 (0.812)	Nebraska		
20 (0.588)	Nevada		
21 (0.421)	Iowa		
22 (0.416)	Ohio		
23 (0.353)	Montana		
24 (0.264)	Texas		
25 (−0.021)	New Mexico		
26 (−0.401)	Alabama		
27 (−0.624)	Hawaii		
28 (−0.786)	Colorado		
29 (−1.043)	North Carolina		
30 (−1.063)	Tennessee		
31 (−1.257)	Idaho		
32 (−1.381)	Mississippi		

NOTE: Score represents the added z-scores of four items.

Table A.33 State ranking and scores on the state nursing facility residents' quality-of-life outcomes scale (2003)

Rank (Score)	State(s)	Rank (Score)	State(s)
1 (5.808)	North Dakota	34 (–0.7020)	West Virginia
2 (5.486)	Nebraska	35 (–0.790)	Virginia
3 (5.245)	Iowa	36 (–0.932)	Maine
4 (5.118)	Minnesota	37(–1.714)	Alabama, Oklahoma
5 (4.979)	Montana	39 (–1.840)	Georgia
6 (4.619)	New Hampshire	40 (–2.103)	Texas
7 (4.438)	Wisconsin	41 (–2.291)	Nevada
8 (4.183)	Wyoming	42 (–2.520)	Tennessee
9 (3.392)	South Dakota	43 (–2.621)	South Carolina
10 (3.308)	Idaho, Vermont	44 (–2.682)	Kentucky
12 (3.252)	Kansas	45 (–2.901)	North Carolina
13 (2.816)	Massachusetts	46 (2.982)	Arkansas
14 (2.257)	Colorado	47 (–3.371)	Hawaii
15 (2.218)	Illinois	48 (–4.103)	Mississippi
16 (2.154)	Missouri	49 (–4.961)	California
17 (2.128)	Connecticut	50 (–6.458)	Louisiana
18 (2.116)	Rhode Island		
19 (1.630)	Utah		

NOTE: Score represents the added z-scores of four items.

Rank (Score)	State(s)
20 (1.615)	New Mexico
21 (1.450)	Michigan
22 (1.270)	Indiana
23 (1.173)	Arizona
24 (1.072)	Ohio
25 (0.336)	Washington
26 (0.254)	New York
27 (0.129)	Delaware
28 (–0.106)	Maryland
29 (–0.250)	Pennsylvania
30 (–0.295)	New Jersey
31 (–0.367)	Oregon
32 (–0.424)	Florida
33 (–0.483)	Alaska

Table A.34 State ranking and rates on average Medicaid nursing facility daily reimbursement (adjusted for state cost of living) (2003)

Rank (Reimbursement)	State(s)	Rank (Reimbursement)	State(s)
1 ($265)	Alaska	36 (90)	New Hampshire, Virginia
2 (156)	Delaware	38 (89)	Georgia, Montana, Wisconsin
3 (141)	Rhode Island	41 (88)	Texas
4 (136)	Maryland	42 (87)	Oklahoma
5 (135)	Hawaii	43 (86)	Utah
6 (131)	West Virginia	44 (79)	Iowa
7 (129)	Florida	45 (78)	Kansas, South Dakota
8 (127)	Ohio	47 (77)	Indiana
9 (125)	Connecticut	48 (74)	Louisiana
10 (121)	New York	49 (73)	Missouri
11 (119)	Arizona	50 (69)	Illinois
12 (118)	Idaho, Pennsylvania		
14 (116)	Alabama		
15 (111)	North Dakota		
16 (110)	California		
17 (109)	Michigan		
18 (107)	Nevada		
19 (106)	Kentucky, Maine, Massachusetts, Minnesota, New Jersey, New Mexico		
25 (104)	Mississippi, Nebraska		
27 (103)	Washington		
28 (102)	Colorado		
29 (101)	Tennessee		
30 (100)	Wyoming		
31 (98)	Arkansas		
32 (95)	North Carolina, Vermont		
34 (94)	South Carolina		
35 (92)	Oregon		

Table A.35 State ranking and amounts on HCBS aged/disabled waivers per 1,000 sixty-five-or-older state residents (2004)

Rank (Expenditure)	State	Rank (Expenditure)	State
1 ($940)	Alaska	34 (105)	Kentucky
2 (585)	Oregon	35 (101)	Alabama
3 (440)	Washington	36 (92)	New Jersey
4 (390)	Vermont	37 (77)	Louisiana
5 (376)	Minnesota	38 (67)	North Dakota
6 (311)	Kansas	39 (55)	South Dakota
7 (296)	Idaho	40 (51)	Michigan
8 (270)	Ohio	41 (45)	Florida
9 (245)	Illinois	42 (40)	Indiana
10 (231)	Texas	43 (37)	New York
11 (225)	Hawaii	44 (29)	Nevada
12 (221)	Nebraska	45 (27)	Massachusetts
13 (213)	Connecticut	46 (24)	California
14 (205)	Wisconsin	47 (22)	Utah
15 (204)	Colorado	48 (16)	Arizona
16 (202)	North Carolina	49 (13)	Mississippi
17 (199)	West Virginia	50 (9)	Tennessee
18 (195)	Rhode Island		
19 (187)	New Mexico		
20 (1800	Georgia		
21 (176)	Oklahoma		
22 (171)	South Carolina		
23 (167)	New Hampshire		
24 (164)	Montana		
25 (149)	Maine		
26 (147)	Virginia		
27 (136)	Wyoming		
28 (135)	Delaware		
29 (125)	Pennsylvania		
30 (116)	Arkansas		
31 (115)	Iowa, Missouri		
33 (111)	Maryland		

Table A.36 State ranking and scores on the recreational lifestyle dimension of SSF

Rank (Score)	State(s)	Rank (Score)	State(s)
1 (10.43)	Nevada	39 (−1.55)	Michigan
2 (9.47)	Hawaii	40 (−1.57)	Pennsylvania
3 (5.79)	Arizona	41 (−1.83)	New York
4 (4.71)	Utah	42 (−1.91)	Mississippi
5 (3.76)	California	43 (−1.92)	Rhode Island
6 (3.68)	Florida	44 (−2.09)	Minnesota
7 (2.68)	New Mexico	45 (−2.18)	Wisconsin
8 (1.47)	Texas	46 (−2.27)	Indiana
9 (1.34)	Delaware	47 (−2.50)	Ohio
10 (1.32)	Colorado	48 (−2.80)	North Dakota
11 (1.14)	South Carolina	49 (−3.01)	Kentucky
12 (1.06)	Maryland	50 (−3.73)	West Virginia
13 (0.49)	Virginia		
14 (0.46)	Georgia		
15 (−0.01)	Idaho, Montana		
17 (−0.06)	North Carolina		
18 (−0.13)	Wyoming		
19 (−0.50)	New Jersey		
20 (−0.55)	Vermont		
21 (−0.64)	Kansas, New Hampshire, Tennessee		
24 (−0.80)	Oregon		
25 (−0.92)	Oklahoma		
26 (−0.94)	Connecticut		
27 (−1.00)	Nebraska		
28 (−1.06)	Washington		
29 (−1.10)	Arkansas		
30 (−1.29)	South Dakota		
31 (−1.31)	Iowa		
32 (−1.35)	Alaska, Louisiana, Maine		
35 (−1.36)	Illinois		
36 (−1.46)	Alabama, Missouri		
38 (−1.52)	Massachusetts		

Table A.37 State ranking and scores on the meaningful contributions and supportive communities dimension of SSF

Rank (Score)	State(s)	Rank (Score)	State(s)
1 (5.54)	Montana	34 (−1.41)	Virginia
2 (5.51)	Minnesota	35 (−2.10)	North Carolina
3 (5.43)	Utah	36 (−2.37)	Arkansas
4 (4.90)	North Dakota	37 (−2.41)	California
5 (4.35)	South Dakota	38 (−2.45)	Nevada
6 (4.21)	Oregon	39 (−2.76)	New Mexico
7 (3.96)	Alaska	40 (−2.86)	Florida
8 (3.74)	New Hampshire	41 (−3.30)	South Carolina
9 (3.67)	Iowa	42 (−3.32)	Louisiana
10 (3.26)	Vermont	43 (−3.49)	Alabama
11 (3.23)	Nebraska	44 (−3.50)	Georgia
12 (3.13)	Wisconsin	45 (−3.77)	West Virginia
13 (2.59)	Kansas	46 (−3.94)	Tennessee
14 (2.30)	Washington	47 (−4.24)	Texas
15 (2.25)	Delaware	48 (4.50)	Kentucky
16 (1.87)	Wyoming	49 (−5.92)	New York
17 (1.74)	Maine	50 (−6.54)	Mississippi
18 (1.20)	Idaho		
19 (1.00)	Ohio		
20 (0.88)	Massachusetts		
21 (0.78)	Colorado		
22 (0.70)	Missouri		
23 (0.40)	Indiana		
24 (0.21)	Michigan		
25 (−0.61)	Hawaii, Rhode Island		
27 (−0.65)	Connecticut		
28 (−0.70)	Pennsylvania		
29 (−0.82)	Maryland		
30 (−0.90)	New Jersey		
31 (−1.20)	Oklahoma		
32 (−1.23)	Arizona		
33 (−1.38)	Illinois		

Table A.38 State ranking and scores on the affordability dimension of SSF

Rank (Score)	State	Rank (Score)	State
1 (6.44)	Mississippi	33 (−1.72)	Minnesota
2 (5.99)	West Virginia	34 (−1.89)	Florida
3 (5.48)	Arkansas	35 (−2.49)	Alaska
4 (4.28)	Kentucky	36 (−2.51)	New Hampshire
5 (4.01)	Montana	37 (−3.00)	Delaware
6 (3.98)	Alabama	38 (−3.05)	Rhode Island
7. (3.90)	North Dakota	39 (−3.17)	Virginia
8 (3.71)	South Dakota	40 (−3.22)	Illinois
9 (3.66)	Louisiana	41 (−3.42)	Colorado
10 (3.59)	Oklahoma	42 (−3.66)	Washington
11 (3.18)	New Mexico	43 (−3.78)	New York
12 (3.10)	Maine	44 (−3.88)	Nevada
13 (3.05)	South Carolina	45 (−4.89)	Massachusetts
14 (2.53)	Tennessee	46 (−5.18)	Connecticut
15 (2.50)	Idaho	47 (−5.53)	Maryland
16 (2.37)	Iowa	48 (−6.32)	California
17 (2.33)	Wyoming	49 (−6.34)	New Jersey
18 (1.97)	North Carolina	50 (−6.38)	Hawaii
19 (1.94)	Vermont		
20 (1.38)	Kansas		
21 (1.25)	Nebraska		
22 (1.23)	Missouri		
23 (1.20)	Indiana		
24 (0.34)	Georgia		
25 (0.25)	Ohio		
26 (0.19)	Wisconsin		
27 (−0.05)	Pennsylvania		
28 (−0.41)	Oregon		
29 (−0.50)	Utah		
30 (−0.64)	Texas		
31 (−0.69)	Arizona		
32 (−0.71)	Michigan		

Table A.39 State ranking and scores on the health and medical care quality dimension of SSF

Rank (Score)	State	Rank (Score)	State
1 (5.47)	New Hampshire	33 (−1.96)	West Virginia
2 (5.03)	Utah	34 (−1.98)	California
3 (4.83)	Oregon	35 (−2.08)	Missouri
4 (4.74)	Hawaii	36 (−2.12)	Nevada
5 (4.32)	Colorado	37 (−2.45)	Tennessee
6 (4.27)	North Dakota	38 (−2.48)	Ohio
7 (4.14)	Maine	39 (−2.84)	Pennsylvania
8 (4.13)	Montana	40 (−3.28)	Alaska
9 (4.05)	Minnesota	41 (−3.50)	Alabama
10 (3.99)	Iowa	42 (−3.51)	New Jersey
11 (3.82)	Vermont	43 (−3.58)	Arkansas
12 (3.61)	Wisconsin	44 (−4.02)	Kentucky
13 (3.49)	Delaware	45 (−4.22)	Georgia
14 (3.40)	Connecticut	46 (−4.45)	Oklahoma
15 (2.71)	Washington	47 (−4.49)	Illinois
16 (2.45)	Virginia	48 (−5.52)	Texas
17 (1.66)	South Dakota	49 (−5.87)	Louisiana
18 (1.61)	Arizona	50 (−5.98)	Mississippi
19 (1.36)	Idaho		
20 (1.25)	Massachusetts		
21 (0.65)	Nebraska		
22 (0.43)	New Mexico		
23 (0.24)	Wyoming		
24 (0.20)	North Carolina		
25 (−0.06)	Rhode Island		
26 (−0.45)	Michigan		
27 (−0.70)	Maryland		
28 (−0.73)	South Carolina		
29 (−1.26)	Indiana		
30 (−1.36)	Kansas		
31 (−1.38)	Florida		
32 (−1.60)	New York		

Table A.40 State ranking and scores on the accessible and high-quality long-term care dimension of SSF

Rank (Score)	State	Rank (Score)	State
1 (9.499)	Rhode Island	33 (−1.101)	Tennessee
2 (5.839)	Connecticut	34 (−1.197)	Delaware
3 (5.454)	North Dakota	35 (−1.356)	Wyoming
4 (5.427)	Massachusetts	36 (−1.949)	Georgia
5 (3.737)	Ohio	37 (−1.993)	Michigan
6 (3.248)	New Hampshire	38 (−2.073)	North Carolina
7 (3.222)	New York	39 (−2.196)	Idaho
8 (2.736)	Indiana	40 (−2.233)	Hawaii
9 (2.678)	Wisconsin	41 (−2.652)	Florida
10 (2.586)	Nebraska	42 (−3.040)	Oregon
11 (2.477)	Pennsylvania	43 (−3.124)	Maine
12 (2.412)	Alaska	44 (−3.366)	South Carolina
13 (2.291)	South Dakota	45 (−3.579)	New Mexico
14 (2.088)	Iowa	46 (−3.680)	Nevada
15 (1.388)	Montana	47 (−3.739)	California
16 (1.232)	New Jersey	48 (−4.021)	Washington
17 (0.944)	Kansas	49 (−4.083)	Utah
18 (0.9090)	Illinois	50 (−6.608)	Arizona
19 (0.615)	Minnesota		
20 (0.590)	Maryland		
21 (0.574)	Louisiana		
22 (0.160)	Alabama		
23 (0.139)	Mississippi		
24 (0.110)	Virginia		
25 (−0.170)	Vermont		
26 (−0.318)	Missouri		
27 (−0.411)	Oklahoma		
28 (−0.594)	Texas		
29 (−0.602)	Kentucky		
30 (−0.839)	Arkansas		
31 (−0.856)	Colorado		
32 (−1.061)	West Virginia		

NOTES

INTRODUCTION

1. Our data are for the period 1995–2000, the most recent five-year span for which data have been disaggregated to the state level. U.S. Census Bureau, *Internal Migration of the Older Population: 1995–2000* (Washington, D.C., U.S. Department of Commerce, 2003).

2. Ruth La Ferla, "Retirees Come Full Circle," *New York Times*, November 28, 2004, 1, 6; E. Litwak, *Helping the Elderly: The Complementary Roles of Informal Networks and Formal Systems* (New York: Guilford Press, 1985); E. Litwak and Charles F. Longino, "Migration Patterns Among the Elderly: A Developmental Perspective," *Gerontologist* 27, no. 3 (1987): 266–72.

3. See Jack Rosenthal, "Wellderly," *New York Times Magazine*, July 22, 2007, 16.

4. Search "baby boom generation," at U.S. Census Bureau, http://census.gov (accessed June 21, 2007).

5. The demographic statistics in this section of the Introduction come largely from Wan He et al., *65+ in the United States: 2005* (Washington, D.C.: Census Bureau, U.S. Department of Commerce and National Institutes of Health, U.S. Department of Health and Human Services, 2005). A few come from volumes, identified in the notes below, that are produced by the AARP's Public Policy Institute, the Administration on Aging, and the Census Bureau.

6. Oregon has worked particularly hard to keep vulnerable older residents "in the community" through these three options rather than institutionalizing them. Remaining in the community is preferred by most older people, and it is also generally less expensive per person served than reliance on a nursing facility.

7. He et al., *65+ in the United States*, 35.

8. See U.S. Census Bureau, *American FactFinder, 2005 American Community Survey*, table C18002, http://census.gov (accessed May 3, 2007). Labor force participation falls off sharply after age sixty-four. In the sixty-five to sixty-nine cohort only 30.2 percent of men and 19.9 percent of women remain.

9. See Nancy Schlossberg, *Revitalizing Retirement: Reshaping Your Identity, Relationships, and Purposes* (Washington, D.C.: American Psychological Association, 2009), and Morley D. Glicken and Brian Haas, *A Simple Guide to Retirement: How to Make Retirement Work for You* (Santa Barbara, Calif.: ABC-CLIO, 2009).

10. Guides that focus on desirable communities represent a limited exception to this generalization. One of the best of these in terms of the range of factors considered and the care of analysis is David Savageau, *Retirement Places Rated: What You Need to Know to Plan the Retirement You Deserve* (New York: Wiley, 2007.)

11. See Isaiah Berlin, *Karl Marx* (Oxford: Oxford University Press, 1978), 121

12. Authors arguing for these trends include Arlie Hochschild, *The Second Shift: Working Parents and the Revolution at Home* (New York: Viking, 1989), or Judith Schor, *The Overworked American* (New York: Basic Books, 1991). For a counterargument, see John P. Robinson and Geoffrey Godbey, *Time for Life: The Surprising Ways Americans Use Their Time* (University Park: Penn State University Press, 2000).

13. Edwin Amenta, Neal Caren, and Sheera Joy Olasky, "Age for Leisure? Political Mediation and the Impact of the Pension Movement on U.S. Old-Age Policy," *American Sociological Review* 70, no. 3 (2005): 516–38.

14. Robert D. Putnam with Robert Leonardi and Raffaella Y. Nanetti, *Making Democracy Work: Civic Traditions in Modern Italy* (Princeton: Princeton University Press, 1993).

15. See U.S. Census Bureau, *2007 Statistical Abstract*, table 408, http://census.gov (accessed August 14, 2007).

16. Ari Houser, Wendy Fox-Grage, and Mary Jo Gibson, *Across the States: Profiles of Long-Term Care and Independent Living* (Washington, D.C.: AARP Public Policy Institute, 2006), R9.

17. He et al., *65+ in the United States,* 97. See also Laurel Breedon and John Rother, *The State of 50+ America* (Washington, D.C.: AARP Public Policy Institute, 2006).

18. See Saadia Greenberg, Donald G. Fowles, and Jennifer Klocinski, *Profile of Older Americans: 2006* (Washington D.C.: Administration on Aging, U.S. Department of Health and Human Services, 2006), 10. See also He et al., *65+ in the United States,* 100.

19. See William H. Walters, "Place Characteristics and Later Life Migration," *Research on Aging* 24, no. 2 (2002): 243–77.

20. The scale has a midpoint of zero. See United Health Foundation, *America's Health: State Health Rankings—2004,* http://unitedhealthfoundation.org (accessed July 5, 2007).

21. We borrow the term "circles of concern" from Dennis McCullough, *My Mother, Your Mother: Embracing "Slow Medicine"—the Compassionate Approach to Caring for Your Aging Loved Ones* (New York: HarperCollins, 2008).

22. The "so-what," or social outcome, variable in each of the first five chapters is the first variable discussed in each chapter's "Additional Indicators" section.

23. See Andrew Karch, "Emerging Issues and Future Directions in State Policy Diffusion Research," *State Politics and Policy Quarterly* 7, no. 1 (2007): 54–80 and Jack L. Walker, "The Diffusion of Innovations Among the American States," *American Political Science Review* 63, no. 3 (1969): 880–99.

CHAPTER 1

1. To the best of our knowledge, this phrase was coined by Charles A. Tiebout, "A Pure Theory of Local Expenditures," *Journal of Political Economy* 64, no. 5 (1956): 416–26. More generally, see Robert F. Wiseman, "Why Older People Move: Theoretical Issues," *Research on Aging* 2, no. 2 (1980): 141–54, and William H. Haas III and William J. Serow, "Amenity Retirement Migration Process: A Model and Preliminary Evidence," *Gerontologist* 33, no. 2 (1993): 212–20.

2. Generally, the shadings on these maps are produced by a quantile system, which is commonly used for atlases. This system produces maps in which roughly ten states are represented by each of five, or occasionally four, shades. Sometimes one or more categories have one or two more or less than ten (or twelve) states as a consequence of rounding numbers or multistate ties. Those maps based on an indicator with plus and minus values employ a forced quantile scheme by which the shadings above zero have roughly an equal number of states and the shadings below zero also have a roughly equal, but perhaps different, number of states.

Additionally, when we speak of "higher" or "top" ranks or "lower" or "bottom" ranks in the text, we generally refer to the top-ten or bottom-ten ranks. Sometimes, the manner in which the fifty states are distributed on an indicator makes the top or bottom ten states more clearly discernible from the tables in the appendix (tables A.1 through A.7 for figs. 1.1 through 1.7) on which a corresponding figure is based than from the figure itself.

3. See the National Climate Data Center of the National Oceanic and Atmospheric Administration of the U.S. Department of Commerce, *Climate Atlas,* http://ncdc.noaa.gov (accessed June 13, 2007).

4. N. E. Rosenthal et al., "Seasonal Affective Disorder: A Description of the Syndrome and Preliminary Findings with Light Therapy," *Archives of General Psychiatry* 41, no. 1 (1984): 72–80.

5. Our data come from the U.S. Census Bureau, American Community Survey via a table created by Ari Houser, Wendy Fox-Grage, and May Jo Gibson, *Across the States: Profiles of Long-Term Care and Independent Living* (Washington, D.C.: AARP Public Policy Institute, 2006), R6.

6. Nationwide, about 1.5 million older citizens are in nursing facilities, another 4.5 million acquire formal assistance through HCBS, and around 8 million are assisted informally by friends

and family. See Robin I. Stone, *Long-Term Care for the Elderly with Disabilities: Current Policy, Emerging Trends, and Implications for the 21st Century* (New York: Milbank Memorial Fund, 2000), and Kaiser Commission on Medicaid and the Uninsured, *Medicaid and Long-Term Care Services* (Washington, D.C.: Kaiser Family Foundation, 2006).

7. Our index of the proportion of a state's sixty-five-or-older population that is disabled draws on data from Houser, Fox-Grage, and Gibson, *Across the States*, R15, R21; and U.S. Census Bureau, *American FactFinder, 2005 American Community Survey,* table C18002, http://census.gov (accessed August 8, 2007).

8. Thomas Frank, *What's the Matter with Kansas? How Conservatives Won the Heart of America* (New York: Henry Holt, 2004).

9. Our data come from U.S. Census Bureau, *The Statistical Abstract of the United States: The National Data Book* (Washington, D.C.: U.S. Department of Commerce, 2007), tables 652 and 1248.

10. Our data come from U.S. Census Bureau, *Internal Migration of the Older Population: 1995–2000* (Washington, D.C.: Department of Commerce, 2003), 4.

11. In the absence of individual-level data, we cannot be certain how thoroughly those who return in their mid-eighties represent those who also left the state early in retirement. But as Ruth La Ferla's article suggests, it is difficult to imagine why someone in her or his mid-eighties would move to Alaska if she or he had not lived there previously and, in all likelihood, had younger family members still living there. See "Retirees Come Full Circle," *New York Times,* November 28, 2004, 1, 6. See also E. Litwak, *Helping the Elderly: The Complementary Roles of Informal Networks and Formal Systems* (New York: Guilford Press, 1985), and E. Litwak and Charles F. Longino, "Migration Patterns Among the Elderly: A Developmental Perspective," *Gerontologist* 27, no. 3 (1987): 266–72.

12. See S. Coren and P. L. Hewitt, "Sex Differences in Elderly Suicide Rates: Some Predictive Factors," *Aging and Mental Health* 3, no. 2 (1999): 112–18.

13. See Centers for Disease Control, *Mortality Rates,* http://webapp.cdc.gov/sasweb/ncipc/mort rate.html (accessed June 17, 2007).

14. See Jean Giles-Sims and Charles Lockhart, "Explaining Cross-State Differences in Elderly Suicide Rates and Identifying State-Level Public Policy Responses that Reduce Rates," *Suicide and Life-Threatening Behavior* 36, no. 6 (2006): 694–708.

15. Emile Durkheim, *Suicide: A Study in Sociology* (New York: Free Press, 1951). This work was originally published in 1897.

CHAPTER 2

1. See Linda L. Barrett, Andrew Kochera, and Audrey Straight, *Beyond 50.05 Survey* (Washington, D.C.: AARP, 2005).

2. See Nancy Schlossberg, *Revitalizing Retirement: Reshaping Your Identity, Relationships, and Purpose* (Washington, D.C.: American Psychological Association, 2009).

3. Phyllis Korkki, "That Spirit of Volunteerism, 60 Million Strong," *New York Times,* June 8, 2008, BU 2.

4. Ibid.; Andrew Kochera et al., *Beyond 50.05: A Report to the Nation on Livable Communities: Creating Environments for Successful Aging* (Washington, D.C.: AARP, 2005), 36; see also Laurel Breedon and John Rother, *The State of 50+ America* (Washington, D.C.: AARP, 2006).

5. Barrett, Kochera, and Straight, *Beyond 50.05 Survey,* 6.

6. Ibid., 17.

7. For instance, see ibid., 27.

8. Nancy's condominium is an "ordinary," open-market variety, and the residents range considerably in age. She considered but eventually decided against a condominium that accepted residents only fifty-five or older as well as against a continuing care retirement community (CCRC)

associated with a group of local nonprofit organizations. The range of housing options for Nancy in Minnesota appears to be more extensive than for the Hestirs in Georgia.

9. Robert Putnam, *Bowling Alone: The Collapse and Revival of American Community* (New York: Simon and Schuster, 2000).

10. See the Saguaro Seminar: Civic Engagement in America, "Access the Data: State Measures," http://bowlingalone.com/StateMeasures.xls (accessed March 7, 2008).

11. Figures 2.1 through 2.7 in this chapter are based on tables A.8 through A.14 in the Appendix. Nevada, the state at the bottom of Putnam's index, but among the leaders in chapter 1 with regard to supporting outdoor social recreation, also has—perhaps not accidentally—the highest rate of suicide, both among seniors and the population generally. See table A.7 in the Appendix.

12. See U.S. Census Bureau, *Social Demographics,* http://census.gov/population/www/socialdemo/voting/cps2004.html (accessed February 18, 2008).

13. Gabriel A. Almond and Sidney Verba, *The Civic Culture: Political Attitudes and Democracy in Five Nations* (Princeton: Princeton University Press, 1963). This relationship has been replicated numerous times since; see, for example, Sidney Verba et al., *Elites and the Idea of Equality: A Comparison of Japan, Sweden, and the United States* (Cambridge: Harvard University Press, 1989).

14. See U.S. Census Bureau, *Economic Statistics,* http://census.gov/hhes/www/incme/histince/state/state4.html (accessed February 14, 2008).

15. See Angus Campbell et al., *The American Voter* (Chicago: University of Chicago Press, 1960), or any of the more recent studies in this vein, such as Michael S. Lewis-Beck et al., *The American Voter Revisited* (Ann Arbor: University of Michigan Press, 2008).

16. See U.S. Census Bureau, *Poverty,* http://pubdb3.census.gov/macro/ 032006/pov/new46_100 125_14.html (accessed February 16, 2008).

17. See particularly Almond and Verba, *The Civic Culture;* Verba et al., *Elites and the Idea of Equality;* Putnam, *Bowling Alone;* Lewis-Beck et al., *The American Voter Revisited;* Kochera et al., *Beyond 50.05.*

18. Scholars interested in culture generally agree that the concept of state political culture refers to the beliefs and values of a particular population. So a state's political culture would involve those beliefs and values of particular relevance to its political life. Some researchers are more inclined to include social institutions as integral aspects of culture; see Michael Thompson, Richard Ellis, and Aaron Wildavsky, *Cultural Theory* (Boulder, Colo.: Westview, 1990). Others are more narrowly focused on beliefs and values; see Hildred Geertz and Clifford Geertz, *Kinship in Bali* (Chicago: University of Chicago Press, 1975).

19. James Madison, *Federalist #10.*

20. Alexis de Tocqueville, *Democracy in America.*

21. See particularly Daniel J. Elazar, *American Federalism: A View from the States* (New York: Thomas Y. Crowell, 1966). The next three paragraphs are based on the second edition of 1972, 100–101.

22. In spite of the age of Elazar's study, a number of scholars find that his cultural assessments exhibit remarkable stability over time. See David R. Moran and Sheilah S. Watson, "Political Culture, Political System Characteristics, and Public Policies Among the American States," *Publius* 21, no. 2 (1991): 32–48. Further, Elazar's schema produces results similar to other, even arguably more sophisticated, measures. See Charles A. Johnson, "Political Culture in the American States: Elazar's Formulation Examined," *American Journal of Political Science* 20, no. 3 (1976): 491–99. Thus the schema continues to be useful for descriptive and explanatory purposes. See, for example, Patrick Fisher and Travis Pratt, "Political Culture and the Death Penalty," *Criminal Justice Policy Review* 17, no. 1 (2006): 48–60; Russell L. Hanson, "Political Culture Variations in State Economic Development Policy," *Publius* 21, no. 2 (1991): 63–81; and Lawrence M. Mead, "State Political Culture and Welfare Reform," *Policy Studies Journal* 32, no. 2 (2004): 271–96.

23. See Donald J. Devine, *The Political Culture of the United States* (Boston: Little, Brown, 1972).

24. Adam Smith, *An Inquiry into the Nature and Causes of the Wealth of Nations.*

25. Mary Douglas, *Cultural Bias* (London: Royal Anthropological Society, 1978); Thompson, Ellis, and Wildavsky, *Cultural Theory.*

26. Thompson, Ellis, and Wildavsky, *Cultural Theory.*

27. Ibid.

28. Our index, running from hierarchy/traditionalistic (low end) to egalitarianism/moralistic (high end), is distinct from, but correlates at 0.96 (technically –0.96) with, Sharkansky's earlier effort, which, unaccountably, runs the other way. See Ira Sharkansky, "The Utility of Elazar's Political Culture," *Polity* 2, no. 1 (1969): 66–83.

29. See Paul Brace et al., "Does State Political Ideology Change Over Time?" *Political Research Quarterly* 57, no. 4 (2004): 529–40.

30. William D. Berry et al., "Measuring Citizen and Government Ideology in the American States," *American Journal of Political Science* 42, no. 1 (1998): 327–48, updated through the archive of the Inter-University Consortium for Political and Social Research at the University of Michigan (ICPSR) (http://icpsr.umich.edu).

31. Charles Barrilleaux, Thomas Holbrook, and Laura Langer, "Electoral Competition, Legislative Balance, and American State Welfare Policy," *American Journal of Political Science* 46, no. 2 (2002): 415–27.

32. The electoral competition data, covering the period 1982–86, come from Thomas H. Holbrook and Emily Van Dunk, "Electoral Competition in the American States," *American Political Science Review* 87, no. 4 (1993): 955–62. The data on Democratic legislative control, covering the period 1981–88, come from John Bibby et al., "Parties in State Politics," in *Politics in the American States,* ed. Virginia Gray, Herbert Jacob, and Robert Albritton, 85–112 (Glenville, Ill.: Scott, Foresman, 1990).

33. Moreover, it is likely that a Minnesota community (Minneapolis) is a more elder-friendly community than a Georgia community (Atlanta). See, for instance, David Hanson and Charles A. Emlet, "Assessing a Community's Elder Friendliness: A Case Example of the Advantage Initiative," *Family and Community Health* 29, no. 4 (2006): 266–78.

34. Elazar, *American Federalism;* Berry et al., "Measuring Citizen and Government Ideology in the American States."'

CHAPTER 3

1. For excellent studies of the economic circumstances of older adults, see James H. Schulz, *The Economics of Aging,* 7th ed. (Westport, Conn.: Greenwood, 2001) and James H. Schulz and Robert H. Binstock, *Aging Nation: The Economics and Politics of Growing Older in America* (Baltimore: Johns Hopkins University Press, 2008).

2. See the story of Ralph and Mildred Pascucci in Caitlin Kelly, "Frugality Can Be Acquired, But It Can't Be Bought," *New York Times,* March 1, 2008, B6. More generally, see William H. Walters, "Place Characteristics and Later Life Migration," *Research on Aging* 24, no. 2 (2002): 243–77.

3. The history of income maintenance in the United States is, naturally, more complex than we imply in this sentence. See Theda Skocpol, *Protecting Soldiers and Mothers: The Political Origins of Social Policy in the United States* (Cambridge: Harvard University Press, 1992).

4. See Michael B. Katz, *In the Shadow of the Poor-House* (New York: Basic Books, 1986).

5. See Wan He et al., *65+ in the United States: 2005* (Washington, D.C.: Census Bureau, U.S. Department of Commerce and National Institutes of Health, U.S. Department of Health and Human Services, 2005), 103.

6. Ibid., 95.

7. Ibid., 96.

8. See Department of Health and Human Services, Assistant Secretary for Planning and Education, "Prior HHS Poverty Guidelines and *General Register* References," http://aspe.hhs.gov/poverty/figures-fed-reg.shtml (accessed March 5, 2008).

9. Other wealthy democracies frequently use 40 percent of the society's median household income as their poverty standard. See Harold L. Wilensky, *Rich Democracies: Political Economy, Public Policy, and Performance* (Berkeley and Los Angeles: University of California, 2002).

10. He et al., *65+ in the United States,* 97.

11. Ibid., 100.

12. Peter Orszag, "Progressivity and Savings: Fixing the Nation's Upsidedown Incentives for Savings," testimony before the House Committee on Education and the Work Force, February 25, 2004, http://brookings.edu/views/testimony/orszag/20040225.pdf (accessed May 28, 2008).

13. He et al., *65+ in the United States: 2005,* 108–9.

14. Jodi Lanet and James W. Meeker, "Subculture Diversity and Fear of Crime and Gangs," *Crime and Delinquency* 46, no. 2 (2000): 497–521.

15. See U.S. Census Bureau, *American FactFinder,* summary file 1, detailed table P2, http://factfinder.census.gov (accessed June 1, 2007).

16. The data underlying figures 3.1 through 3.7 appear in tables A.15 through A.21, respectively, in the Appendix.

17. See the Bureau of Labor Statistics, *Bureau of Labor Statistics News,* January 22, 2004, http://bls.gov/ro7/cexmwst.htm (accessed March 3, 2008).

18. He et al., *65+ in the United States,* 111.

19. Ibid., 113.

20. See U.S. Census Bureau, *American FactFinder, Housing, Financial Characteristics,* http://census.gov (accessed June 3, 2007).

21. For FMAP data, see the Department of Health and Human Services, http://aspe.hhs.gov/health/fmap05.htm (accessed June 1, 2007).

22. See, for instance, Paul E. Peterson and Mark C. Rom, *Welfare Magnets: The New Case for a National Welfare Standard* (Washington, D.C.: Brookings Institution, 1990).

23. Our data come from U.S. Census Bureau, American Community Survey, 2005, table B19049 as organized by Ari Houser, Wendy Fox-Grage, and Mary Jo Gibson, *Across the States: Profiles of Long-Term Care and Independent Communities* (Washington, D.C.: AARP Public Policy Institute, 2006), R9.

24. See William D. Berry, Richard C. Fording, and Russell L. Hanson, "An Annual Cost of Living Index for the American States, 1960–1995," *Journal of Politics* 62, no. 2 (2000): 550–67. This index is updated annually (although there is a lag time). Updates are available through the data archive of the Inter-University Consortium for Political and Social Research (ICPSR) at the University of Michigan (http://icpsr.umich.edu).

25. See Shannan M. Catalano, "Criminal Victimization, 2005," *Bureau of Justice Statistics Bulletin,* September 2006, 4, 7, http://ojp.usdoj.gov/bjs (accessed June 15, 2007).

26. Ibid.

27. See the Bureau of Justice Statistics, *Homicides by State and Age, 2004,* http://bjsdata.ojp.usdoj.gov/dataonline/Search/Homicide/State/RunHomOneYearofData.cfm (accessed June 4, 2007).

28. See the Disaster Center, *Property Crime Rates,* http://disastercenter.com/crime (accessed June 13, 2007).

CHAPTER 4

1. See Atul Gawande, "The Cost Conundrum: What a Texas Town Can Teach Us About Health Care," *New Yorker,* June 1, 2009, 36–44.

2. For an overview of these state aspects, see Andrew Karch, "Emerging Issues and Future Directions in State Policy Diffusion Research," *State Politics and Policy Quarterly* 7, no. 1 (2007): 54–80.

3. See Centers for Disease Control, *The State of Health and Aging in America 2007* (Washington, D.C.: Department of Health and Human Services, 2007), http://cdc.gov/aging/pdf.saha_2007.pdf (accessed on May 7, 2007).

4. Figures 4.1 through 4.7 are based on tables A.22 through A.28 in the Appendix.

5. See Stephen F. Jencks, Edwin D. Huff, and Timothy Cuerdon, "Change in the Quality of Care Delivered to Medicare Beneficiaries, 1998 to 2000–2001," *Journal of the American Medical Association* 289, no. 3 (2003): 305–12. The data on which this study is based originate with the Centers for Medicare and Medicaid Services (CMS), but these data have been laboriously collected and analyzed by Jencks, Huff, and Cuerdon (http://content.healthaffairs.org/cqi/reprint/hlthaff.w4.184vl.pdf). We draw on only their overall state rankings.

6. See Denise Grady, "Cancer Patients, Lost in a Maze of Uneven Care," *New York Times,* July 29, 2007, 1, 18–19.

7. Once again, these data originate with CMS, but the basis for our rank-ordering appears in Katherine Baicker and Amitabh Chandra, "Medicare Spending, the Physician Workforce, and Beneficiaries' Quality of Care," *Health Affairs,* http://content.healthaffairs.org/cqi/reprint/hlthaff.W5.526vl.pdf, W4-184 (April 7, 2004) (accessed September 24, 2004).

8. This orientation is called "slow medicine" by some of its advocates. See Dennis McCullough, *My Mother, Your Mother: Embracing "Slow Medicine"; The Compassionate Approach to Caring for Your Aging Loved Ones* (New York: HarperCollins, 2008); Abigail Zuger, "For the Very Old, a Dose of 'Slow Medicine,'" *New York Times,* February 26, 2008, D12; and Jane Gross, "For the Elderly, Being Heard About Life's End," *New York Times,* May 5, 2008, A1, A14. For an example of the chaos that can ensue from having a number of specialists involved with a patient, see Sandeep Januhar, "Many Doctors, Many Tests, No Rhyme or Reason," *New York Times,* March 11, 2008, D5.

9. See Dartmouth Institute, the *Dartmouth Atlas of Health Care,* http://dartmouthatlas.org (accessed May 23, 2008).

10. Indeed, this list does not exhaust the relative deficiencies of high-spending regions. See John D. Wennberg et al., "Evaluating the Efficiency of California Providers in Caring for Patients with Chronic Illness," *Health Affairs* (online version), W5-526-43 (November 16, 2005) (accessed July 17, 2008), and Elliott S. Fisher, et al., "The Implications of Regional Variations in Medicare Spending," pt. 1, "The Content, Quality, and Accessibility of Care," *Annals of Internal Medicine* 138, no. 4 (2003): 273–87, and pt.2, "Health Outcomes and Satisfaction with Care," *Annals of Internal Medicine* 138, no. 4 (2003): 288–98.

11. Gawande, "The Cost Conundrum."

12. McCullough, *My Mother, Your Mother.*

13. Susan Sontag, as described by David Rieff, *Swimming in a Sea of Death: A Son's Memoir* (New York: Simon and Schuster, 2007), appears to have been the former type of patient.

14. This reversed indicator correlates at 0.48 (statistically significant) with *Forbes* "Best Places to Die Index," http://forbes.com/2004/08/11/b2dieland.html (accessed June 11, 2007).

15. See Dartmouth Institute, *The Dartmouth Atlas of Health Care,* http://dartmouthatlas.org/data/download/2005_eol_medpar_state.xls, p. 5 (accessed June 13, 2008).

16. Indeed, the ICU/CCU indicator also correlates positively with the three indicators to be introduced below in this chapter. Further, in only one of these three instances is the correlation not statistically significant. That exception is the number of physicians per one hundred thousand state residents, for which the correlation, while positive, is a meager 0.02. This low correlation may serve as a subtle indicator of resistance among physicians to abstaining from dramatic end-of-life therapies.

17. See Ruth La Ferla, "Retirees Come Full Circle," *New York Times,* November 28, 2004, 1, 6.

18. Thus we use quality of life (e.g., the CDC's healthy aging index) as a predictor for quantity of life. We are, in effect, saying, If you live better, you live longer. This seems more appropriate than reversing the imputed causality.

19. Our 2000 data are from Centers for Disease Control, *Life Expectancy,* http://wonder .cdc.gov/WONDER/help/populations/population-projections/MethodsTable2.xls (accessed May 2, 2008). The life expectancy statistic projects into the future. In previous work on this issue we had used the Centers for Disease Control, National Center for Health Statistics (NCHS) 1989–91 calculation of lifespan, http://cdc.gov/nchs/data/lifetables/life89ia.pdf (accessed June 21, 2007). From e-mail exchanges with NCHS staff we gained the impression that this latter statistic, also calculated at decennial intervals, drew retrospectively on experience of the recent past. We are uncertain about why the NCHS has shifted from lifespan to life expectancy. However, for our purposes the shift does not matter much. The current life expectancy data correlate at 0.90 with the 1989–91 lifespan data. Further, the 1989–91 data correlate at 0.93 with the corresponding data for 1979–81. So while Americans are living longer with each passing decade, state rank-ordering on length of life appears relatively stable across time and measures.

20. See United Health Foundation, *America's Health: State Health Rankings—2004,* http://unit edhealthfoundation.org/shr2004/Findings.html (accessed July 5, 2007).

21. U.S. Census Bureau, *Statistical Abstract of the United States: The National Data Book* (Washington, D.C.: U.S. Department of Commerce, 2007), Health and Nutrition, table 154. We use total state population, rather than state residents sixty-five-or-older, in this figure since, even though seniors draw on physicians' services more routinely than do younger adults, they still have to compete with the rest of the population, particularly children, in obtaining access to physicians.

22. Registered nurses distribute themselves in a roughly similar pattern. See Bureau of Labor Statistics, *Registered Nurses* http://bls.gov (accessed August 8, 2008).

23. On this last point, see *Forbes,* "Best Places to Die," http://forbes.com/2004/08/11/b2dieland .html (accessed June 11, 2007).

CHAPTER 5

1. See U.S. Census Bureau, *American FactFinder, 2005 American Community Survey,* table C18001, http://census.gov (accessed March 10, 2008).

2. See Robin I. Stone, *Long-Term Care for the Elderly with Disabilities: Current Policy, Emerging Trends and Implications for the 21st Century* (New York: Milbank Memorial Fund, 2000), and Kaiser Commission on Medicaid and the Uninsured. *Medicaid and Long-Term Care Services* (Washington, D.C.: Kaiser Family Foundation, 2006).

3. On contemporary long-term care costs and services, see Charles Duhigg, "At Many Homes, More Profit and Less Nursing," *New York Times,* September 23, 2007, 1, 20–21; Jane Gross, "Study Finds Higher Outlays for Caregivers of Older Relatives," *New York Times,* November 19, 2007, 15; and Laurie Tarkan, "Doctors Say Medication is Overused in Dementia," *New York Times,* June 24, 2008, D1, 6.

4. Robert Mollica and Heather Johnson-Lamarche, *State Residential Care and Assisted Living Policy: 2004* (Washington, D.C.: U.S. Department of Health and Human Services, 2005), 1-41–42.

5. See James Button and Walter Rosenbaum, "Gray Power, Gray Peril, or Gray Myth? The Political Impact of the Aging in Local Sunbelt Politics," *Social Science Quarterly* 71, no. 1 (1990): 25–38, and Nina Glasgow, "Retirement Migration and Use of Services in Nonmetropolitan Counties," *Rural Sociology* 60, no. 2 (1995): 224–43.

6. For which states employ which methods, see also Mollica and Johnson-Lamarche, *State Residential Care and Assisted Living Policy,* 1-41–42.

7. Medicare, for instance, supports nursing facility and related care only for short periods involving recuperation or physical therapy following hospitalization.

8. For another example of American exceptionalism, see F. James Davis, *Who Is Black? One Nation's Definition* (University Park: Penn State University Press, 2001).

9. See Beatrix Hoffman, "Tell Me Again: Why Is There No National Health Insurance in the United States?" *Journal of Health Politics, Policy and Law* 31, no. 4 (2006): 839–47. It is also the case that medical care policy suffers to some degree from a "trilemma": only any two of three central goals (universal access, incorporating cutting-edge care improvements, and limited expenditures) can be achieved at once. See Charles Lockhart, *The Roots of American Exceptionalism: Institutions, Culture, and Policies* (New York: Palgrave/St. Martin's, 2003).

10. See Charles Lockhart, Jean Giles-Sims, and Kristen Klopfenstein, "Comparing States' Medicaid Nursing Facility and HCBS Long-Term Care Programs: Quality and Fit with Inclination, Capacity, and Need," *Journal of Aging and Social Policy* 21, no. 11 (2009): 52–74.

11. See Mollica and Johnson-Lamarche, *State Residential Care and Assisted Living Policy,* and Brian Burwell, Kate Sredl, and Steve Eiken's annual memos *Medicaid Long-Term Care Expenditures;* for these memos, see Home and Community-Based Services, *Medicaid Long-Term Care Expenditures,* http://hcbs.org/moreInfo-php/type_tool/129/sby/Date/doc/1260 and http://hcbs.org/moreInfo-php/type_tool/129/sby/Date/doc/1254 (accessed June 23, 2009).

12. See, for example, Vincent Mor et al., "The Quality of Quality Measurement in U.S. Nursing Homes," in "Challenges in Nursing Home Care," special issue, *Gerontologist* 43, supp. 2 (2003): 37–46.

13. See Lockhart, Giles-Sims, and Klopfenstein, "Comparing States' Medicaid Nursing Facility and HCBS Long-Term Care Programs."

14. Most nursing facility beds nationwide carry a dual Medicaid/Medicare certification. A small portion (less than 5 percent) carry Medicare certification only. These latter beds are generally in recuperation and rehabilitation facilities. A few of these facilities are self-standing independent entities, but most are housed in a portion of a hospital or a nursing facility. In the latter instance, they are apt to represent a fairly small proportion of the facility's total beds. Technically, the former, dual-certified beds can be used for either purpose (i.e., long-term care or short-term recuperation and rehabilitation), but most such beds have the former residents most of the time. A relatively small proportion (less than 10 percent) of nursing facility beds carry only Medicaid certification. An uncertain but relatively small proportion of nursing facility beds nationwide are not certified by either Medicaid or Medicare. See Charlene Harrington, Helen Carrillo, and Cynthia Mercado-Scott, *Nursing Facilities, Staffing, Residents, and Facility Deficiencies, 1998 Through 2004* (San Francisco: Department of Social and Behavioral Sciences, University of California, 2005), table 5.

15. Figures 5.1 through 5.7 are based on data in tables A.29 through A.35 in the appendix. Data for 2003 on nursing facility beds come from Harrington, Carrillo, and Mercado-Scott, *Nursing Facilities, Staffing, Residents and Facility Deficiencies,* table 2. Data on states' sixty-five-or-older populations come from table 20 of the online version of the *Statistical Abstract of the United States* for 2005. See U.S. Census Bureau, *Statistical Abstract,* http://census.gov (accessed October 17, 2007).

16. These latter and usually younger persons are generally residents of intermediate care/mental retardation facilities rather than the nursing facilities that focus on older persons.

17. Our data, for 2003 in this instance, come from table 110 of the 2005 *Health Care Financing Review: Medicare and Medicaid Statistical Supplement,* an annual volume published by the U.S. Department of Health and Human Services.

During this time period, Arizona supported a range of activities that in other states were paid for by federal-state Medicaid cost sharing through a peculiar waiver whereby the federal and state funds employed were not technically part of the Medicaid program. Our thanks go to Gina Flores and Alan Schafer of the Arizona Health Care Cost Containment System for providing expenditure data on this anomalous approach.

18. Jerry Cromwell, Sylvia Hurdle, and Rachel Schurman, "Defederalizing Medicaid: Fair to the Poor, Fair to the Taxpayers?" *Journal of Health Politics, Policy and Law* 12, no. 1 (1987): 1–34.

19. Our data for 2003 come from table 110 of the 2005 *Health Care Financing Review: Medicare and Medicaid Statistical Supplement* and table 20 of the online version of the *Statistical Abstract of*

the United States. (See notes 17 and 15, respectively, above.) Thanks again to Gina Flores and Alan Schafer for data on Arizona.

20. Harrington, Carrillo, and Mercado-Scott, *Nursing Facilities, Staffing, Residents, and Facility Deficiencies,* tables 7 and 8.

21. See, for instance, David R. Zimmerman et al., "Development and Testing of Nursing Home Quality Indicators," *Health Care Financing Review* 16, no. 4 (1995): 107–27.

22. See, for instance, Katherine Berg et al., "Identification and Evaluation of Existing Nursing Home Quality Indictors," *Health Care Financing Review* 23, no. 4 (2002): 19–36; David C. Grabowski, Joseph H. Angelelli and Vincent Mor, "Medicaid Payment and Risk-Adjusted Nursing Home Quality Measures," *Health Affairs* 23, no. 5 (2004): 243–52; Bita A. Kash, Catherine Hawes, and Charles D. Phillips, "Comparing Staffing Levels in the Online Survey and Reporting (OSCAR) System with the Medicaid Cost Report Data: Are Differences Systematic?" *Gerontologist* 47, no. 4 (2007): 480–89; Mor et al., "The Quality of Quality Measurement in U.S. Nursing Homes"; and Dana B. Mukamel and C. A. Brower, "The Influence of Risk Adjustment Methods on Conclusions about Quality of Care in Nursing Homes Based on Outcome Measures," *Gerontologist* 38, no. 6 (1998): 695–703.

23. Our data for 2003 come from Harrington, Carrillo, and Mercado-Scott, *Nursing Facilities, Staffing, Residents, and Facility Deficiencies,* table 36.

To derive a scale score for each state, we transform these percentages into z-scores, or units of standard deviation, in order to achieve a standard metric (avoiding adding apples and oranges). Then we add a state's z-scores for the four criteria together. The alpha or reliability reading for the resulting scale is 0.78.

24. See Lockhart, Giles-Sims, and Klopfenstein, "Comparing States' Medicaid Nursing Facility and HCBS Long-Term Care Programs."

25. Our data, for 2003, come from Harrington, Carrillo, and Mercado-Scott, *Nursing Facilities, Staffing, Residents, and Facility Deficiencies,* tables 18, 15, 14, and 21. The alpha for this scale is 0.83.

26. See Charles Lockhart and Jean Giles-Sims, "Cross-State Variations in Conceptions of Quality of Nursing Facility Long-Term Care for the Elderly," *Journal of Aging and Social Policy* 19, no. 4 (2007): 1–19.

27. For journal publications designed to engage in both scientific description and explanation, we routinely adjust all variables expressed in currency amounts for state cost of living. These adjustments generally have the effect of modestly reducing levels of association among variables of interest. In this book, which is generally focused on description, we think that this adjustment is an unnecessary complication. While the consequences of applying the adjustment in this instance turn out to be relatively minor, we were persuaded that it was an appropriate adjustment to make in the instance of small-scale economic entities such as nursing facilities.

Reimbursement-rate data come courtesy of Janet G. Freeze at the Centers for Medicare and Medicaid (CMS). The state cost-of-living adjustment is provided by William D. Berry, Richard C. Fording, and Russell L. Hanson, "An Annual Cost of Living Index for the American States, 1960–1995," *Journal of Politics* 62, no. 2 (2000): 550–67, as updated through the data archive of the Inter-University Consortium for Political and Social Research (ICPSR) at the University of Michigan (http://icpsr.umich.edu).

28. See also Grabowski et al., "Medicaid Payment and Risk-Adjusted Nursing Home Quality Measures," who find mixed results.

29. The comparison is rough, for instance, because outside an institutional setting—that is, a hospital or nursing facility—Medicaid does not pay for room and board. States resort to various strategies to help extremely poor HCBS recipients pay for these necessities. See Mollica and Johnson-Lamarche, *State Residential Care and Assisted Living Policy,* 1-47–55.

30. Thanks to Steve Eiken. See the Burwell, Sredl, and Eiken annual *Medicaid Long-Term Care Expenditures* (see note 11 above).

31. Thanks again to Gina Flores and Alan Schafer for data on Arizona.

CHAPTER 6

1. As we mentioned in the Introduction, David Savageau's *Retirement Places Rated: What You Need to Know to Plan the Retirement You Deserve* (New York: Wiley, 2007) seems to be particularly well thought out.

2. See William W. Lammers and David Klingman, *State Policies and the Aging: Sources, Trends, and Options* (Lexington, Mass.: D. C. Heath, 1984); Penny H. Feldman et al., *A Tale of Two Older Americas: Community, Opportunities, and Challenges* (New York: Center for Home Care Policy and Research, 2004); and particularly Marc Miringoff and Marque-Luisa Miringoff, *The Social Health of the Nation: How America Is Really Doing* (New York: Oxford University Press, 1999).

3. A few of these indicators (e.g., our quality of state nursing facility processes scale) are already expressed in z-scores, that is, units of standard deviation, so they need no further conversion.

4. An unusually low correlation between climate and not being disabled (0.08) is largely responsible for the low alpha.

5. See the Saguaro Seminar: Civic Engagement in America, "Access the Data: State Measures," http://bowlingalone.com/StateMeasures.xls (accessed May 10, 2007).

6. See Centers for Disease Control, *The State of Health and Aging in America 2007,* http://cdc.gov/aging/pdf.saha_2007.pdf (accessed May 7, 2007).

7. Stephen F. Jencks, Edwin D. Huff, and Timothy Cuerdon, "Change in the Quality of Care Delivered to Medicare Beneficiaries, 1998–1999 to 2000–2001," *Journal of the American Medical Association* 289, no. 3 (2003): 305–12.

8. See Katherine Baicker and Amitabh Chandra, "Medicare Spending, the Physician Workforce, and Beneficiaries' Quality of Care," *Health Affairs,* http://content.healthaffairs.org/cqi/reprint/hlthaff.W4.184vl.pdf, W4-184 (April 7, 2004) (accessed September 24, 2004).

9. This was done in table 3.1.

10. The strong positive correlation between the meaningful contributions, supportive communities, and health and high-quality medical care dimensions of 0.79 creates a potential multicollinearity problem for table 6.3. When the meaningful contributions and supportive communities dimension is removed from the five-dimensional analysis, the results are largely unchanged. When the health and high-quality medical care dimension is removed from the five-dimensional analysis, the effects of the meaningful contributions, supportive communities dimension on state cost of living (reversed) and life expectancy at birth rise considerably. But in each of these four-dimensional analyses, the adjusted R squares are remarkably similar to the five-dimensional model. It appears as if the health and high-quality medical care dimension draws influence away from the meaningful contributions and supportive communities dimension when the two are used together as they are in table 6.3.

A similar but less pronounced situation affects the relations between the recreational lifestyle dimension and both the affordability and the accessible, high-quality long-term care dimensions. Once again, the adjusted R squares for the four-dimensional analyses remain much the same, but the accessible, long-term care dimension appears to draw influence away from the recreational lifestyle dimension, particularly in the instances of state cost of living (reversed) and state nursing facilities residents' quality-of-life outcomes, when the two are used together as they are in table 6.3.

11. See Andrew Karch, "Emerging Issues and Future Directions in State Policy Diffusion Research, *State Politics and Policy Quarterly* 7, no. 1 (2007): 54–80.

12. All four of the factors that Karch mentions can be measured by several different variables. Our choices, Elazar-Douglas-Wildavsky state political culture in this instance, are based on the following considerations: (1) keeping the total number of independent variables within the range that our fifty cases can support, (2) reducing multicollinearity problems among our independent variables to a minimum, and (3) relying on specific variables that other research in this general area suggests are the most appropriate for our current purpose.

Our data for culture are based on Daniel J. Elazar, *American Federalism: A View from the States* (New York: Thomas Y. Crowell, 1966). A good source for ideology would be William D. Berry et al., "Measuring Citizen and Governmental Ideology in the American States, 1960–1993," *American Journal of Political Science* 42, no. 1 (1998): 327–48 (updated through the data archive of the ICPSR at the University of Michigan).

13. On this point, see Charles Barrilleaux, Thomas Holbrook, and Laura Langer, "Electoral Competition, Legislative Balance, and American State Welfare Policy," *American Journal of Political Science* 46, no. 2 (2002): 415–27. The most widely employed index of party competition is Ranney's. See Austin Ranney, "Parties in State Politics," in *Politics in the American States: A Comparative Analysis*, 3rd ed., ed. Herbert Jacob and Kenneth Vines, 61–99 (Boston: Little, Brown, 1965). Our data on the Ranney index are from John F. Bibby and Thomas M. Holbrook, "Parties and Elections," in *Politics in the American States*, 8th ed., ed. Virginia Gray and Russell L. Hanson, 62–99 (Washington, D.C.: Congressional Quarterly Press, 2004).

14. For tax-capacity data (with states indexed to the national average), see National Center for State Higher Education and Policy Making Analysis, *Tax Capacity*, http://higheredinfo.org (accessed August 7, 2007). The particular concept of state fiscal solvency that we use ([total state revenues]—[total state expenditures] / [total state expenditures]) was developed by Francis Stokes Berry and William D. Berry, "The Politics of Tax Increases in the States," *American Journal of Political Science* 38, no. 3 (1994): 855–59. Data can be obtained from the online version of the *Statistical Abstract*. Our median state sixty-five-or-older household income data come from the U.S. Census Bureau through tables drawn up by Mary Jo Gibson et al., *Across the States: Profiles of Long-Term Care* (Washington, D.C.: AARP Public Policy Institute, 2004), R8. We adjust state median sixty-five-or-older household income for state cost of living. See William B. Berry, Richard C. Fording, and Russell L. Hanson, "An Annual Cost of Living Index for the American States, 1960–1995," *Journal of Politics* 62, no. 2 (2000): 550–67 (updated through the data archive of the ICPSR at the University of Michigan).

15. See the U.S. Census Bureau, *Statistical Abstract*, http://census.gov (accessed May 11, 2007).

16. Anne Schneider and Helen Ingram, "Social Construction of Target Populations: Implications for Politics and Policy," *American Political Science Review* 87, no. 2 (1993): 334–48.

17. See also Fay Lomax Cook and Edith J. Barrett, *Support for the American Welfare State* (New York: Columbia University Press, 1992).

18. For example, see Greg J. Duncan, Kathleen Mullan Harris, and Johanne Boisjoly, "Times Limits and Welfare Reform: New Estimates of the Number and Characteristics of Affected Families," *Social Services Review* 74, no. 1 (2000): 55–75; Martin Gilens, *Why Americans Hate Welfare: Race, Media, and the Politics of Antipoverty Policy* (Chicago: University of Chicago Press, 1999); Jill Quadagno, *The Color of Welfare: How Racism Undermined the War on Poverty* (New York: Oxford University Press, 1994); and Joe Soss et al., "Setting the Terms of Relief: Explaining State Policy Choices in the Devolution Revolution," *American Journal of Political Science* 45, no. 2 (2001): 378–403.

19. See Gibson et al., *Across the States*, R7.

20. Jack L. Walker, "The Diffusion of Innovations Among the American States," *American Political Science Review* 63, no. 3 (1969): 880–99.

21. Our state generosity of seniors' residential property tax abatement variable correlates statistically significantly with the following SSF dimensions: meaningful contributions and supportive communities at 0.29, affordability at –0.43, and health and high-quality medical care at 0.30. But it is virtually unrelated to the recreational lifestyle (0.14) and accessible, high-quality long-term care (–0.5) dimensions.

22. Our data on home ownership, income, and taxes come from Wan He et al., *65+ in the United States* (Washington, D.C.: Census Bureau, U.S. Department of Commerce and National Institutes of Health, U.S. Department of Health and Human Services, 2005).

23. As with Karch's factors, there are multiple ways to measure this concern. We formulate our measure of the average generosity of the senior residential property tax abatement policies of a

state's contiguous neighbors from data in David Baer, *State Programs and Practices for Reducing Residential Property Taxes* (Washington, D.C.: AARP Public Policy Institute, 2003). On regional distinctiveness in the United States, see also V. O. Key, *Southern Politics in State and Nation* (New York: Knopf, 1949), and Robert S. Erikson, Gerald C. Wright, and John P. McIver, *Statehouse Democracy: Public Opinion and Policy in the American States* (New York: Cambridge University Press, 1993).

24. See Robert D. Putnam, with Robert Leonardi and Raffaella Y. Nanetti, *Making Democracy Work: Civic Traditions in Modern Italy* (Princeton: Princeton University Press, 1993), and Edwin Amenta, Neal Caren, and Sheera Joy Olasky, "Age for Leisure? Political Mediation Theory and the Impact of the Pension Movement on U.S. Old-Age Policy, *American Sociological Review* 70, no. 3 (2005): 516–38.

25. See Charles Lockhart, Jean Giles-Sims and Bayliss Camp, "States' Senior Residential Property Tax Abatements: Uncontroversial Benefit or Looming But Unrecognized Problem," *Politics and Policy* 38, no. 4 (2010): 677–704.

26. Unfortunately, this is not an unusual research finding. See Robert D. Putnam, "*E Pluribus Unum:* Diversity and Community in the Twenty-first Century: The 2006 Johan Skytte Prize Lecture," *Scandinavian Political Studies* 30, no. 2 (2007): 137–74.

27. See Elazar, *American Federalism;* Mary Douglas, *Cultural Bias* (London: Royal Anthropological Society, 1978); and Michael Thompson, Richard Ellis, and Aaron Wildavsky, *Cultural Theory* (Boulder, Colo.: Westview, 1990).

28. Elazar-Douglas-Wildavsky culture and our contiguous states' average senior residential property tax abatement index correlate at a statistically significant 0.53.

29. See Charles Lockhart, Jean Giles-Sims, and Kristen Klopfenstein, "Cross-State Variation in Medicaid Support for Older Citizens in Long-Term Care Nursing Facilities," *State and Local Government Review* 40, no. 3 (2008): 173–85.

EPILOGUE

1. However, New Mexico ranks forty-third on property crime, reminding us that no state scores well on all the factors contributing to SSF.

2. A number of authors have recently addressed how changes in both the private and public sectors have shifted increasing financial burdens onto households, particularly at crucial junctures in life, such as retirement. See, for example, Peter Gosselin, *The Precarious Financial Lives of American Families* (New York: Basic Books, 2008); Steven Greenhouse, *Tough Times for the American Worker* (New York: Knopf, 2008); Jacob S. Hacker, *The Great Risk Shift: The New Economic Insecurity and the Decline of the American Dream,* revised and expanded ed. (New York: Oxford University Press, 2008); Elisabeth Jacobs, "The Politics of Economic Security," *Issues in Government Studies,* issue paper 10 (Washington, D.C.: Brookings, 2007), Brookings Institution, *Papers,* www3.brookings.edu/views/papers.jacobs20070913.pdf (accessed July 6, 2008); Alicia H. Munnell and Steven A. Sass, *Working Longer: The Solution to the Retirement Income Challenge* (Washington, D.C.: Brookings Institution, 2008); and Christopher Newfield, *Unmaking the Public University: The Forty-Year Assault on the Middle Class* (Cambridge: Harvard University Press, 2008).

3. See Dennis McCullough, *My Mother, Your Mother: Embracing "Slow Medicine"; The Compassionate Approach to Caring for Your Aging Loved Ones* (New York: HarperCollins, 2008).

4. Richard H. Thaler and Cass R. Sunstein, *Nudge: Improving Decisions About Health, Wealth, and Happiness* (New Haven: Yale University Press, 2008).

SELECTED READINGS

RECREATIONAL LIFESTYLE

Gillon, Steven M. *Boomer Nation: The Largest and Richest Generation Ever, and How It Changed America.* New York: Free Press, 2004.

Green, Kelly. "When It Comes to Finding a New Place to Live, Today's Retirees are Looking for Something Completely Different." *Wall Street Journal,* October 2, 2006.

La Ferla, Ruth. "Retirees Come Full Circle." *New York Times,* November 28, 2004.

Longino, Charles F., Jr. and Don E. Bradley. "A First Look at Retirement Migration Trends in 2000." *Gerontologist* 43, no. 6 (2003): 904–7.

McGuire, Francis A., Roseangela Boyd, and Raymond E. Tedrick. *Leisure and Aging: Ulyssean Living in Later Life.* 3rd ed. Champaign, Ill.: Sagamore, 2004.

Savageau, David. *Retirement Places Rated: What You Need to Know to Plan the Retirement You Deserve.* New York: Wiley, 2007.

MEANING AND COMMUNITY

AARP. *Reimagining America: AARP's Blueprint for the Future.* Washington, D.C.: AARP, 2005.

Caro, Francis G., ed. *Family and Aging Policy.* New York: Haworth, 2006.

Cutler, Neal E., Nancy A. Whitelaw, and Bonita L. Beattie. *American Perceptions of Aging in the 21st Century: Myths and Realities of Aging Chartbook.* Washington, D.C.: National Council on the Aging, 2002.

Friedman, Marc. *Prime Time: How Baby Boomers Will Revolutionize Retirement and Transform America.* New York: Public Affairs Press, 2002.

Schlossberg, Nancy. *Revitalizing Retirement: Reshaping Your Identity, Relationships, and Purpose.* Washington, D.C.: American Psychological Association, 2009.

Vaillant, George E. *Aging Well.* Boston: Little, Brown, 2002.

AFFORDABILITY AND SAFETY

Altman, Stuart H., and David Schatman, eds. *Policies for an Aging Society.* Baltimore: Johns Hopkins University Press, 2002.

Clark, Robert L., Richard V. Burkhauser, Marilyn Moon, Joseph F. Quinn, and Timothy M. Smeeding. *Economics of an Aging Society.* Malden, Mass.: Blackwell, 2004.

Glicken, Morley D., and Brian Haas. *A Simple Guide to Retirement: How to Make Retirement Work for You.* Santa Barbara, Calif.: ABC-CLIO, 2009.

Lee, Sunwah, and Lois Shaw. *Gender and Economic Security in Retirement.* Washington, D.C.: Women's Policy Research, 2003.

Munnell, Alice H., and Steven A. Sass. *Working Longer: The Solution to the Retirement Income Challenge.* Washington, D.C.: Brookings Institution, 2008.

Schulz, James H., and Robert H. Binstock. *Aging Nation: The Economics and Politics of Growing Older in America.* Baltimore: Johns Hopkins Press, 2008.

HEALTH AND HIGH-QUALITY MEDICAL CARE

Centers for Disease Control. *The State of Health and Aging in America 2007.* Washington, D.C.: U.S. Department of Health and Human Services, 2007.

Hudson, Robert B. *The New Politics of Old Age Policy.* Baltimore: Johns Hopkins Press, 2005.

Jencks, Stephen F., Edwin D. Huff, and Timothy Cuerdon. "Change in the Quality of Care Delivered to Medicare Beneficiaries, 1998 to 2000–2001." *Journal of the American Medical Association* 289 (January 15, 2003): 305–12.

McCullough, Dennis. *My Mother, Your Mother: Embracing "Slow Medicine"—the Compassionate Approach to Caring for Your Aging Loved Ones.* New York: Harper and Row, 2008.

Rowe, John W., and Robert L. Kahn. *Successful Aging.* New York: Pantheon, 1998.

Schoen, Cathy, and Barbara S. Cooper. *Medicare's Future: Current Picture, Trends, and the Prescription Drug Policy Debate.* New York: Commonwealth Fund, 2003.

ACCESSIBLE, HIGH-QUALITY LONG-TERM CARE

Binstock, Robert H., Linda K. George, Stephen J. Cutler, Jon Hendricks, and James H. Schulz, eds. *Handbook of Aging and the Social Sciences.* 6th ed. New York: Academic Press, 2006.

Harrington, Charlene, Helen Carrillo, and Brandee Woleslagle Blank. *Nursing Facilities, Staffing, Residents, and Facility Deficiencies, 2000 Through 2006.* San Francisco: University of California, San Francisco, 2007.

Kaiser Commission on Medicaid and the Uninsured. *Medicaid and Long-Term Care Services.* Washington, D.C.: Kaiser Family Foundation, 2006.

Kane, Robert L., and Rosalie A. Kane. "What Older People Want from Long-Term Care, and How They Can Get It." *Health Affairs* 20, no. 6 (2001): 114–27.

Mollica, Robert, and Heather Johnson-Lamarche. *State Residential Care and Assisted Living Policy: 2004.* Washington, D.C.: U.S. Department of Health and Human Services, 2005.

Stone, Robin I. *Long-Term Care for the Elderly with Disabilities: Current Policy, Emerging Trends, and Implications for the 21st Century.* New York: Milbank Memorial Fund, 2000.

INDEX